LEGENDARY LOCALS

OF

CASTRO VALLEY, HAYWARD, AND SAN LORENZO

CALIFORNIA

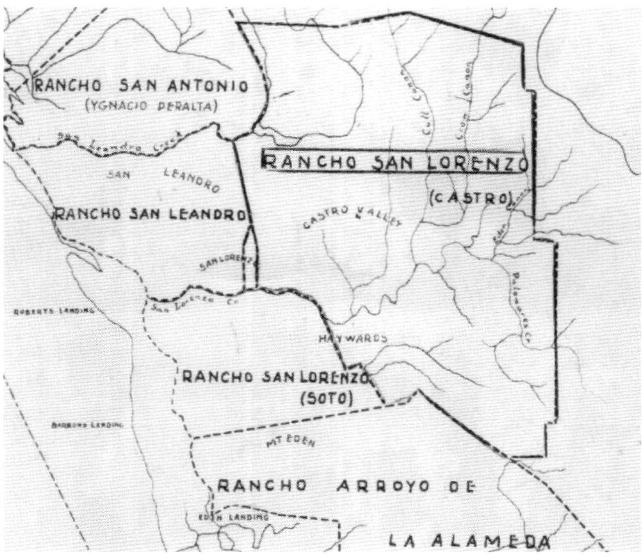

I0806118

Page 2: **Mexican Rancheros**

This partial map of Alameda County shows the Mexican land grants that form present-day Castro Valley, Hayward, and San Lorenzo. (Courtesy of the Hayward Area Historical Society.)

LEGENDARY LOCALS OF CASTRO VALLEY, HAYWARD, AND SAN LORENZO CALIFORNIA

DORIS MARCIEL AND THE
HAYWARD AREA HISTORICAL SOCIETY

LEGENDARY LOCALS

ISBN 978-1-4671-0065-6

Legendary Locals is an imprint of Arcadia Publishing
Charleston, South Carolina

Printed in the United States of America

Library of Congress Control Number: 2012951004

For all general information, please contact Arcadia Publishing:
Telephone 843-853-2070
Fax 843-853-0044
E-mail sales@arcadiapublishing.com
For customer service and orders:
Toll-Free 1-888-313-2665

Visit us on the Internet at www.arcadiapublishing.com

Dedication

This book is dedicated to the legendary locals not included due to the lack of space that have also made the Castro Valley, Hayward and San Lorenzo areas a great place to live and work.

On the Cover: From left to right:
(TOP ROW) Don Guillermo Castro, owner of Rancho San Lorenzo (Courtesy of the Hayward Area Historical Society; see page 11), William Fletcher, auto mechanic (Courtesy of the Hayward Area Historical Society; see page 65), Frank Goulart, amateur historian (Courtesy of Frank Goulart; see page 81), Esther Jorgensen, homes association board member (Courtesy of Esther Jorgensen; see page 112), William Meek, largest landowner (Courtesy of the Hayward Area Historical Society; see page 111).
(MIDDLE ROW) Lucille Lorge, Castro Valley historian (Courtesy of Lucille Lorge; see page 41), Alden Oliver, salt harvester (Courtesy of the Hayward Area Historical Society; see page 59), Matt Jimenez, Hayward fire chief (Courtesy of the Hayward Area Historical Society; see page 73), James Harvey Strobridge, railroad supervisor (Courtesy of the Hayward Area Historical Society; see page 17), Gail Steele, elected official (Courtesy of Doris Marciel; see page 89).
(BOTTOM ROW) Frank Denevi, photographer (Courtesy of Frank Denevi; see page 121), Sung Han Lee, green business owner (Courtesy of Doris Marciel; see page 123), John Lewelling, horticulturalist (Courtesy of the Hayward Area Historical Society; see page 96), Suzanne Barba, community activist (Courtesy of Suzanne Barba; see page 36), Harry Rowell, rodeo promoter and rancher (Courtesy of the Hayward Area Historical Society; see page 26).

CONTENTS

ACKNOWLEDGMENTS

This book is possible because of two special people from the Hayward Area Historical Society: Diane Curry, curator and archivist, and John Christian, assistant archivist. They obtained information and pictures, scanned the photographs, and critiqued the captions. I also want to thank Lucille Lorge and Frank Goulart for suggesting legends and organizations. I thank those who gave me information and photographs, especially Dale Harder, Leonard Hancock, Suzanne Barba, Gerry Osborne, Erma Smith, Maryann Francis, Lucille Lorge, Charlotte Lusschen, Gale Steele, Frank Goulart, Nels Nelson, David Kolm, Doris Rodriguez, Maria Ochoa, Samira Hamid, Edward Martins, Robert Vejby, Barbara Kuhns, Beverly Bras Ford, Maybelle Rasmussen, Dorothy Partridge, John King, Frank Denevi, Nancy Van Huffel, Donna McCarty, Sung Lee, Mary Bossley, Tom and Cathy Clements, Esther Jorgensen, Tom Vierra, Keith Barros, Dr. Dennis Byas, Diane Bordi, Tom Longaker, Allan Fishman, Joe Espina, Barney Mooney, Richard Krause, Dennis Waespi, Steve Ontiveros, Lola Gianelli, Charlotte Lusschen and Stephanie Bigelow of the Castro Valley Women's Club, Marcene Willard, Bud Critzer, Claire McKibben, Bonnie Peterson, and Bob and Erica Campisi. Special thanks goes to Arcadia editors Tiffany Frary and Amy Perryman for their patience and understanding.

Unless otherwise noted, all images appear courtesy of the Hayward Area Historical Society.

INTRODUCTION

Close to the San Francisco–Oakland area of California are the two unincorporated towns of Castro Valley and San Lorenzo. The city of Hayward, known as the "Heart of the Bay," borders these towns. All three are in Alameda County and, as a group, are often referred to as the Hayward area.

Castro Valley is nestled in a valley surrounded by tree-covered rolling hills. In the early days, redwood trees were harvested and taken by horse-drawn wagons to Roberts' Landing in San Lorenzo, where they were shipped across the bay to San Francisco. Some areas of Castro Valley still have a rural atmosphere with lots of open land and privately owned horse stables.

In the early 1900s, Castro Valley was known for its chicken ranches and was one of the largest egg-producing centers in California. As more people began moving to this area in the 1940s and 1950s, poultry ranching faded, and the land was subdivided for residences. The community workers commuted to their jobs in surrounding areas. As an unincorporated area, it is governed by the Alameda County Board of Supervisors, with the Alameda County Sheriff's Department and Fire Department providing services. Castro Valley has its own school district.

Hayward's total area is about 64 square miles with about 19 square miles of water. Much of the coastal area contained productive salt ponds. It is the sixth largest city in the San Francisco Bay Area and third largest in Alameda County. It is located between Castro Valley and Union City with the eastern section containing the Hayward–San Mateo Bridge, which crosses San Francisco Bay to San Mateo. The San Lorenzo Creek runs through the western section of the city.

Hayward has its own fault, the Hayward fault, which runs mostly along Mission Boulevard. The first great earthquake along the fault occurred on the morning of October 21, 1868. It was approximately a 7.0 magnitude earthquake lasting for about 40 seconds, leaving the small community with damage to homes and businesses, but no one was killed. Hayward rebuilt and carried on. The threat of another devastating earthquake lingers to this day

Prior to World War II, agriculture was the main industry in Hayward, and Hunt Brothers Cannery, which canned much of the local produce, employed a large percentage of the population. Following the war, Hayward saw a huge economic and population boom. Now, Hayward has a large number of manufacturing businesses and corporate headquarters including high-tech companies, a Bay Area Rapid Transit System, and many housing developments.

There are four parks administered by the East Bay Regional Park District. Other parks and recreational areas are administered by the Hayward Area Recreation and Park District. Hayward is the home of California State University, East Bay, and Chabot College. Within the city limits, Hayward is governed by a city council and mayor with its own police and fire department. The unincorporated sections are governed by the Alameda County Board of Supervisors. Hayward has enhanced its downtown area with murals on buildings and utility boxes for beautification and to combat graffiti.

San Lorenzo probably was named for the Mexican land grant Rancho San Lorenzo or the San Lorenzo Creek when, in 1854, the federal government accepted it as a post office station in the San Lorenzo House, a hotel owned by the first postmaster, Albert E. Crane.

Before the David D. Bohannon organization purchased farmland south of the San Lorenzo Creek in 1944 to make the planned community housing tract for workers in the East Bay's war industry, San Lorenzo was a framing and resort town. It grew up at the "Four Corners" of Main Street (now Lewelling Boulevard) and Telegraph Road (now Hesperian Boulevard). Many people arrived on weekends and vacations from San Francisco by ship to Oakland and took a streetcar and a trolley car to stay at its two hotels, the Willows and the San Lorenzo House. They purchased the farm crops and used the recreation areas.

The San Lorenzo Grove—an eight-acre natural park with oak trees, a pavilion, picnic grounds, an outdoor bandstand, and a concession area—was a major recreation center. The Village Hall was a meeting place for socials and medicine shows. It also contained the first Alameda County Library organized in 1910. The first church, built in 1875, still stands today across from the San Lorenzo Pioneer Cemetery, established in 1853.

The San Lorenzo School District is one of the oldest continuously operated school systems in the state of California. It began in 1850 with only six students and a tiny portable schoolhouse shared with Hayward. The first permanent school was built in 1859 across from the cemetery. There are now nine elementary, three middle, and three high schools in the San Lorenzo Unified School District. Five schools are leased.

Other features in town included the Trojan Powder Company factory, the former California Packing Corporation cannery, and the Southern Pacific Railroad Station. Flower nurseries were established by Japanese and Italian families.

The town changed along with the farmland. The library and post office were moved to the village, and stores were built along with the 1947 Lorenzo Theater.

The neighboring cities of Hayward and San Leandro annexed a large part of the San Lorenzo area. The Alameda County Board of Supervisors, govern the remaining area and the San Lorenzo Village has a homes association. Historical Lewelling Boulevard sidewalks from Hesperian Boulevard to Meekland Avenue have 10 embedded plaques telling the story of the former and remaining Main Street sites. San Lorenzo is a unique town.

CHAPTER ONE

Castro Valley

This unincorporated community is nestled in a shallow valley between the cities of Hayward and San Leandro. It is named for Don Guillermo Castro, an officer in the Mexican army. He was awarded a grant of 26,722 acres of land, including Hayward and part of San Lorenzo. Castro Valley was where his cattle grazed for part of the year.

The first American settlers came in the early 1850s, purchasing land from Castro. In the following decades, more settlers came to the valley and purchased vast acreage. Their names live on in the street names throughout the town. William Cull, John Proctor, John Jamison, and the Jensen brothers are a few. James Harvey Strobridge and Michael Stanton settled here after making their fortunes in building the transcontinental railroad that connected California to the rest of the nation. All of these early pioneers found the land fertile where they could grow profitable crops or raise cattle, sheep, and horses. One enterprising pioneer, Isaac Parsons, not only grew orchards but also established a model dairy farm while being involved in civic organizations in neighboring Hayward.

Not all early settlers operated farms and ranches. The first commercial business was Thomford's Exchange, established by Henry A. Thomford, in the 1870s. The exchange was located at the corner of two roads leading into Castro Valley and out to Hayward. It was a crucial stopping point in the transportation routes connecting the Hayward area to communities in the Livermore Valley.

An early development that had a lasting impact on the landscape was a huge water project built in the northern section of the valley by water pioneer Anthony Chabot. The Chabot dam and lake provided water to the surrounding communities and is now a major recreation area for Castro Valley residents and neighboring areas. It is one of the most beautiful locations in the valley.

By the 1920s, not only did orchards and farms dot the landscape but also chicken ranches. In fact, Castro Valley was the second largest egg-producing region in California next to Petaluma. The growth of the poultry industry spurred the development of a downtown commercial district along what is now Castro Valley Boulevard. Early businesses such as Pete's Hardware, established in 1926 by Pete Selmeczki, catered to the needs of poultry farmers who did not want to go into Hayward for supplies. One of the longest-operating chicken hatcheries in town, the California State Hatchery, was started by Cyril Lorge and operated into the 1950s by his sons Ray and Jim Lorge. The Lorge family's connection to Castro Valley runs very deep. Ray's wife, Lucille Lorge, keeps Castro Valley history alive today with presentations and exhibits.

After World War II, like many communities in California, farms began fading away as more people moved to the area and more homes were built. Forward-thinking men, like Arnold Anderson, saw the opportunities available in Castro Valley and worked to bring major development to the town, such as persuading Al Nunes, whose family owned land along Castro Valley Boulevard, to sell some prime acres in the center of town for a shopping center.

As the community grew, so did its need for education, Castro Valley had several schools by the end of the 19th century but saw growth in the 1940s and 1950s under the direction of Supt. Alfred Bowman

Morris. His successor, Marvin Smith, oversaw the creation of the Castro Valley Unified School District, which brought all the elementary schools and the new high school into one district.

Castro Valley residents are focused now on building community. Many individuals and service organizations, such as the Hayward Castro Valley Moose Lodge, the Women's Club, and Veterans of Foreign Wars (VFW), work to make Castro Valley a better place. People like Dale Harder, Leroy Pegis, Leonard Hancock, Brian Morrison, Suzanne Barba, Gerry Osborne, and Harry Francis volunteer or have volunteered their time to improve Castro Valley and help others. Some individuals make very large contributions, such as Erma Smith and Terry Leibowitz who helped raise funds to establish the Castro Valley Arts Foundation, which finances the Center for the Arts with the school district. Owen and Erma Smith also donated to the Smith Center for Private Enterprise Studies at California East Bay University.

The one-time grazing land is now a thriving community of more than 60,000 people. It is the legacy of those early pioneers, 20th-century visionaries, and community-minded individuals that make Castro Valley what it is today.

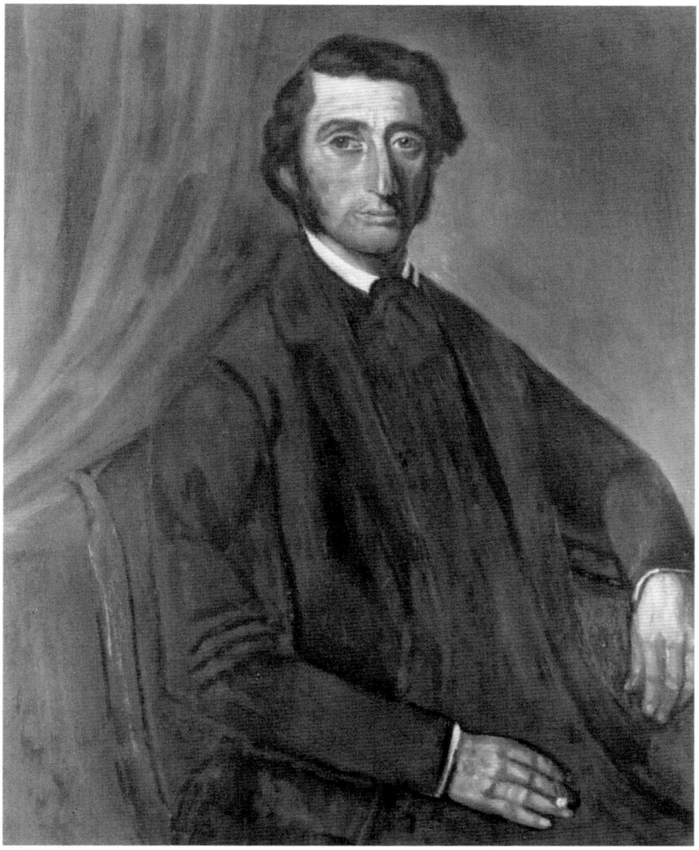

Castro's Valley

Don Guillermo Castro was born in 1810 and grew up near the original Pueblo San Jose in the Santa Clara Valley. In the early 1830s, Guillermo joined the Mexican army and, by 1837, was a lieutenant. The following year, he became a land surveyor for the Mexican government. In 1831, Guillermo married Maria Luisa Peralta at Mission Santa Clara. At the time of their marriage, Guillermo received a herd of cattle from his father-in-law as a wedding gift. This gift was the beginning of Guillermo's later cattle ranch. In 1839, Guillermo came to what would become Hayward and built a home. He then submitted an application for a land grant to the Mexican governor. He was granted 26,722 acres of land, called Rancho San Lorenzo Alta, covering what is now most of Hayward, Castro Valley, and Cull, Crow, and Palomares Canyons in 1841 and 1843. Guillermo received his land grant because of his military service, his serving as a government land surveyor, his family's (and that of his wife's) standing in the community, and his family's political connections. He used his land for grazing a large herd of cattle and horses. Castro Valley and the canyons were seasonal pastureland. William Hayward came to the canyon area in 1851 and went to work for Guillermo. He allowed Hayward to build a small stage stop and boardinghouse that would eventually become the Hayward's Hotel at about the corner of A and Main Streets. Hayward purchased 60 acres of land from Guillermo in 1853. A year earlier, Guillermo lost money during a trip to Southern California to purchase new animal stock. Most sources claim he lost the money gambling. In 1856, he mortgaged his estate for the first time and then made a series of bad investments. By the early 1860s, Guillermo was engaged in legal action with about 80 squatters who were occupying his land and, by 1864, he lost the last of his land. It was auctioned off at the county courthouse in San Leandro. Guillermo and most of his family left for South America. Although he never returned, his name remains attached to the valley that he once owned.

Rancher
William S. Cull, a native of Kentucky, came across the Plains to California by wagon train in 1849 to find gold. He met Daniel Luce along the way. They went to the mines around Sonora. Finding mining not too profitable, they went into the wagon freighting business. In 1853, they returned to Kentucky and the following year returned to California. In a Castro Valley canyon, they purchased 2,200 acres of land to begin their ranching partnership until 1880. After dissolving the partnership, Cull kept the ranch buildings and 1,111 acres. Luce kept 1,089 acres and moved to Hayward. William was the first settler to plant fruit orchards of pears, cherries, and apricots on the higher slopes of the canyon. He died in 1896 at age 67. His sons continued the ranching operations. The canyon is known as Cull Canyon.

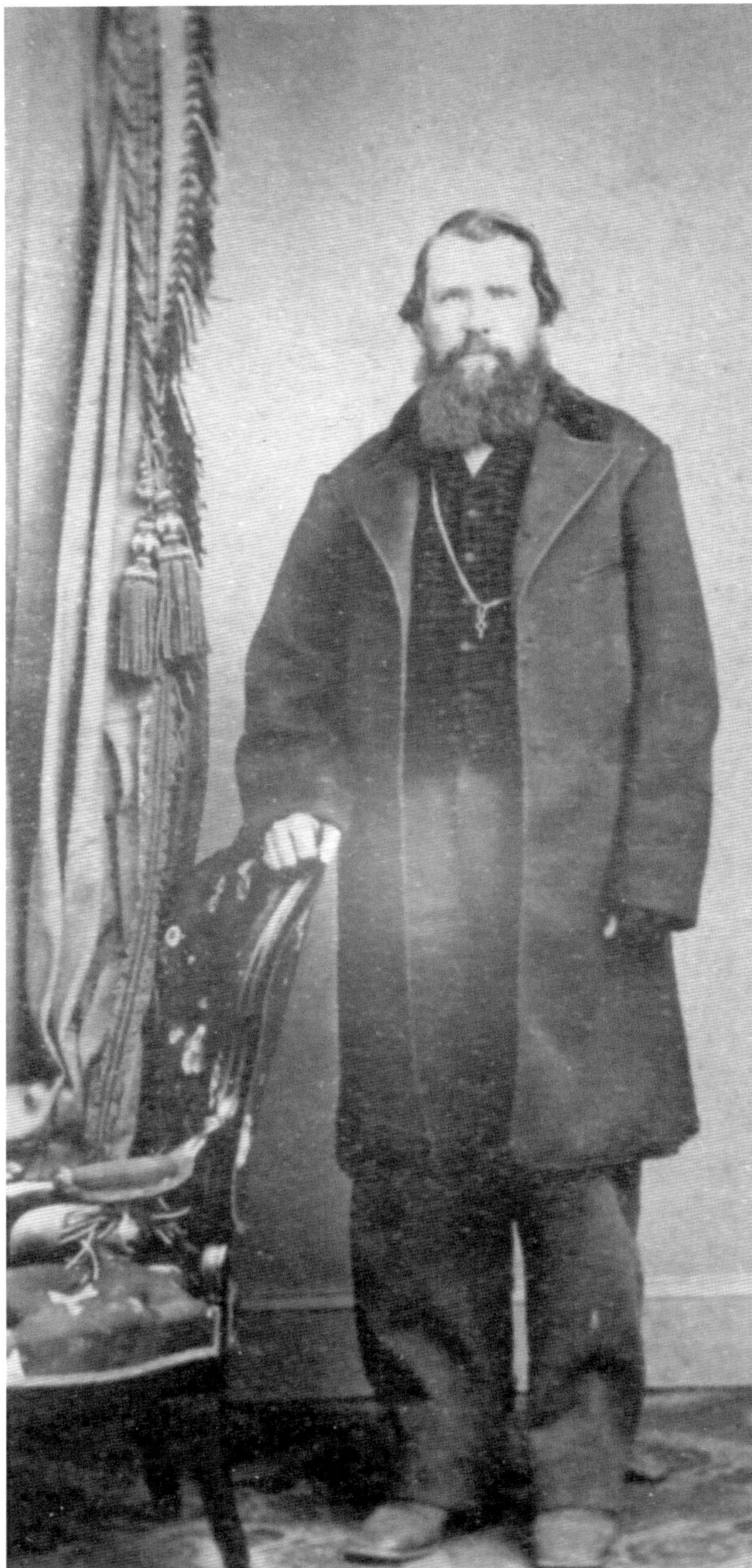

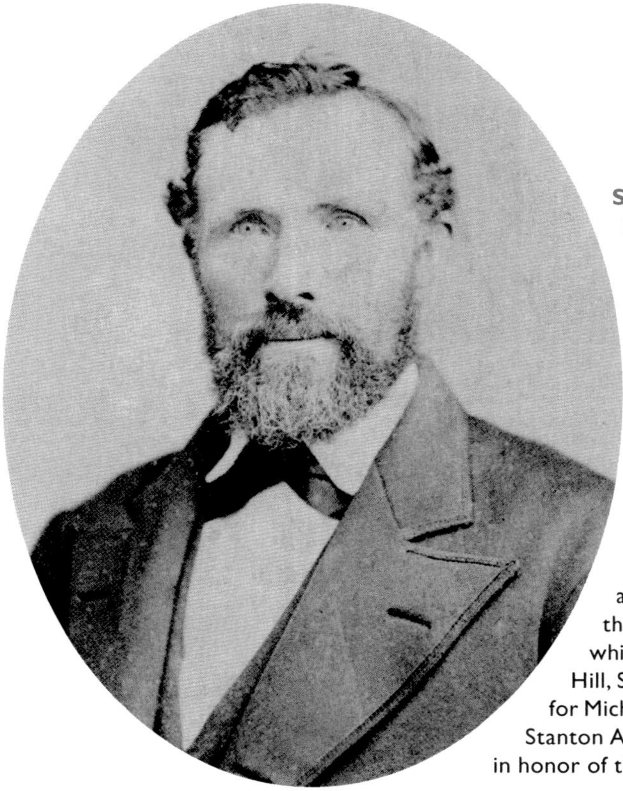

Stanton Family Legacy

Born in Ireland in 1829, Michael Stanton left home in the late 1840s. He traveled by ship to San Francisco and settled in San Jose where he met his wife, Mary. Michael worked with J.H. Strobridge on the construction of the transcontinental railroad. In 1871, he purchased 500 acres in Castro Valley from William Mattox. A large house, pictured below, already existed on the property and became known as Stanton House. The house has been moved several times and is now used as offices. The family's legacy lives on in the form of streets named for the family, which are found throughout town. Stanton Hill, Santa Maria, and San Miguel were named for Michael and Mary. John Drive, Anita Avenue, Stanton Avenue, and Stanton School were named in honor of their son John and his wife, Anita.

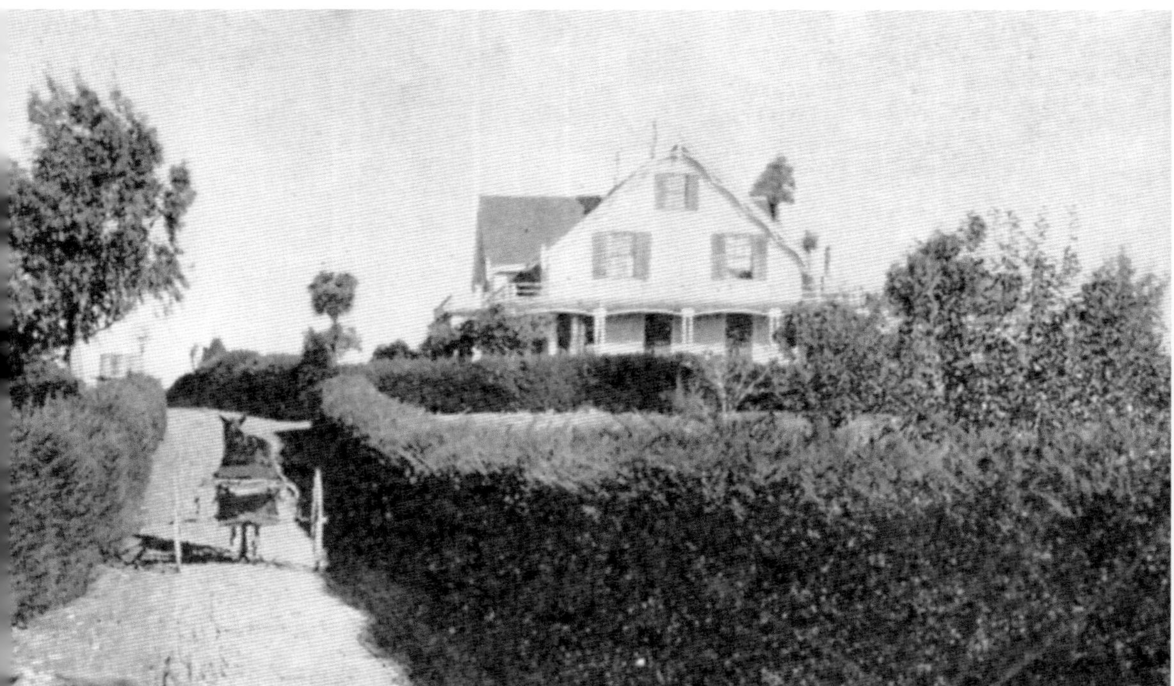

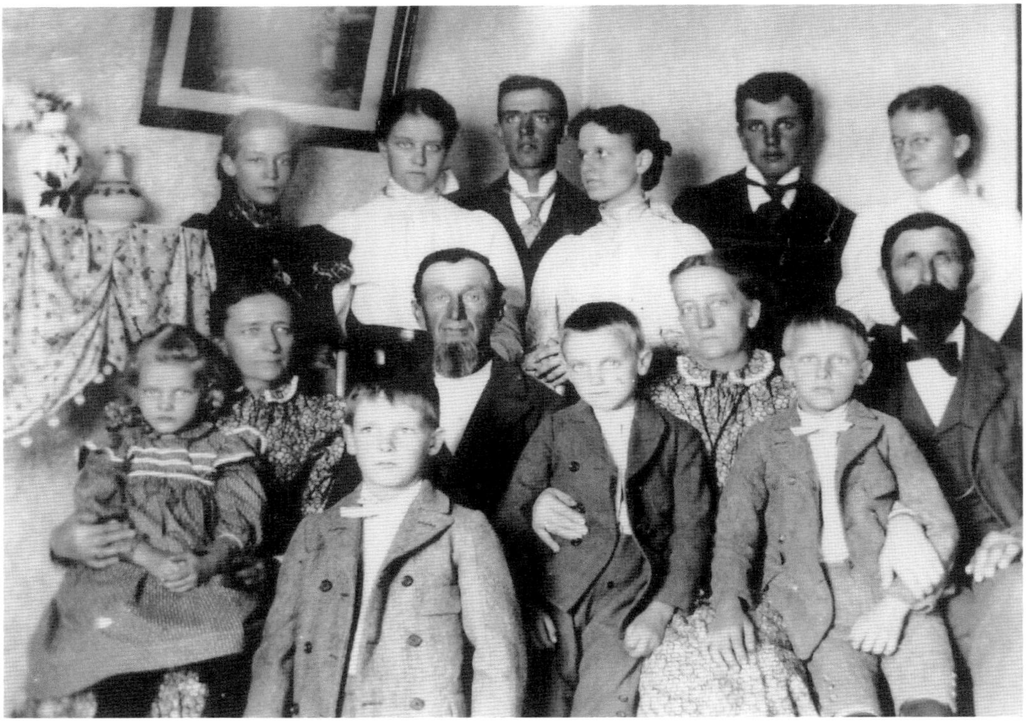

Danish Family

Erich R. Jensen from Schleswig-Holstein Denmark arrived in 1860 in San Francisco Bay after a two-month voyage around Cape Horn. He worked on dairy farms and grain ranches in the area of Alvarado, San Leandro, and Bloomfield by Petaluma where other Danish and German immigrants lived. In 1864, his brother Jens Christian Jensen arrived via the Isthmus of Panama. The brothers saved money and, in 1867, purchased 450 acres of grazing and grain land at the end of a lane along a ridge, which became Jensen Road in Castro Valley. They built barns, fences, sheds, a blacksmith shop, and a farmhouse. Erich returned to Denmark in 1872 and married Christiane Heinsen. Upon returning to California, he sent for his widowed mother and her seven children, the oldest was 11 years old. In 1876, Emilie Heinsen came from Denmark to visit her sister Christiane. She married Jens Christian Jensen. They had 10 children, five sons and five daughters. Christiane and Erich never had any children and helped raise their nieces and nephews. In this photograph, the adults pictured are, from left to right, Christiane, Erich, Emilie, and Jens Jensen with all of Emilie and Jens's children. Jens was active in Hayward-area civic affairs. He was an Alameda County supervisor, a road superintendent for 20 years, and a trustee for the Independent Primary School Board and Hayward Union High School Board. Erwin, grandson of Jens Jensen, was a member of the Hayward Area Historical Society. His wife, Edith, chaired the committees that recorded the grave markers and burial information for the San Lorenzo Pioneer Cemetery and Mount Eden Cemetery. The Jensen Ranch School is located on the family's former ranch. In 1999, Erwin and Edith Jensen donated the Jensen History Collection to the California State University, East Bay Library. The collection chronicles the lives of these early immigrants to Castro Valley. It describes the farming, ranching, and daily activities of the pioneer family. Among the items are photographs, drawings, books, and ledgers. The couple decided the collection would be of value to the students of history. They donated some of the antique farm machinery to the University of California, Davis, and had other items transferred to California State University, East Bay. (Courtesy of Lucille Lorge.)

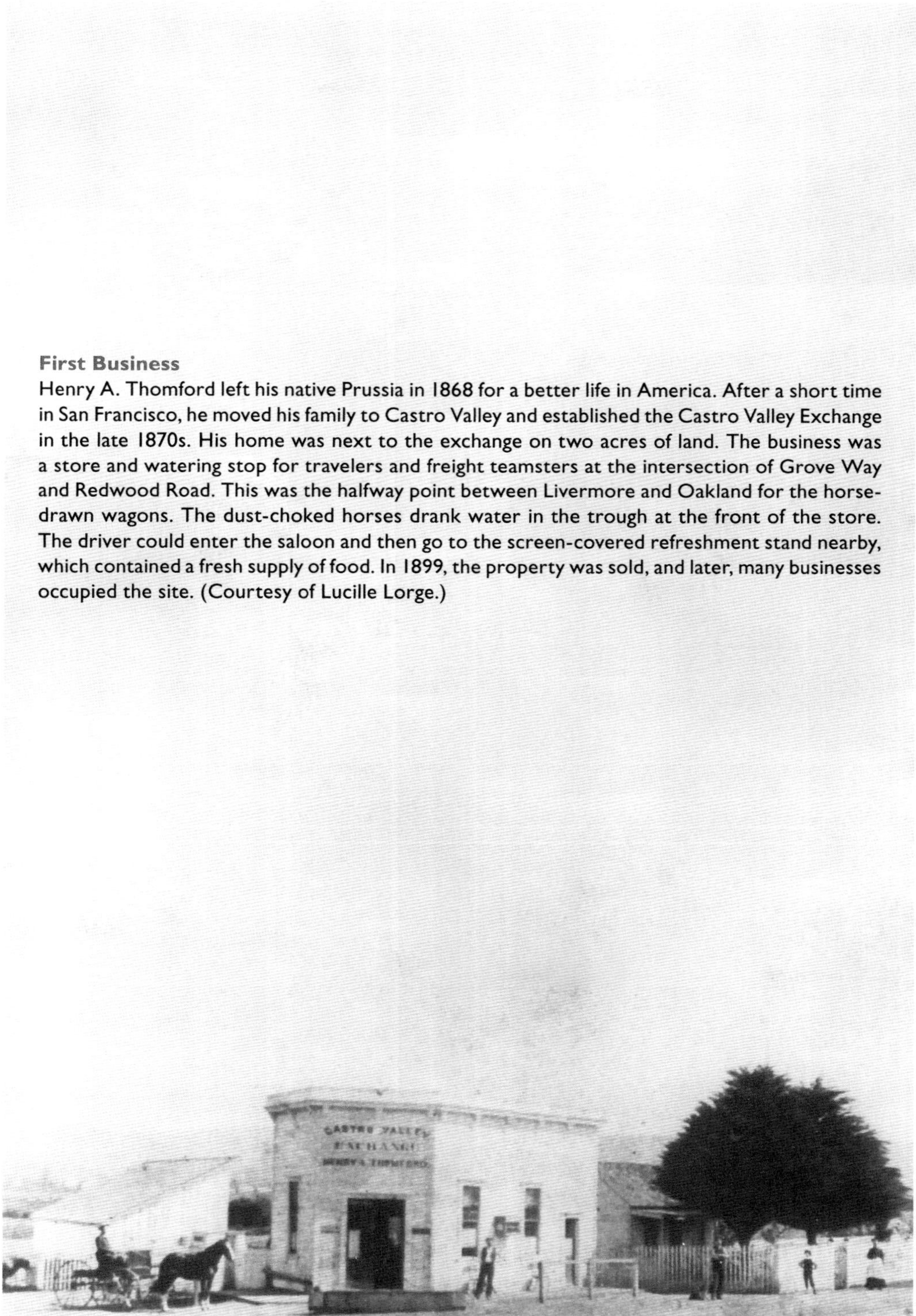

First Business

Henry A. Thomford left his native Prussia in 1868 for a better life in America. After a short time in San Francisco, he moved his family to Castro Valley and established the Castro Valley Exchange in the late 1870s. His home was next to the exchange on two acres of land. The business was a store and watering stop for travelers and freight teamsters at the intersection of Grove Way and Redwood Road. This was the halfway point between Livermore and Oakland for the horse-drawn wagons. The dust-choked horses drank water in the trough at the front of the store. The driver could enter the saloon and then go to the screen-covered refreshment stand nearby, which contained a fresh supply of food. In 1899, the property was sold, and later, many businesses occupied the site. (Courtesy of Lucille Lorge.)

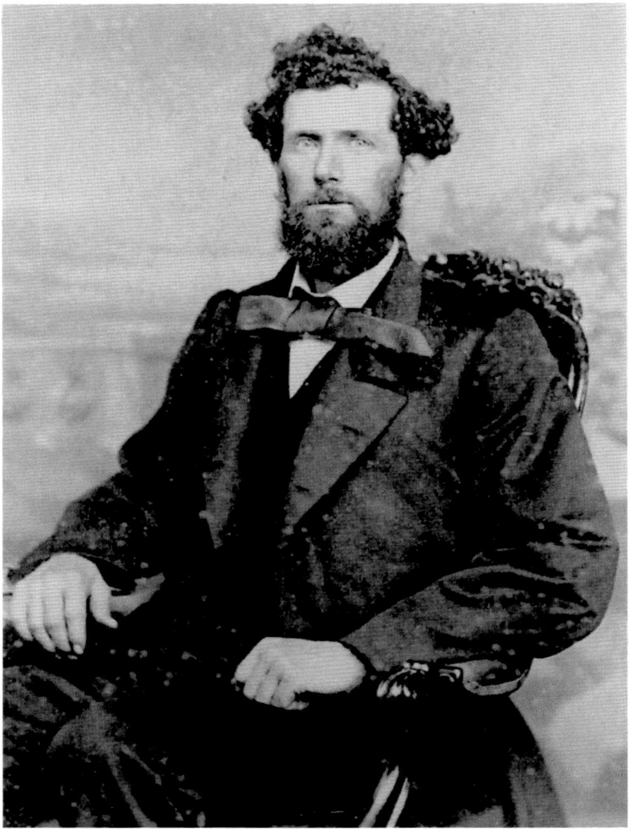

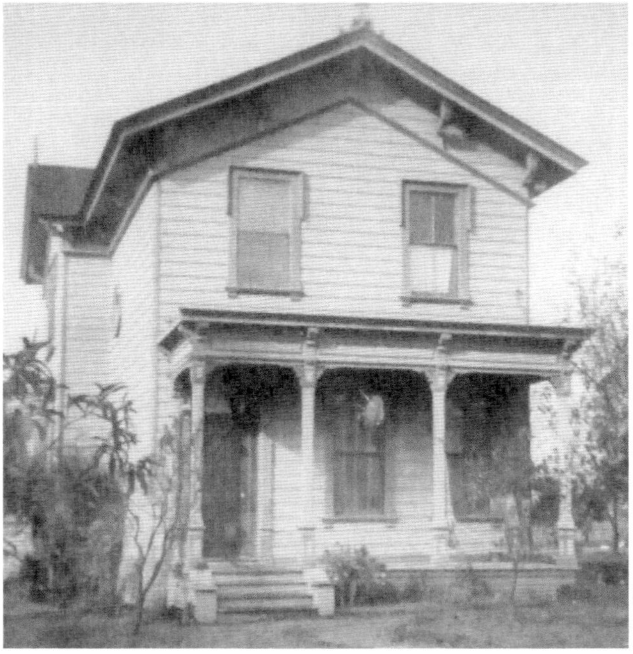

Oldest Resident in the 1800s

J.W. Jamison was born in Missouri and came around Cape Horn to California in 1853. He bought 129 acres of land from Guillermo Castro in the area of the Redwood Road and Castro Valley Boulevard intersection. In 1854, Jamison bought 125 acres at $60 an acre from his stepfather, Zachariah Hughes (one of the earliest pioneers to Castro Valley), where he built his home, pictured below, and lived until his death. In 1862, Jamison married Jennie Hamilton. They had four children. J.W. Jamison was one of the oldest members of the Hayward Methodist Church and San Leandro Masonic Lodge. When he passed away at age 76 in 1901, he was the oldest resident of Castro Valley at the time. He is buried in the family plot at the San Lorenzo Pioneer Cemetery.

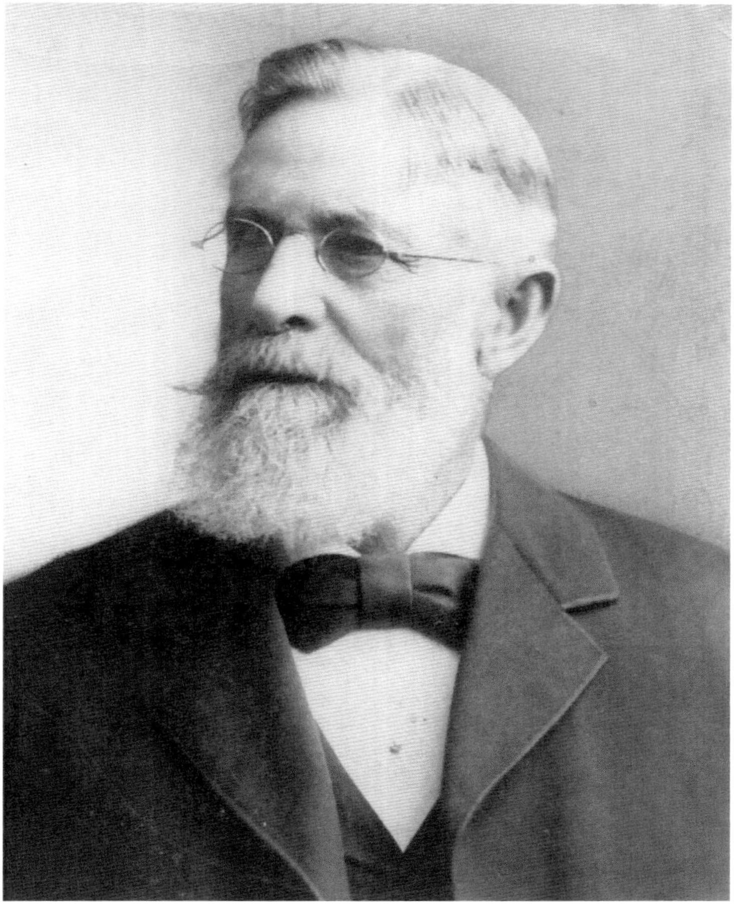

The Railroad Supervisor

Born in Vermont in 1827, James Harvey Strobridge left his family farm at age 16 to work as a tracklayer on the Boston & Fitchburg Railroad. Later, he became the foreman of construction crews specializing in grading and excavations for the Vermont Central Railroad. At age 22, Strobridge sailed for the California gold country via Cape Horn, landing in San Francisco. He went to Sacramento to work in a hay and feed yard and then developed a freighting line with E.M. Pitcher, carrying supplies to the mines in Placerville while doing some placer mining. In 1849, Strobridge used his construction experience in Dutch Flats to build the Placer County Canal used for hydraulic mining. Completing this project, he went to San Francisco to supervise the excavation of the Bernal Heights Cut for the San Francisco & San Jose Railroad. The project's success was brought to the attention of Charles Crocker and the Central Pacific Railway Company. They were building the first 15 miles of the transcontinental route from Sacramento to Newcastle. Strobridge became the superintendent of construction for the entire project. He lived with his wife, Maria, whom he met in 1860 while working at Dutch Flat, in a boxcar parked along the railroad line so he could give his entire attention to the progress of the work. When the construction work was completed in 1869, Strobridge participated in the famous "Golden Spike" ceremony at Promontory Point in Utah. Soon after, he purchased 500 acres of land between Castro Valley and the town of Hayward. There, he built a ranch house and became a prominent agriculturalist, known for his Bartlett pears and fine horses. He continued working in the railroad industry for many years until his eyesight got too bad, and he was forced to retire in 1890. Strobridge was married three times and adopted six children: two orphaned children of a friend and the others were nieces and nephews of two of his wives. Strobridge died in 1921 at age 94.

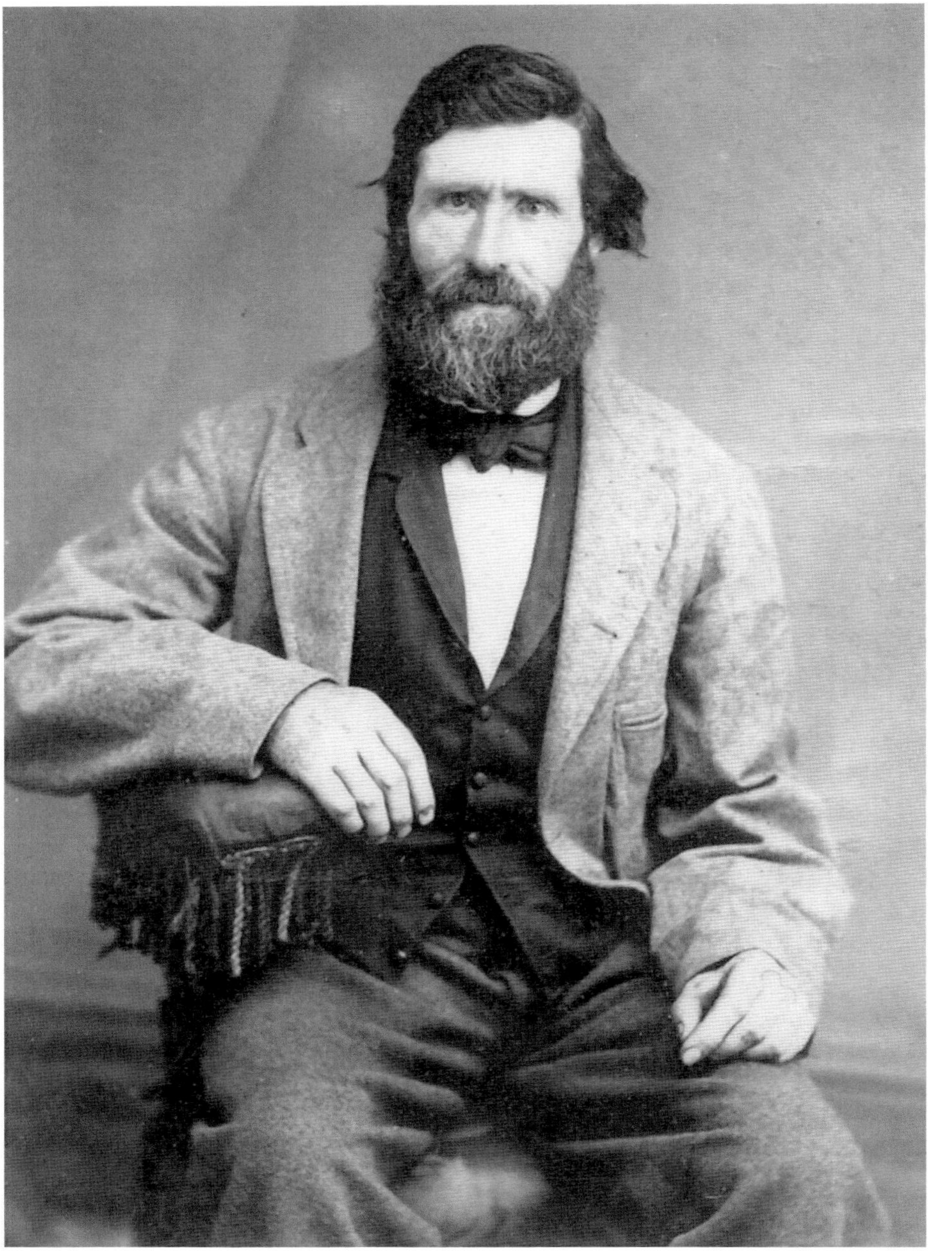

Pioneer Rancher

William Stewart was born in Glasgow, Scotland, in 1824. At age 24, he came to California looking for gold. After a three-month voyage around Cape Horn, William arrived in San Francisco in 1848. Eager to find gold, he went to the Sierra mining camp at Hangtown. When William was blinded in one eye by a faulty blasting cap, he returned to San Francisco for treatment. In the late 1850s, he bought a 740-acre ranch in Cull Canyon where he raised grain and grazed cattle in the hills. Along the creek he planted apricots, pears, and cherry trees. There, he lived with his wife, Ann Boyce, and had six children. In 1893, William purchased and moved to 37 acres in the San Lorenzo area; he died there in 1919 at age 95.

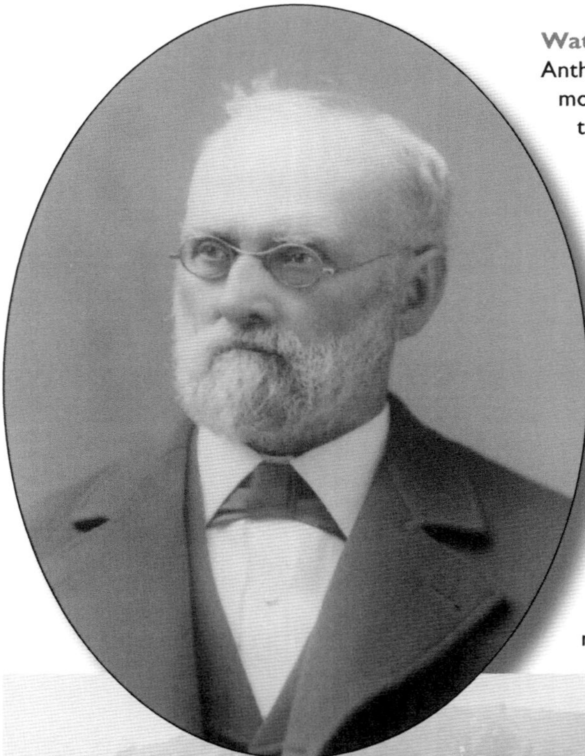

Water Baron

Anthony Chabot was born in Canada in 1814. He moved to the United States where he spent years trying his hand at different businesses. When he arrived in California in the 1850s, he pioneered hydraulic mining and made much of his fortune. With his knowledge of hydraulic mining, he began building waterways for various cities. In 1874, Anthony began a project that would transform Castro Valley and the East Bay with the construction of a reservoir, later named Lake Chabot (pictured below in 1909), which took 18 years to complete. Some 800 Chinese laborers lived and worked on the project under difficult conditions. The completed reservoir provided water to the surrounding communities. However, it was not until 1966 that Lake Chabot was opened to the public for recreational use. The lake has become one of Castro Valley's main landmarks.

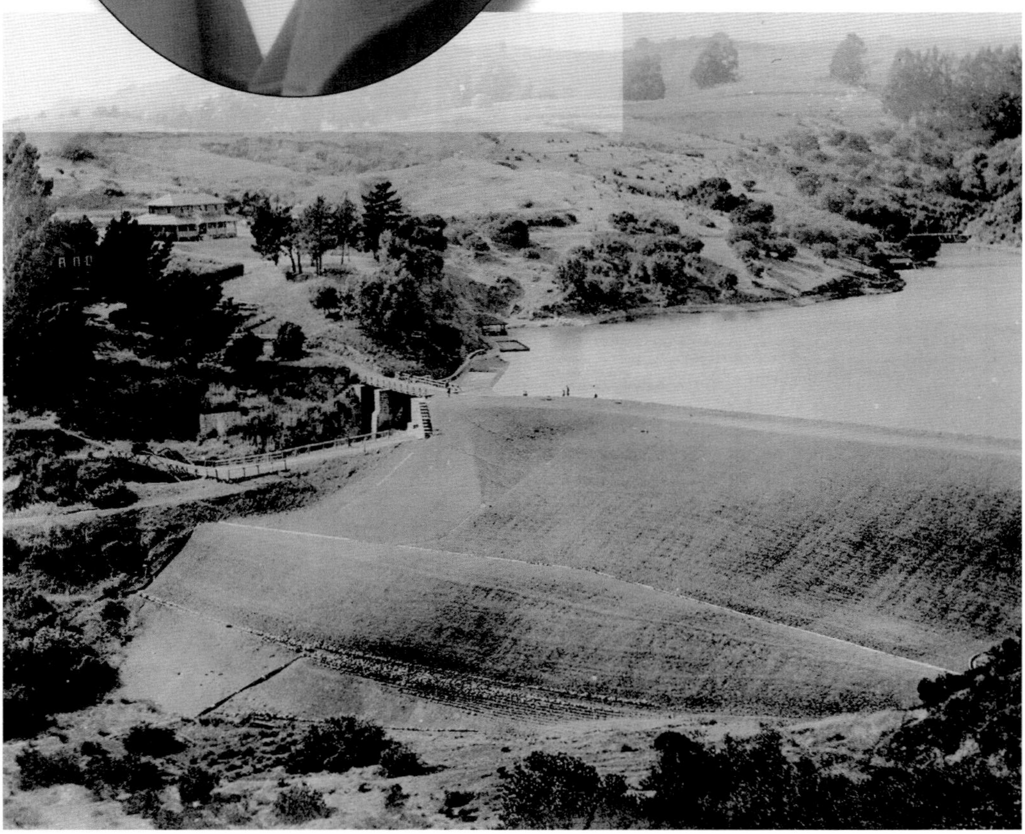

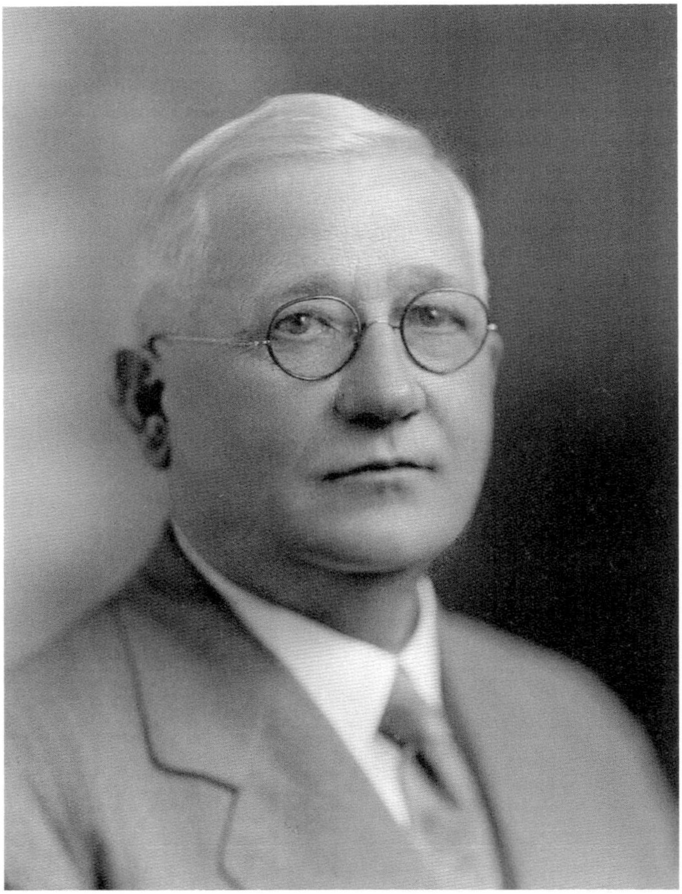

School Trustee
Isaac B. Parsons was born in New York in 1860. After graduating from the Annapolis Naval Academy in 1877, he served at a base in Shanghai. Upon his return to the United States, he passed through Hayward. Liking what he saw here, he returned to the region with his bride and bought 40 acres of land in Castro Valley. Later, Isaac bought additional land on Seven Hills Road for his model dairy farm, pictured below. In 1891, Isaac became one of the first trustees of the new Hayward Union High School District, which built the first four-room high school in Hayward. Isaac remained a trustee for more than 50 years. He was associated with many civic organizations, such as the Hayward Rotary for most of his career, and was president of the Bank of Haywards from 1907 until his death in 1948.

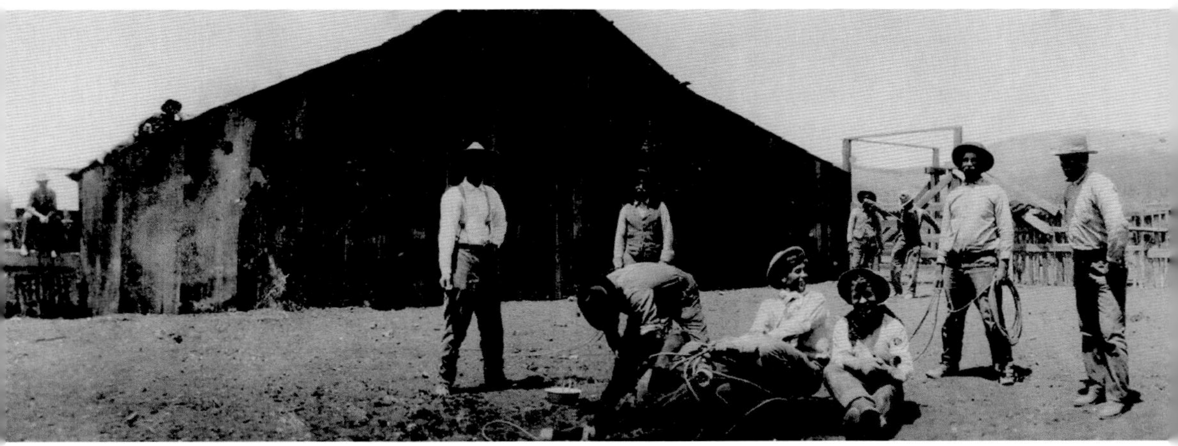

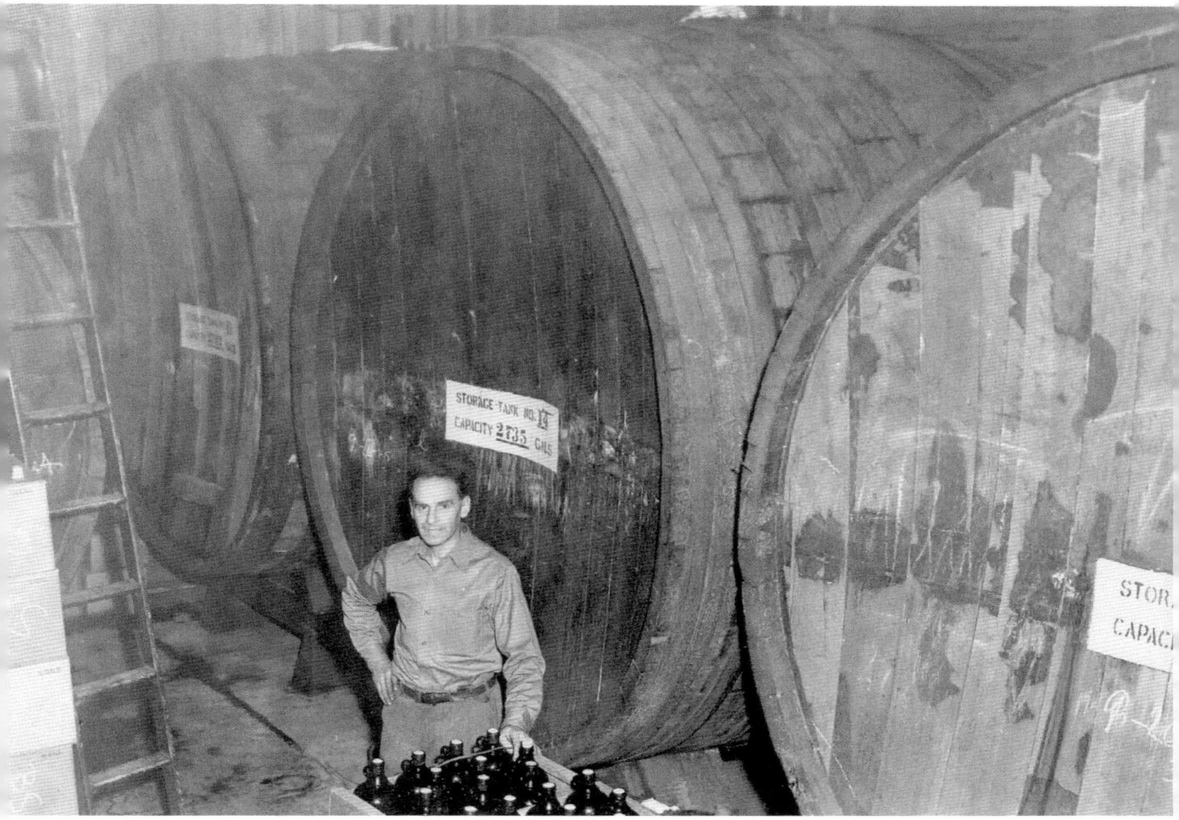

The First Winery

Paul Rhodes operated Castro Valley's first winery between 1937 and 1965. Paul was more than a vintner. He served on the Eden Hospital Board of Directors for more than 25 years. On the board, Paul was often described as a "minority of one," staunchly defending his conservative views. A gag rule was put into place by the board before Paul had finished serving a single year. Paul also served on the Castro Valley school board and ran unsuccessfully for county supervisor in 1958, all while staying true to his trademark brashness. Despite this, Paul earned the respect of his colleagues. A fellow hospital board member said, "He was my teacher, he was my mentor, he was my tormentor." Despite his reputation, Paul Rhodes's legacy is one of community service in Castro Valley.

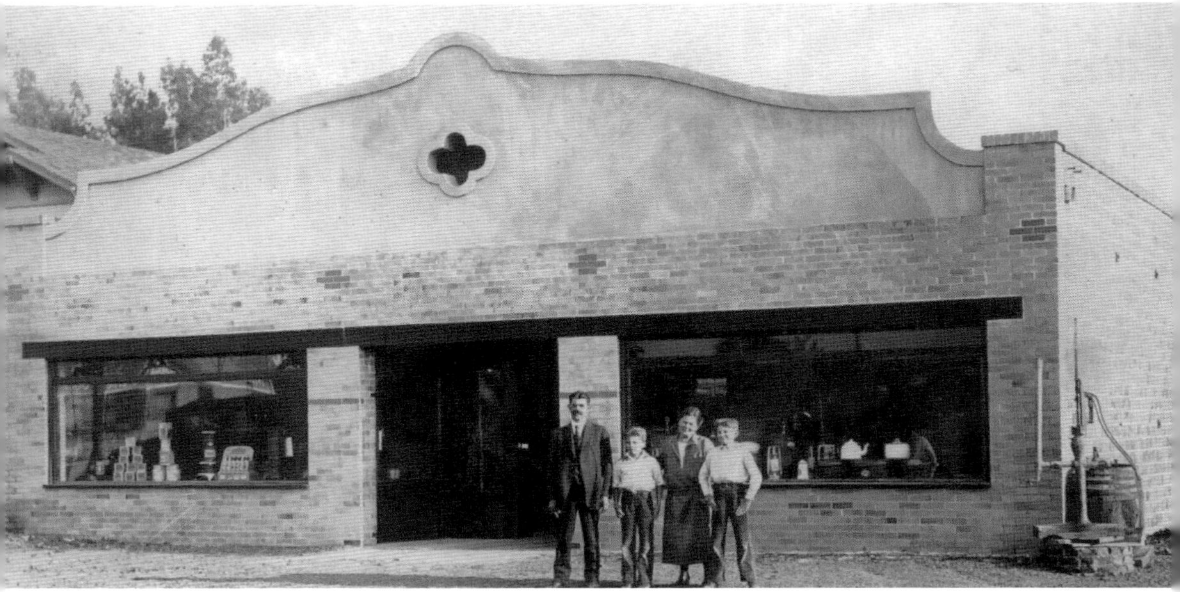

Pete's Hardware

Pete Selmeczki was a Hungarian immigrant who came to the United States before World War I. He first settled in Connecticut, where his son Ernie was born in 1917. Pete came to Oakland and opened a business, called First Class Automobile & Carriage Painter. In 1921, he moved to Hayward to continue his business for four years. Pete was impressed with Castro Valley, and although he knew nothing about the hardware business, decided to open a store. He built the store in front of his home in 1926, which was the center of the community along Castro Valley Boulevard. It has been in the same location and the family business ever since. The old store was replaced with a modern one in 1970, and the house was removed. In the early days, Pete's Hardware catered to agricultural businesses, such as chicken, rabbit, and dairy ranchers and fruit farmers. Today, the store serves contractors, do-it-yourself people, and anyone else with a hardware or garden need. After Pete's death, his sons Ernie and Frank continued the business until Frank's death in 1975. Ernie attributed his father's philosophy of "service and knowledge" as the reason for the success of the business. Ernie passed away in 2006 leaving a legacy that his daughter Linda Roark and her daughter Jennifer continue.

Superintendent

Alfred Bowman Morris was born in Sacramento in 1892. His family moved to Hayward in 1902. He graduated from Hayward Grammar School but did not attend high school. Alfred managed to obtain admission to the Western Normal School in Stockton and qualified to teach grammar school after obtaining the highest score on a teacher exam. While visiting his parents, he met his future wife, Elsie Comstocke. They built a home in Castro Valley. Alfred took a teacher-principal position at Redwood School, later becoming superintendent of the district. Alfred promoted the Adobe Community Building as a project behind the Castro Valley Elementary School, which was completed in 1938. It is now the A.B. Morris Adobe Art Center. When he retired in 1956, there were 13 schools in Castro Valley.

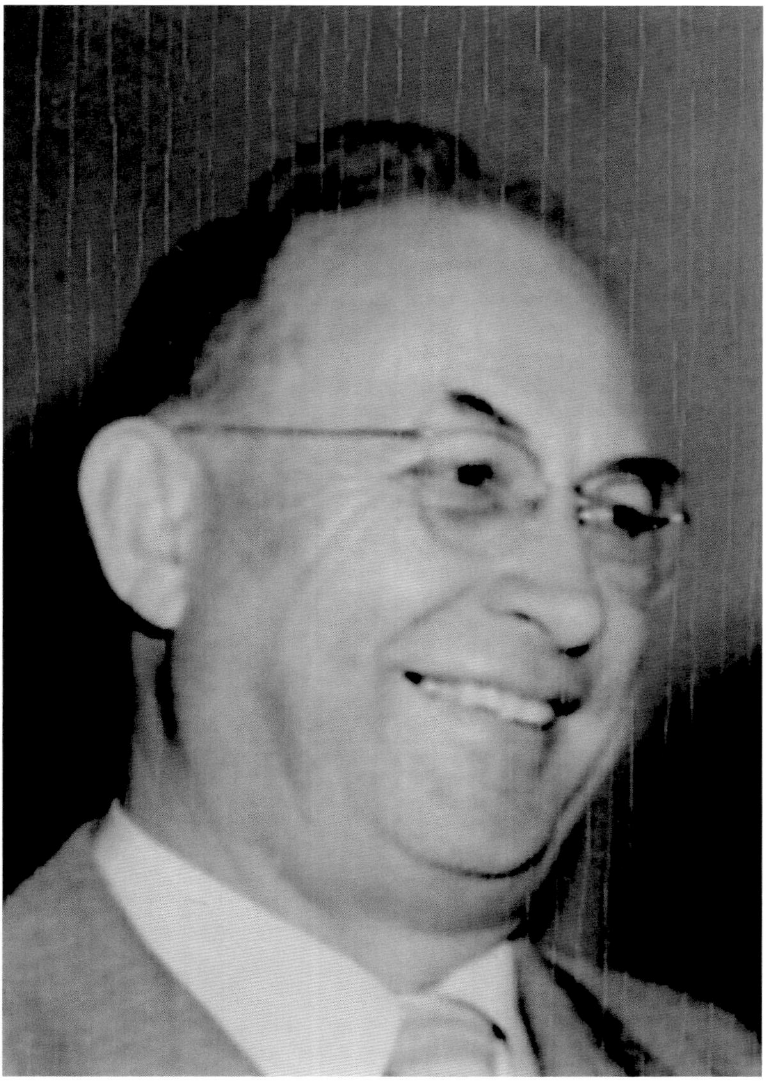

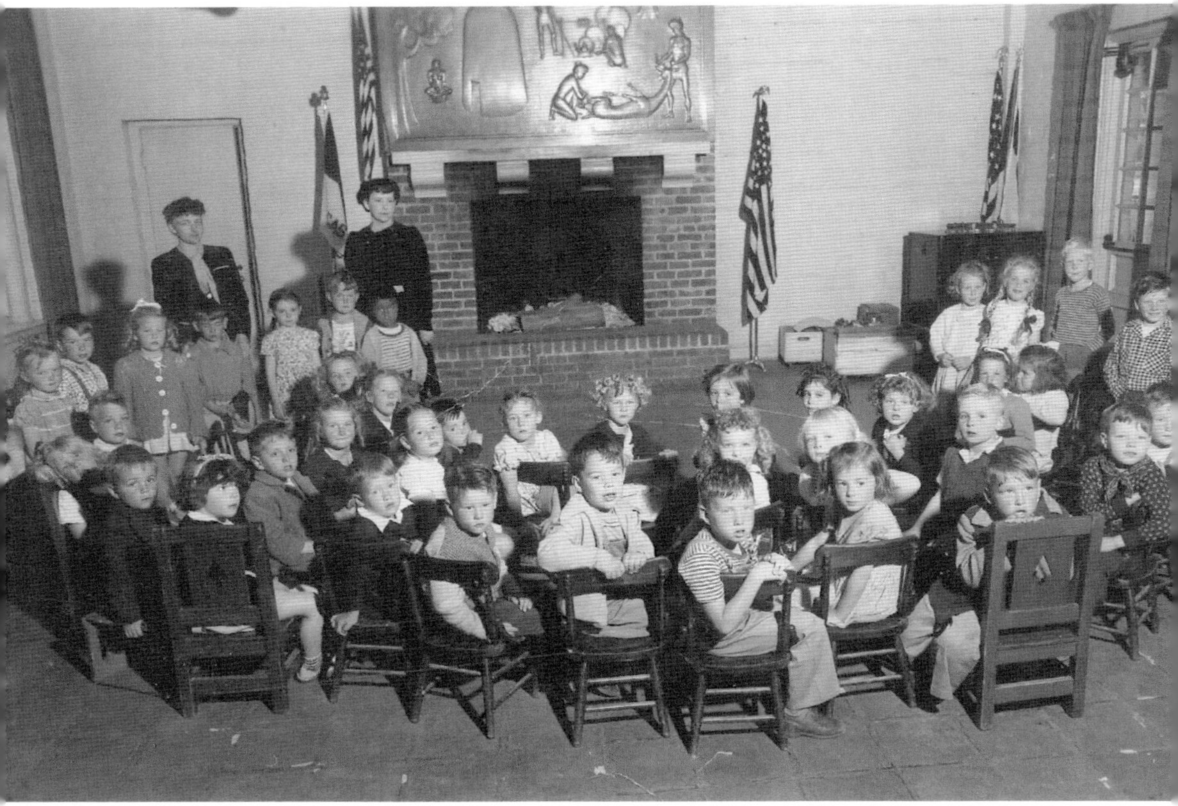

First Kindergarten Teacher

Beatrice Hampton was born and raised in Canada. After completing elementary school, her family moved to Washington State. Upon graduation from high school, her parents moved to California, where she attended college to become a teacher. In 1935, Beatrice and her husband, Henry, moved to Hayward. Henry became the vice principal at Hayward Union High School. In 1939, they moved to Castro Valley, where Beatrice became the first kindergarten teacher. She taught at the newly built Adobe Center. Beatrice is pictured (back row, right) with fellow teacher Grace Niemcziek (left) and one of her kindergarten classes. Later, she moved to the Castro Valley Grammar School. Her kindergarten had 45 students in the morning and 45 students in the afternoon. Beatrice retired from teaching in 1965. (Courtesy of Grace Niemcziek.)

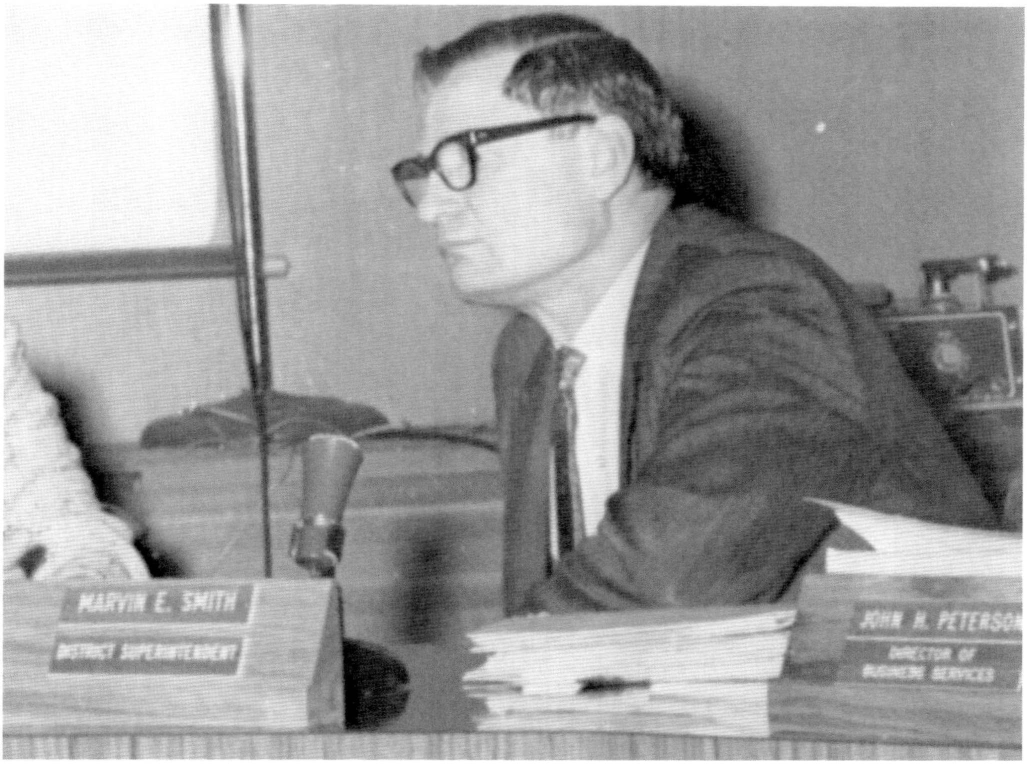

Castro Valley Educator for All Ages

Marvin Smith, longtime educator, was invited to come to Castro Valley from Roseburg, Oregon, in 1955 after he applied for the superintendent of schools position. He worked with Supt. A.B. Morris as his assistant. In 1965, the Castro Valley Elementary School District became the Castro Valley Unified School District, and Marvin became its first superintendent. When he retired, he became the principal of Castro Valley Adult School. At 75, he was the unofficial historian of Castro Valley, teaching local history at the adult school for two years. Marvin compiled the information from guest speakers and self-published it as the *Castro Valley Magazine* for the class. In 1994, he wrote and edited the book *Castro Valley School Stories*.

The Rodeo King

James Henry "Harry" Rowell was born in 1891 in Peterborough, Northamptonshire, England. In 1904, he joined the British navy. At age 21, he and a shipmate were on the HMS *Shearwater* surveying the Inland Passage when they decided to jump ship in British Columbia on Thanksgiving Day 1912. Harry entered the United States through Vancouver and found his way to California with little money. Rowell's first job was on a dairy in Berkeley milking cows. He entered boxing matches to earn money and won a heavyweight event in Oakland. Next, he drove a tallow wagon for the West Coast Soap Company. Settling in Castro Valley and raising chickens to sell eggs, Harry found there was more money hauling dead animals. In 1921, he established a slaughterhouse on Mattox Road and Foothill Boulevard in Hayward. He began organizing rodeos on his Mattox Road ranch that same year and produced a show on the Bret Harte School grounds in Hayward. In 1924, Harry bought land in the Dublin Canyon area of Castro Valley to construct a meatpacking plant, holding corrals, ranch house, office, and bunkhouse for ranch hands. He and his wife, Bertha, settled there and eventually moved the rodeo to the Dublin Canyon ranch. It became one of the biggest events in the Hayward area and a popular stop on the Professional Rodeo Cowboys Association tour. A parade held prior to the weekend rodeo in Hayward later moved to Castro Valley. In 1936, Bertha Condon Rowell died, and Harry married Margaret "Maggie" Tryon in 1938. When Harry Rowell died in 1969, horsemen from all the Western states mourned. The streets of Hayward were roped off as hundreds of mounted riders paid their last respects. Maggie Rowell continued the rodeo in Harry's memory. Following her death in 1975, the Hayward Area Recreation and Park District took over the rodeo. The Hayward Rodeo in 1978 was renamed Rowell Ranch Rodeo in honor of Harry and Maggie.

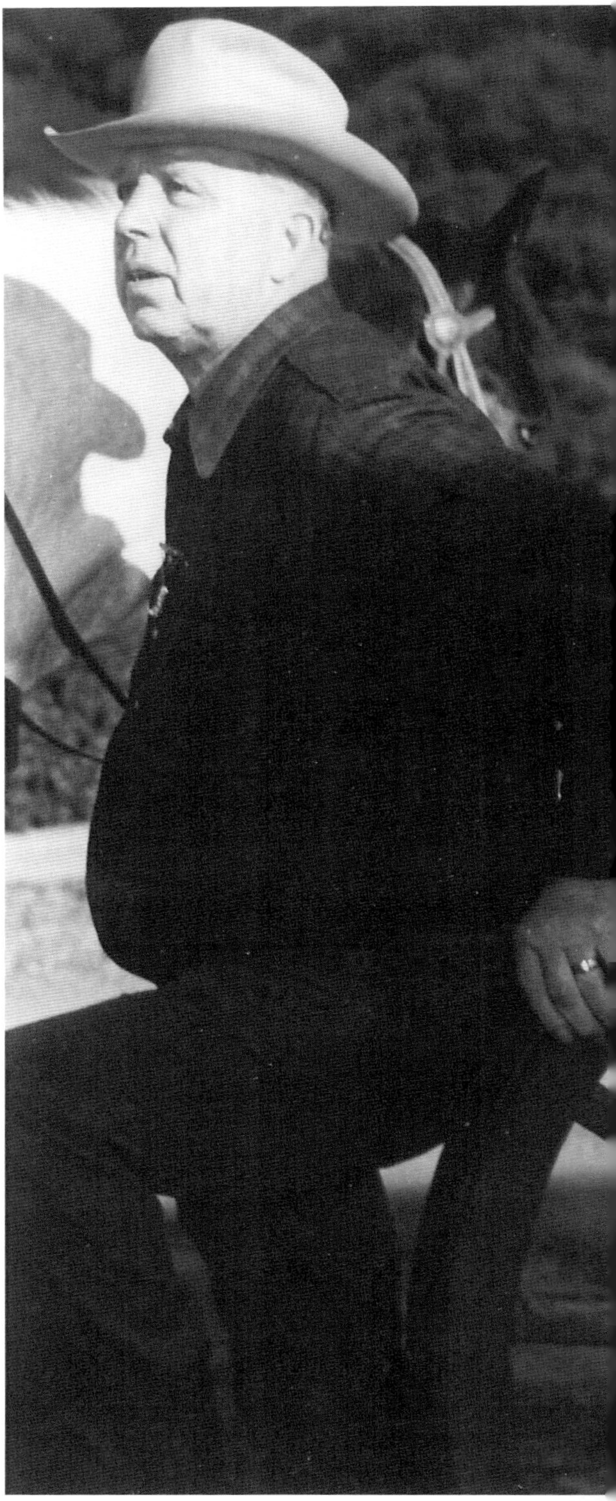

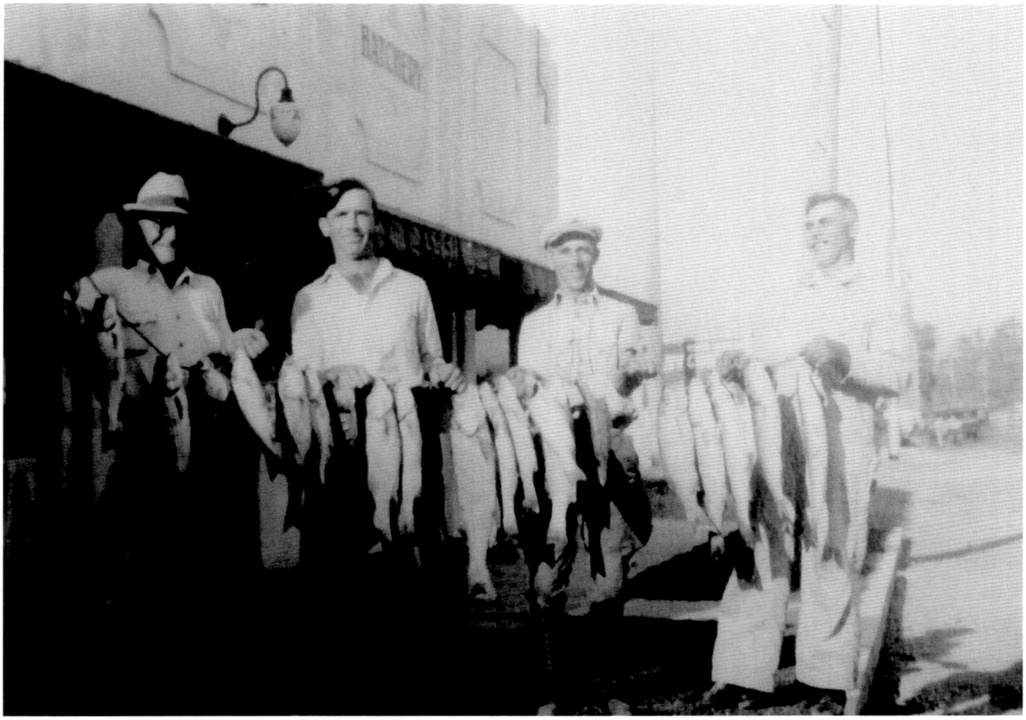

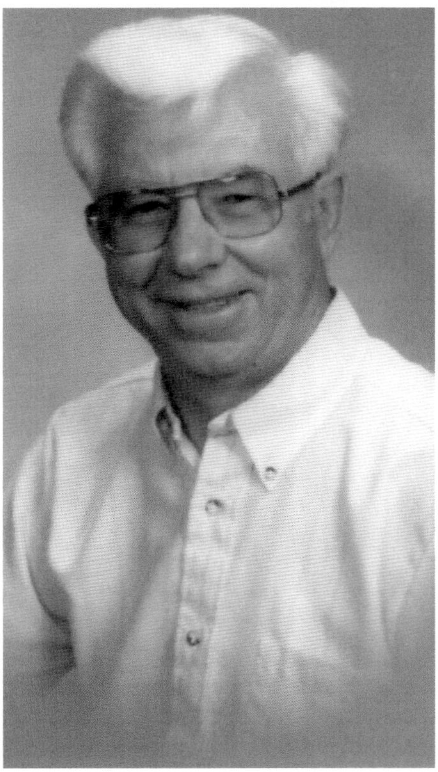

"We're Crowin' Cuz We're Growin'"

This was Castro Valley's slogan when it was known for chicken hatcheries. By 1925, the chicken population was 800,000, and the human population under 5,000. There were 12 poultry hatcheries and many chicken farms. Poultry ranches replaced farmland. Many tracks of land were divided into six-acre parcels. Castro Valley became known as the "Chicken Ranch of Alameda County." After World War II, the small landowners found it more profitable to eliminate all poultry production to sell or subdivide the land. In the 1920s, the Rio-Linda Hatchery was operated by Cyril Lorge and Jack and Ed Perry. The above photograph shows (from left to right) Ed, an unidentified friend, Cyril, and Pete Selmeczki in front of the hatchery after a fishing trip. In 1934, the name changed to the California State Hatchery. Cyril's sons Ray, pictured at left, and Jim eventually became owners of the hatchery, which was the last hatchery to close in Castro Valley. Today, it is the site of a business. (Both, courtesy of Lucille Lorge.)

Castro Valley Developer

Born in Oakland in 1913, Arnold Anderson and his family bought a chicken ranch in Castro Valley in 1922. After World War II, he partnered with his mother and brother in a real estate business. They set up a storefront along Castro Valley Boulevard. Across the street was a tomato patch. Arnold purchased this large chunk of property from Al Nunes and began to design and develop the Castro Village shopping center. The village has been the heart of the unincorporated valley ever since. The conceptual drawing for the shopping center can be seen in the background of this photograph. Arnold is the second man from the left. Arnold also pushed for street widening and sidewalk installation along Castro Valley Boulevard. He organized business owners and the Castro Valley Chamber of Commerce to better work with Alameda County. He also served on several boards, most notably the Bay Area Rapid Transit District Board for 16 years, and helped locate Eden Hospital in Castro Valley. Summing up his career Arnold said, "There was a lack of leadership in Castro Valley at this time, and I found myself getting into everything." Arnold helped forge Castro Valley's postwar identity. He passed away in 2012 at age 99.

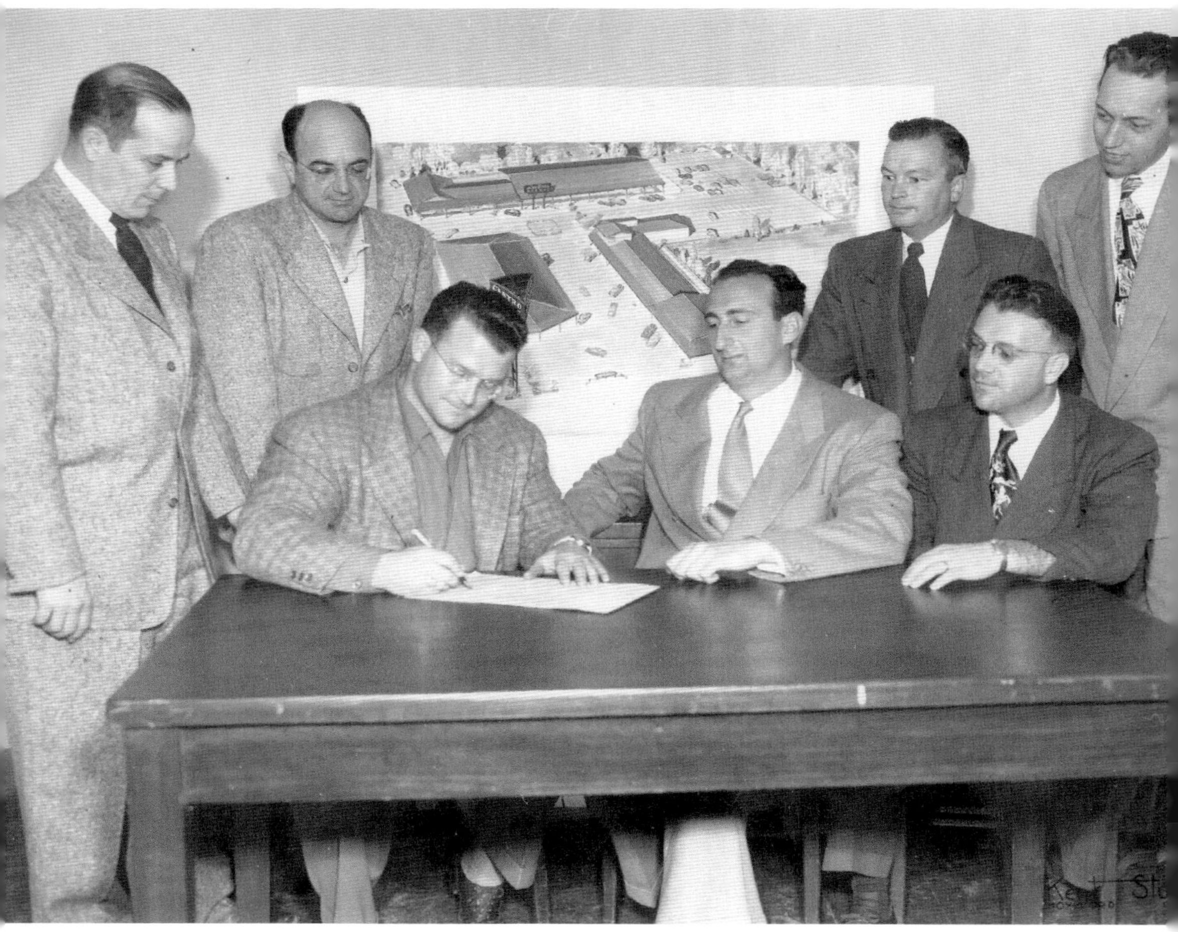

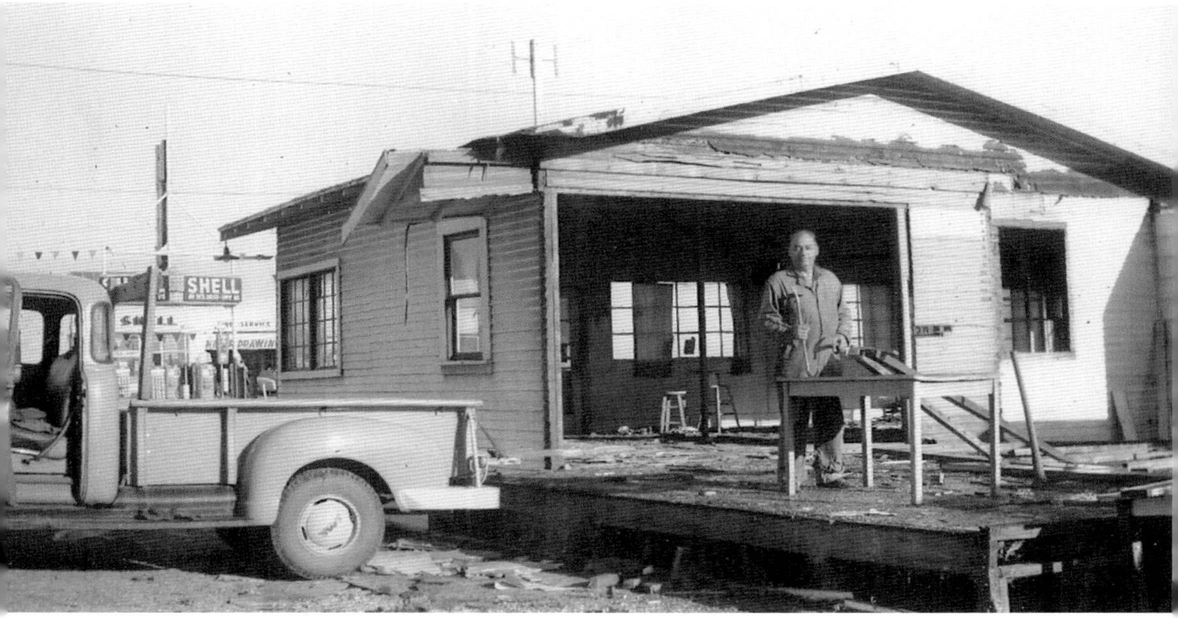

Castro Valley Farmer

Al Nunes grew up in Castro Valley in the early 20th century, at the time when there were only a handful of farming families in the area. He worked on his father's farm starting at a young age, attending only one year of high school. Like his father, Al also went into business threshing and harvesting the fields of farmers throughout the area. In Castro Valley, he continued to farm and owned property along Castro Valley Boulevard, including the land where Castro Village Shopping Center now sits. He remained in Castro Valley his entire life, witnessing the town's transformation from farmland into a bustling suburban community. In this photograph, Al is working on an addition to one of his properties on Castro Valley Boulevard.

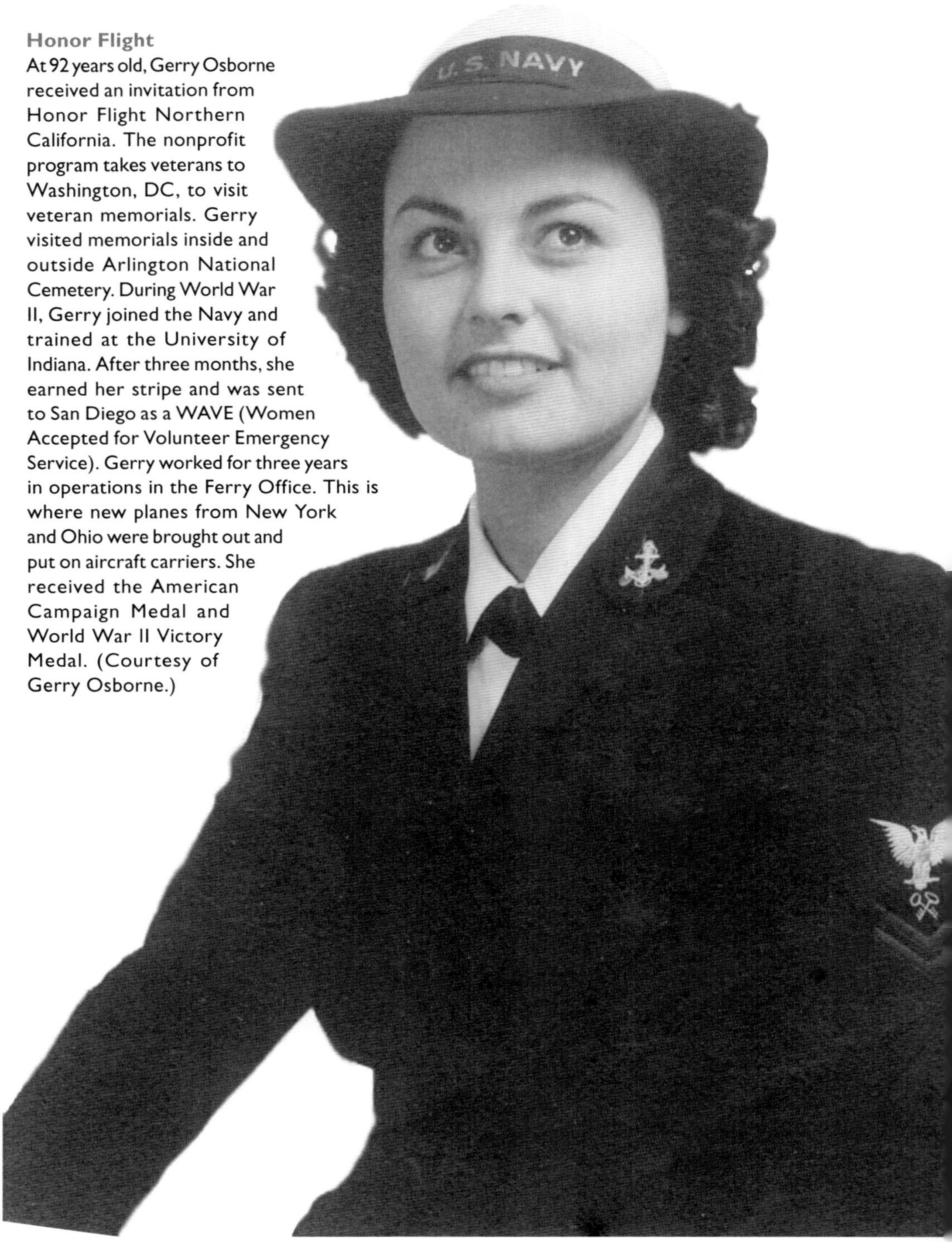

Honor Flight

At 92 years old, Gerry Osborne received an invitation from Honor Flight Northern California. The nonprofit program takes veterans to Washington, DC, to visit veteran memorials. Gerry visited memorials inside and outside Arlington National Cemetery. During World War II, Gerry joined the Navy and trained at the University of Indiana. After three months, she earned her stripe and was sent to San Diego as a WAVE (Women Accepted for Volunteer Emergency Service). Gerry worked for three years in operations in the Ferry Office. This is where new planes from New York and Ohio were brought out and put on aircraft carriers. She received the American Campaign Medal and World War II Victory Medal. (Courtesy of Gerry Osborne.)

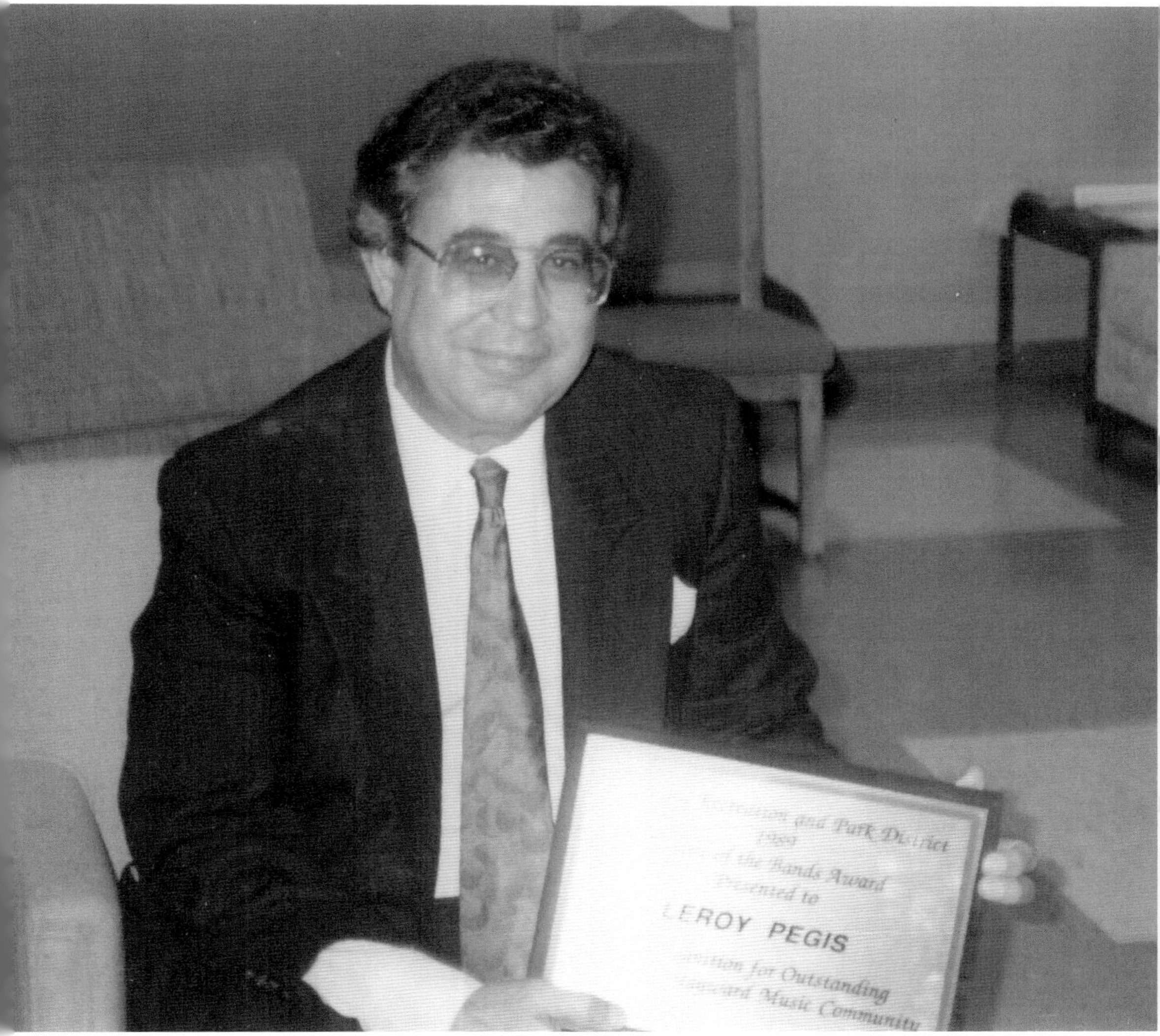

Battle of the Bands

LeRoy Pegis graduated from Hayward Union High School in 1955 and moved to Castro Valley when he married Dorothy Rubio. His love of music began when he played the drums for the Portuguese festivals. Later, he formed his group called the Escorts, a well-known dance band. After graduating college with a recreation degree, LeRoy began working at the Hayward Area Recreation and Park District as a playground leader. Soon, he became the teenage supervisor and originated the Hayward Area Recreation and Park District's "Battle of the Bands" in 1963. This competition for teenagers in bands is known throughout Northern California. LeRoy retired as the superintendent of recreation in 1989. Proud of his Portuguese heritage, he was a member of Irmandade do Divino Espirito Santo (IDES), Faro-Hayward Sister City Committee, and Centro Social M. Julio Martins Foundation. He will always be remembered for the Battle of the Bands. (Author's collection.)

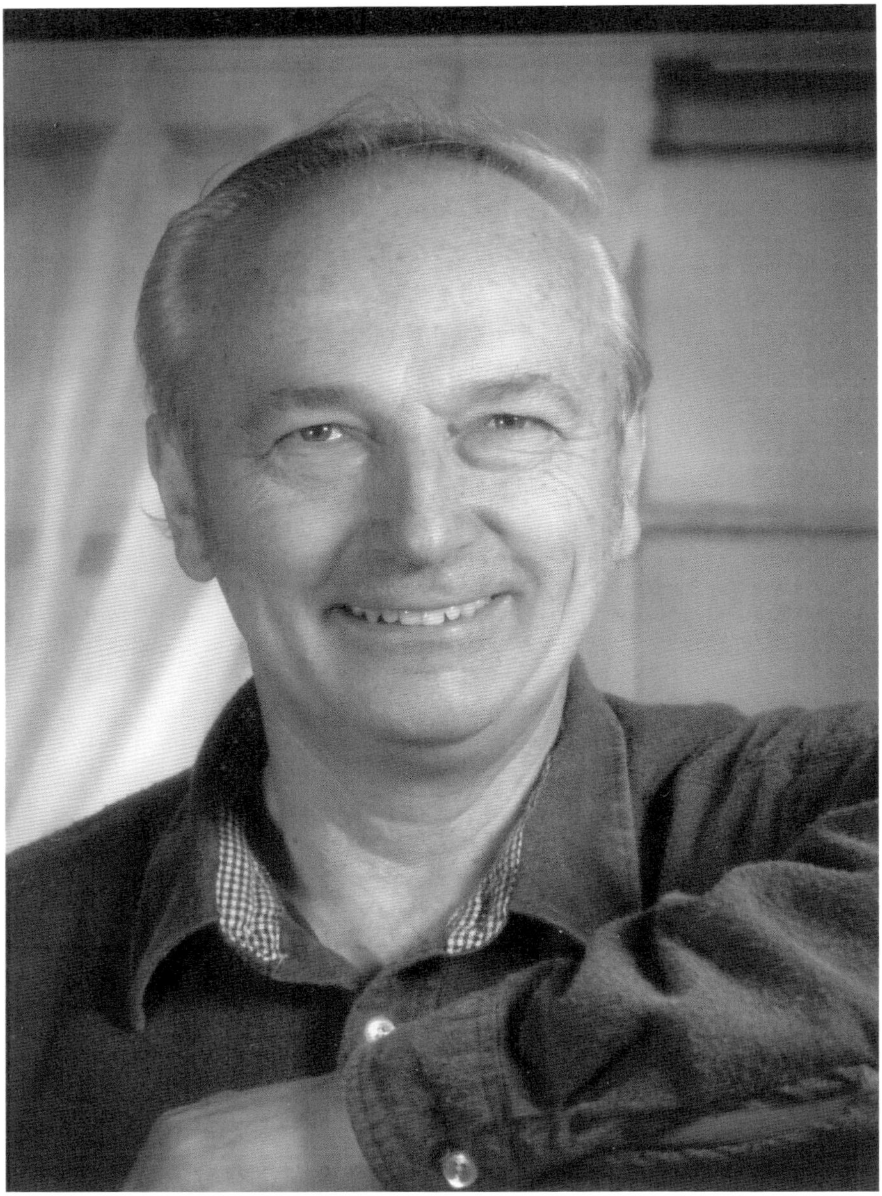

Games and Strength

Dale Harder, a retired educator, developed a new spelling game called "Smarty" because he was bored with the limitations of other commercial word games. The game contains two dice with vowels and four with consonants; players can also add letters. Another word game Dale developed uses letters he selects for the participants to make the longest noncapitalized word up to 18 letters using at least four of the letters for a score. As a retired math teacher, he has developed Frac Jack, Decimal Blackjack, and Math Blackjack. Dale is considered a leading authority on strength sports. He participates and writes articles for his "Strength and Speed Newsletter." With his hand dynamometer, he measures people's strength. In 2002, Dale entered the World's Scottish Highland Games and won in his age group. He has authored more than 60 books. (Courtesy of Dale Harder.)

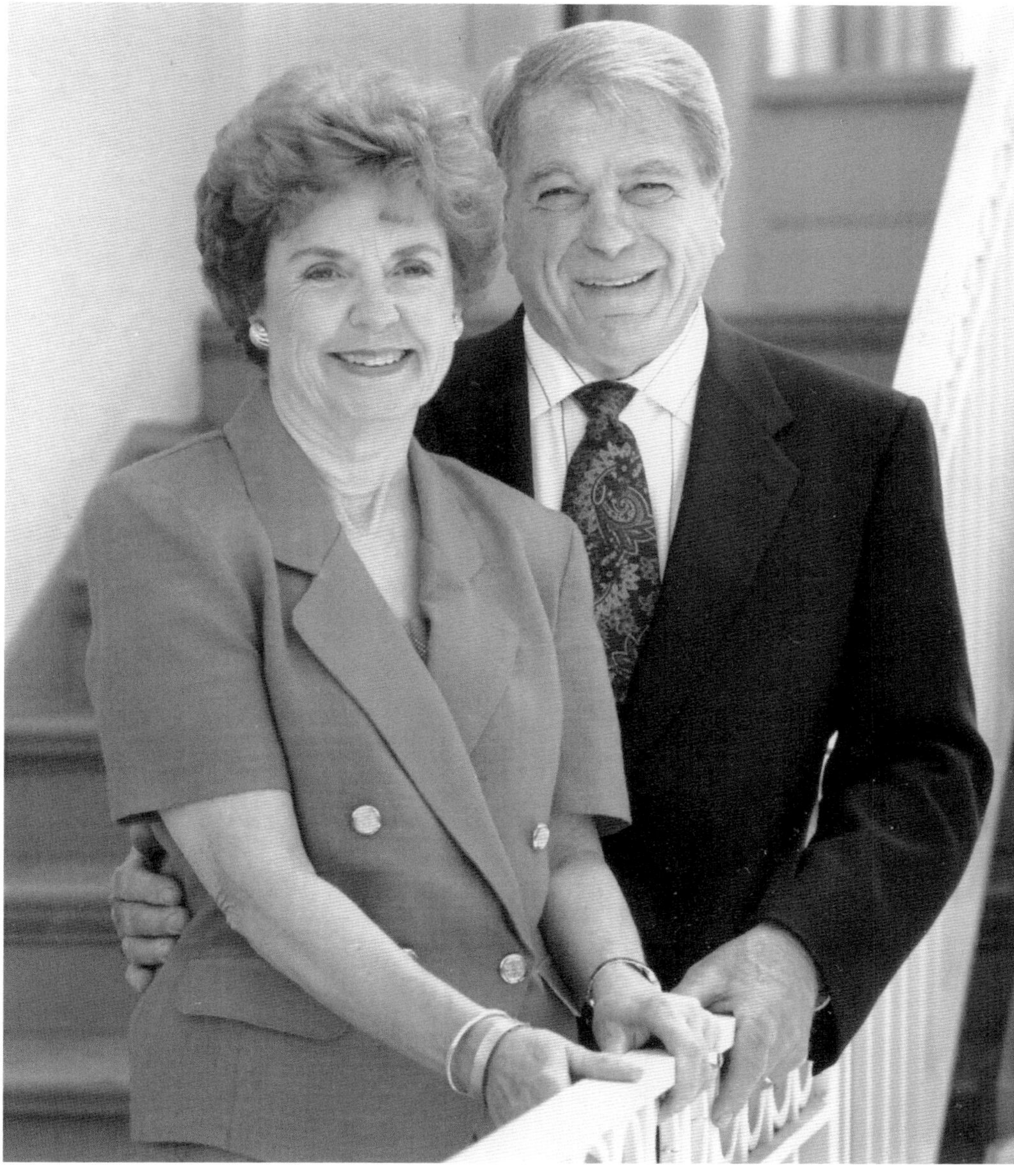

Private Enterprise Studies
Castro Valley residents Owen R. and Erma F. Smith have been entrepreneurs and business owners for 50 years. Grateful for the freedom to choose, they gave $1 million to California State University, East Bay, for establishing the Smith Center for Private Enterprise Studies to increase awareness and understanding of the principles of property rights, entrepreneurship, limited government, and free markets. The center sponsors lectures, research, seminars, conferences, and courses for future leaders to learn how the principles of free enterprise build a strong economy. Programs explore concepts of private property, voluntary exchange, economic and civil liberties, constitutional law, financial markets, entrepreneurship, and new venture management. The center has also sponsored high school essay contests, awarded prizes for outstanding entrepreneurs, and presented outstanding speakers of national prominence. (Courtesy of Erma Smith.)

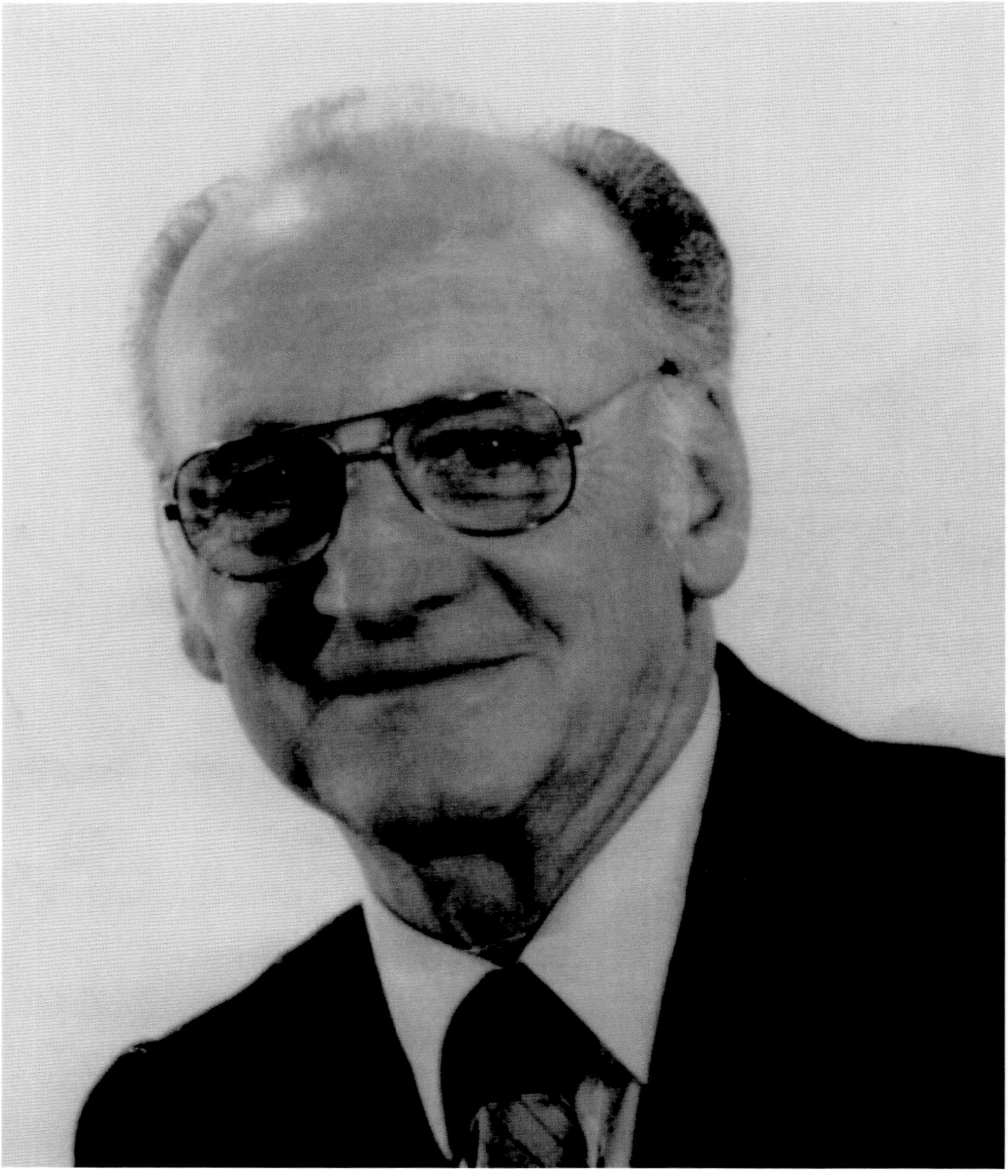

Retired Educator Volunteer

Leonard Hancock, born in 1923, participated in the Pals Program at Stanton Elementary School from 2003 until his death in 2012. Hancock and his granddaughter volunteered weekly in classrooms to help students who needed extra time to catch up on their schoolwork. Leonard graduated in 1941 from Fremont High School in Oakland. After serving in the Army Air Force during World War II, he attended the University of California, Berkeley, earning bachelor and master's degrees and a K-12 administration certificate. He spent 30 years in the San Lorenzo School District, first as a high school English teacher and then as the first principal of the San Lorenzo Adult School. His other community service included the Castro Valley School Advisory Council and annual Thanksgiving food program. He also was a volunteer in his church. (Author's collection.)

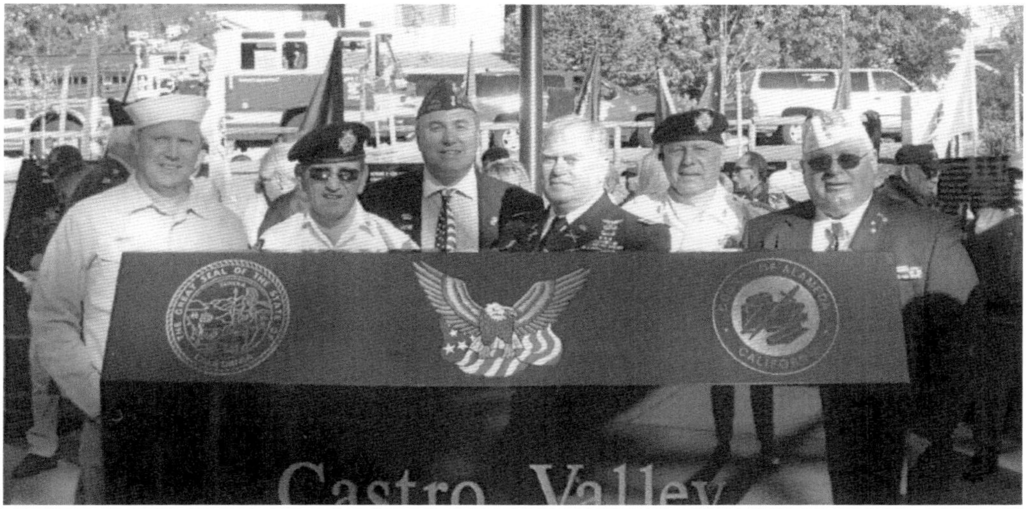

Salute To Veterans

Veterans of Foreign Wars Post No. 9601 initiated the construction of the Castro Valley Veterans Memorial, which opened in 2012. It was accomplished with the support and contributions of individuals, businesses, and organizations. Each branch of the military—Army, Air Force, Marines, Merchant Marine, Coast Guard, and Navy—has a granite monument inscribed with names of veterans. On the ground are paving stones inscribed with messages from individuals and organizations. The memorial has meaning to so many! (Courtesy of Michael Emerson.)

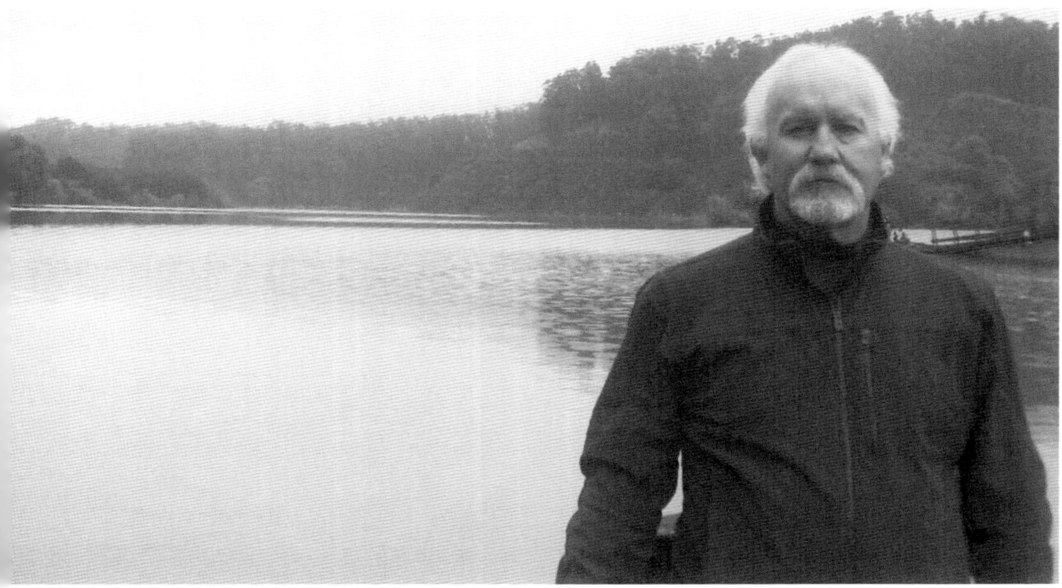

Champion of Parks and Recreation

Dennis Waespi spent 38 years as a ranger and firefighter with the East Bay Regional Park District. Elected to the Castro Valley Sanitary District Board of Directors in 1999, he promoted recycling and sustainability programs. He served on the Alameda County Parks, Recreation, and Historical Commission from 1999 until 2011 and was elected to the Hayward Area Recreation and Park District Board of Directors in 2008. (Courtesy of Dennis Waespi.)

Community Activist and Volunteer

Suzanne Barba and her family migrated to Castro Valley from Southern California 32 years ago, where she was a community activist. In Castro Valley, she continued her community activism and volunteered in the school district. Her first job was as a stringer for a section in the *Daily Review* newspaper that focused on Castro Valley. She received 25¢ per column inch for her articles. Next, she became the events coordinator for the Castro Valley Chamber of Commerce. In the 1980s, she worked as an administrative assistant at Eden Hospital. When she left for another job with Chabot College, she ran for the hospital board and was elected. That made Suzanne her old boss's boss because the chief executive officer reports to the board. She served on the board for 16 years. Even though Suzanne had full-time jobs, she kept up her community activism and was involved in three different unsuccessful attempts to convince Castro Valley voters to incorporate the town as a city. She also served on the Castro Valley General and Specific Plan Committee. In 2000, Suzanne retired from the Alameda County Office of Education after 14 years, where she managed the Teacher of the Year celebration, planned numerous educational events, and was liaison to the Alameda County School Boards Association. Suzanne has devoted many hours to the League of Women Voters as president, newsletter editor, and chaired numerous state and national league studies. She also gave many presentations on state propositions and chaired local educational programs. For 28 years, she has been a board member of the Hispanic Community Affairs Council, which has given more than $1 million in scholarships to more than 800 students in Alameda County. In 2012, Suzanne began tutoring a group of adults to improve their reading and writing skills to assist with career and citizenship goals. She serves on the Alameda County Measure A Oversight Committee and on the Chabot-Los Positas Community College Oversight Committee. In 2010 and 2011, she served on the Alameda County Grand Jury. (Courtesy of Suzanne Barba.)

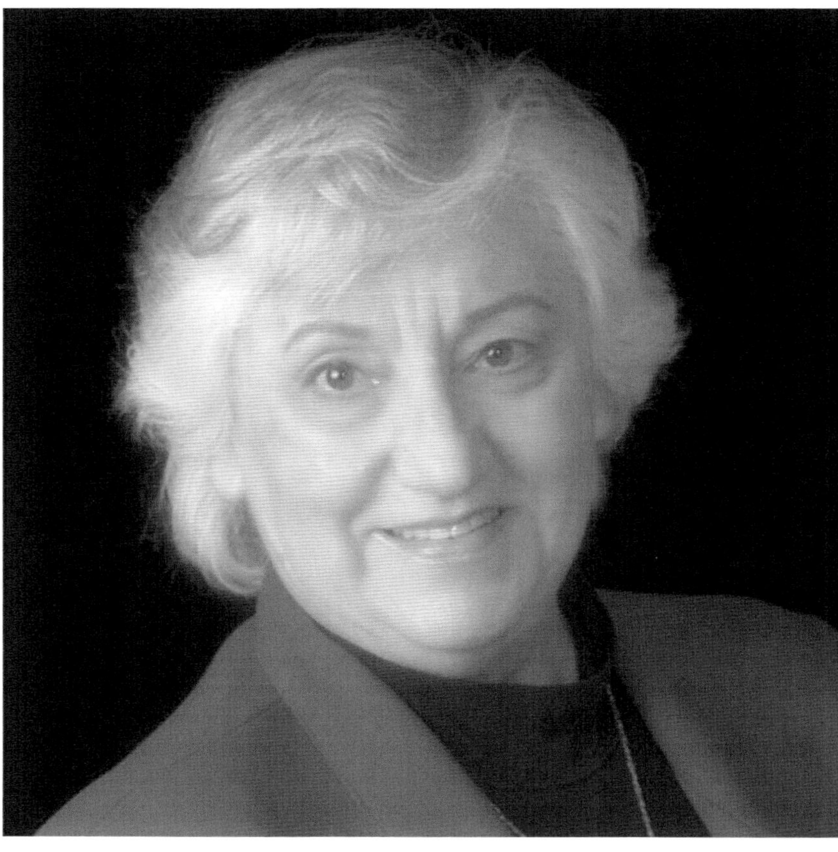

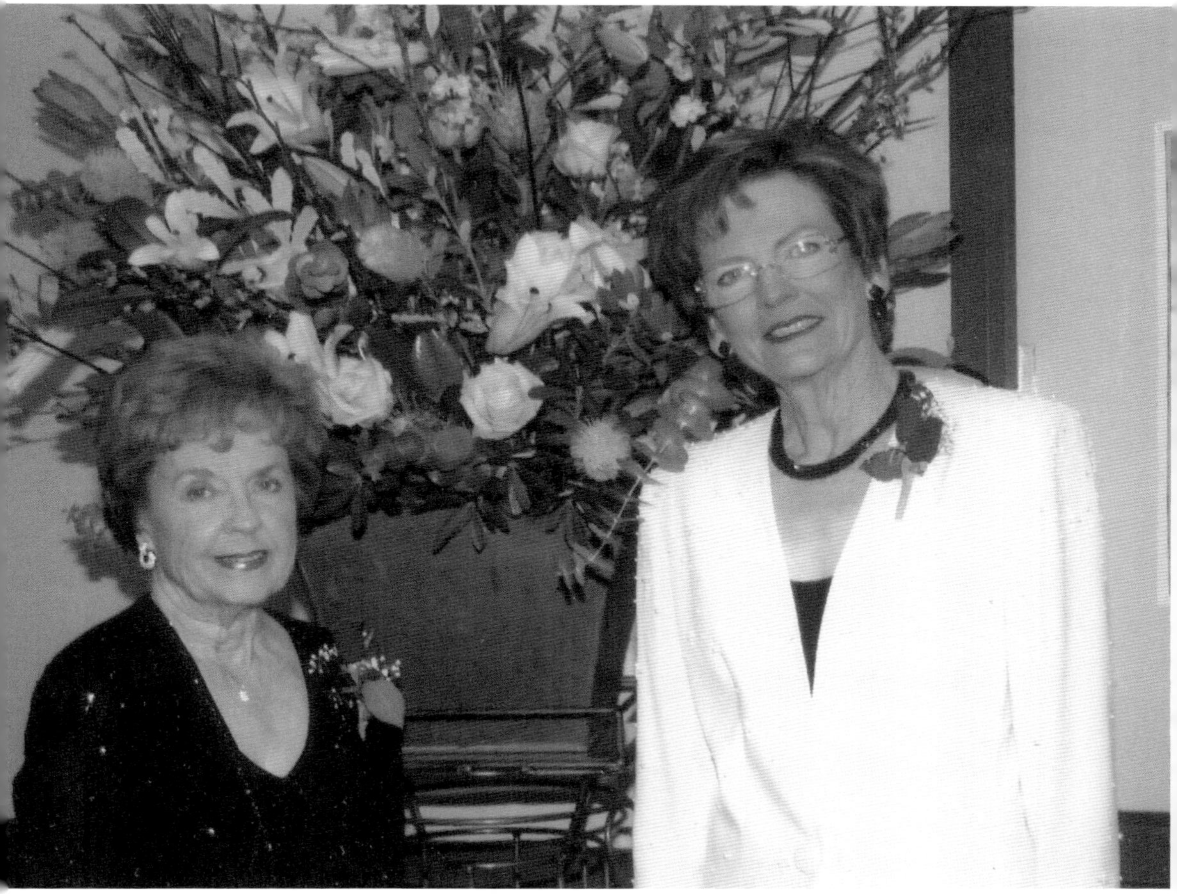

Center for the Arts

The Castro Valley community's dream to establish a Center for the Arts was promoted and kept alive by Erma Smith (right) and Terry Liebowitz (left). With the partnership between the school district and community, the center opened in 2006 on the Castro Valley High School campus. Erma and Terry organized many successful fundraisers for the center support and spearheaded the establishment of the Castro Valley Arts Foundation. The Foundation helps fund operations, provides additional equipment, sponsors productions, oversees a group of volunteers and box office staff, and arranges art exhibits. It also provides students and the community with artistic experiences that educate, enrich, and entertain by securing resources for the center. Erma and Owen Smith and her family gave $500,000 to start a permanent endowment to support the center. The Smith Theater was named in memory of Erma's parents. (Courtesy of Erma Smith.)

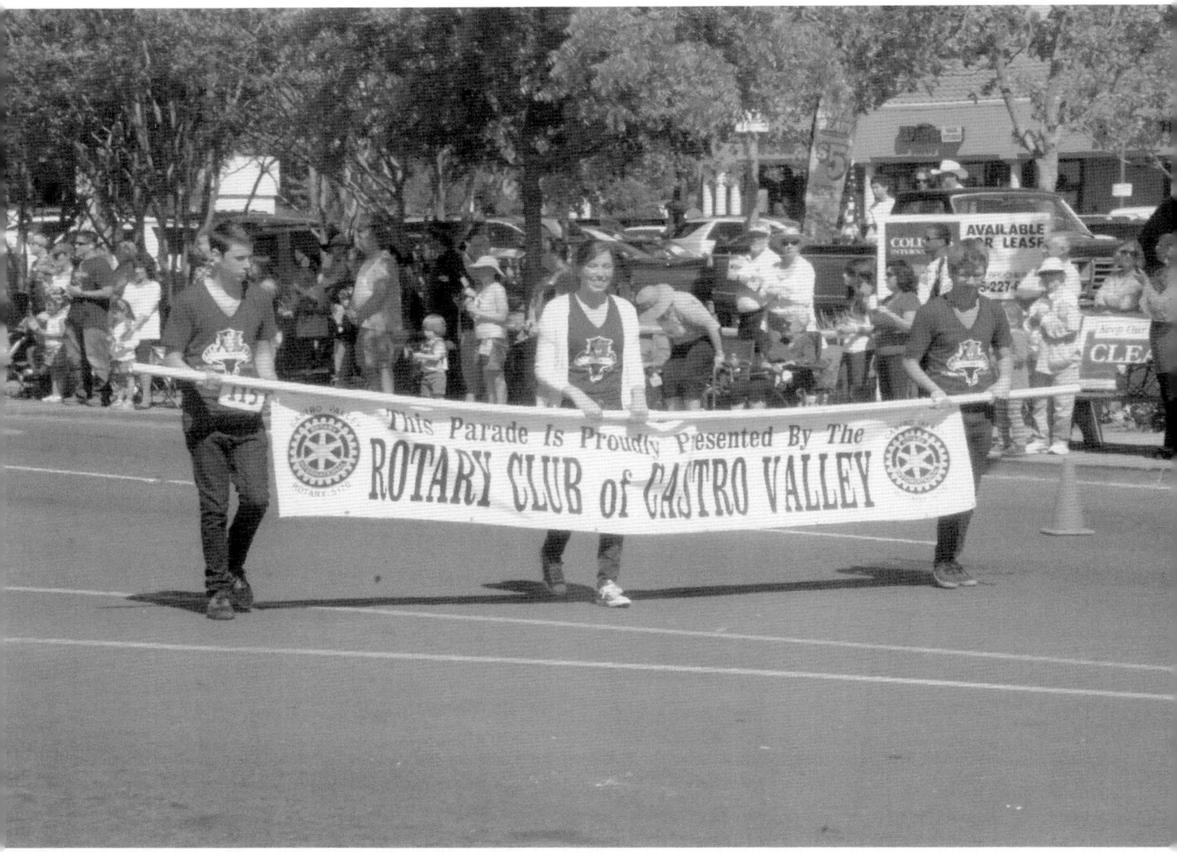

Rotary Club of Castro Valley

Since 1953, Castro Valley Rotarians have been putting the Rotary International's motto "Service Above Self" into action. Rotary is a network of people, more than one million worldwide, that get together to exchange ideas, grow their businesses, and make new friends. They volunteer to help their communities. Annually, Castro Valley Rotarians put on events that bring the town together like the Castro Valley Chili Cook Off, the Rowell Ranch Rodeo Parade (pictured), the Valley Blues Festival, and many more. These fundraisers are fun, and they help the Rotary Club of Castro Valley provide grants to other community groups and sponsor local students through scholarships. (Courtesy of Steve Ontiveros.)

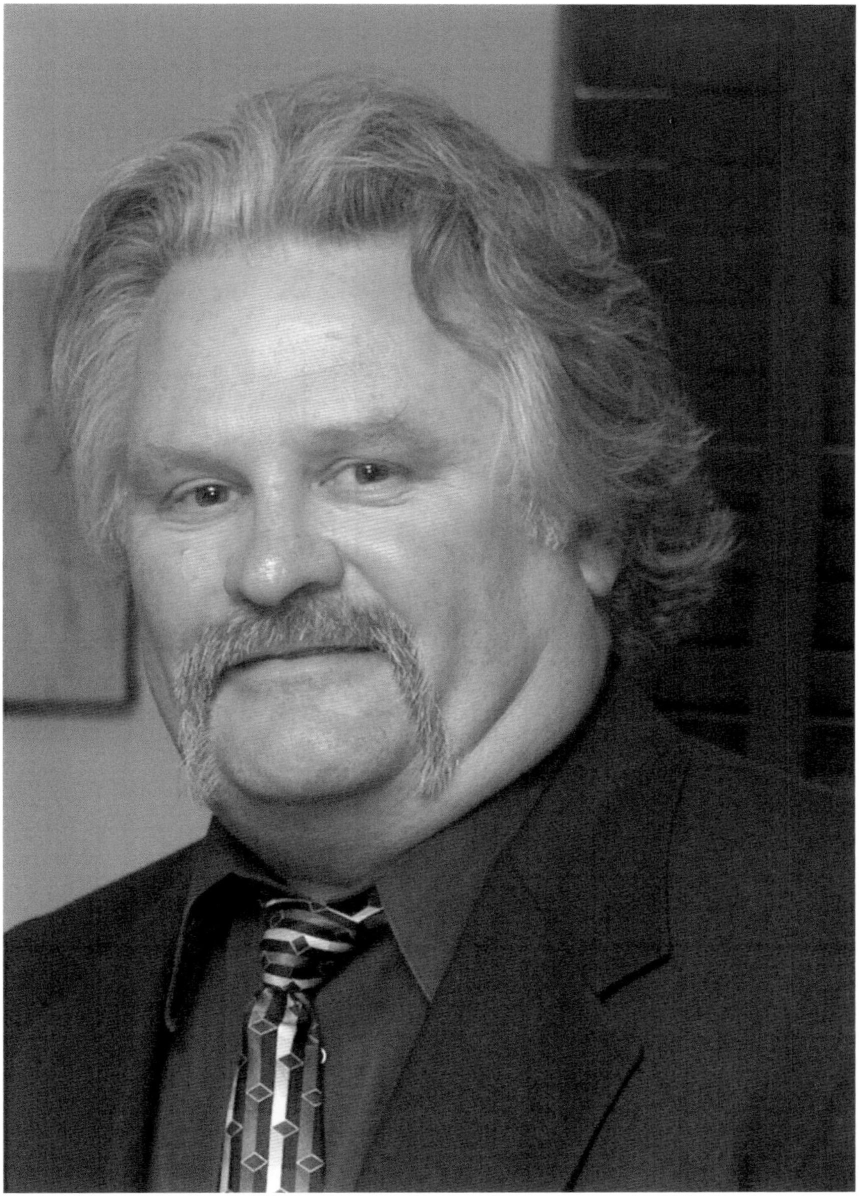

Mr. Castro Valley
Brian Morrison was born in Oakland but has spent his entire life within the unincorporated Hayward area communities. Brian has taken a keen interest in the welfare of Castro Valley. He has served on multiple boards and committees ranging from the Castro Valley Chamber of Commerce to the Boys & Girls Club of Castro Valley. In 1990, Brian started his own heating, ventilation, and air-conditioning (HVAC) and contracting business. He chose the site of the Nesbitt Feed Store in old town Castro Valley and rehabilitated the space. He won a Historic Preservation Award for his work on the building from the Hayward Area Historical Society. Brian has also been active in the politics of the area. In 2002, he ran for Castro Valley City Council and won a seat; however, the Castro Valley incorporation measure failed. Although it was a symbolic victory, it demonstrated the high regard many residents hold for Brian.

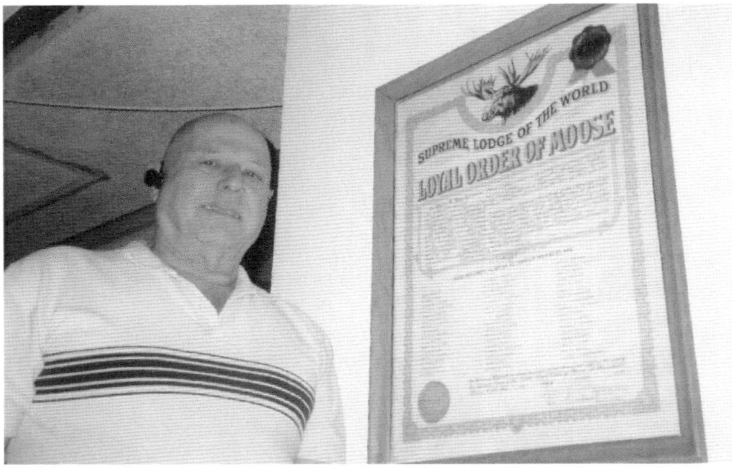

Moose Lodge

In March 1948, the Moose Lodge began in Hayward. When it moved to Castro Valley and purchased a building, it became the Hayward Castro Valley Moose Lodge No. 1491. Robert "Bob" Pirone (pictured) is currently the administrator of this nonprofit fraternal organization, open to men and women. He was previously the governor. The officers are elected every year. There are 776 members, which includes 175 women. The organization is dedicated to bringing individuals from various communities together through meetings, events, and charity services on a worldwide basis. They give scholarships to high school seniors and sponsor benefits, family events, and Bingo. The Boy Scouts, 4-H, Home School Groups, VFW, American Legion, Buon Tempo, Garden Club, and others use their facility. Moose Lodge International support Moose Heart for children and Moose Haven in Florida for retired members. (Author's collection.)

Women's Club

In December 1948, a group of Castro Valley women got together to establish the Castro Valley Women's Club. No one woman lead the movement, but pictured are some of the club's first officers. From left to right are Barbara Russell, Betty Eads, Ruth Dingman, and Helen Fowler, the first club president. The club was devoted to programs involving philanthropy, drama, art, and gardening. The tradition continues today with scholarships to local students and donations to causes like Operation Smile. (Courtesy of Charlotte Lusschen.)

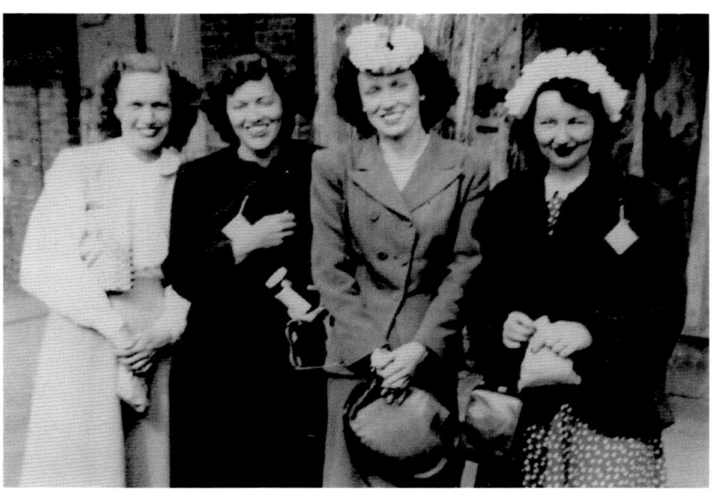

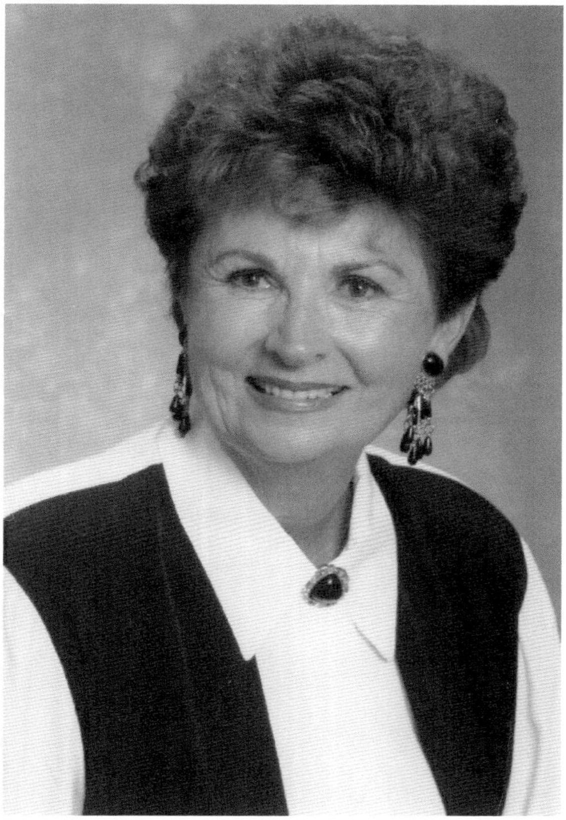

Community Historian

Lucille Thomford Lorge was born and raised in the house her father built in 1924 on the former William Meek property in Cherryland. She attended local schools, married Ray Lorge, and has lived in Castro Valley ever since, as have her three children. Ray was part owner of the California State Hatchery, which opened in 1934, when Castro Valley was the second largest egg-producing area. Her great-grandfather Henry Thomford opened the Castro Valley Exchange. Today, Trader Joe's is located on the same corner where Lucille placed photographs of old Castro Valley on their hallway walls and local farmers donated farm equipment to display. In 1985, Lucille realized no one was collecting the old photographs and stories of Castro Valley, so she collected over 200 photographs, which she copied into slides for presentations to schoolchildren and local organizations. Local history became her passion. Lucille coauthored Images of America: *Castro Valley*. When the new library was going to be built, she thought a local history section should be added, so she mailed more than 200 letters asking for donations and received over $21,000. A display case and changing television slide show are now part of the library. Lucille was on the Hayward Area Historical Society Board for many years. As the McConaghy House director from 1975 until 2010, she opened a store in the house and a store at the Hayward Area Historical Society Museum. Lucille has received many awards. They include Project Eden, Castro Valley Rotary Club's Paul Harris Award, Hayward Lions Club's Distinguished Citizen of the Year, Hayward Area Historical Society's John Sandoval Award, Castro Valley Business Person of the Year, Hayward Area Recreation and Park District's 2006 Award, Alameda Fire Commissions Award for 17 years of service on the board, and she was the Rowell Rodeo Parade marshal. Lucille said, "The greatest award of all has been the joy of doing something of service that you truly enjoy." Her additional community involvement has been with Parent-Teacher Association (PTA), Chabot Swim Club, Girl Scout leader, church schoolteacher, Jobs Daughters Council, Eden Hospital Foundation Fundraiser, Hill and Valley Women's Club, Fairmont Animal Shelter, and Questers. (Courtesy of Lucille Lorge.)

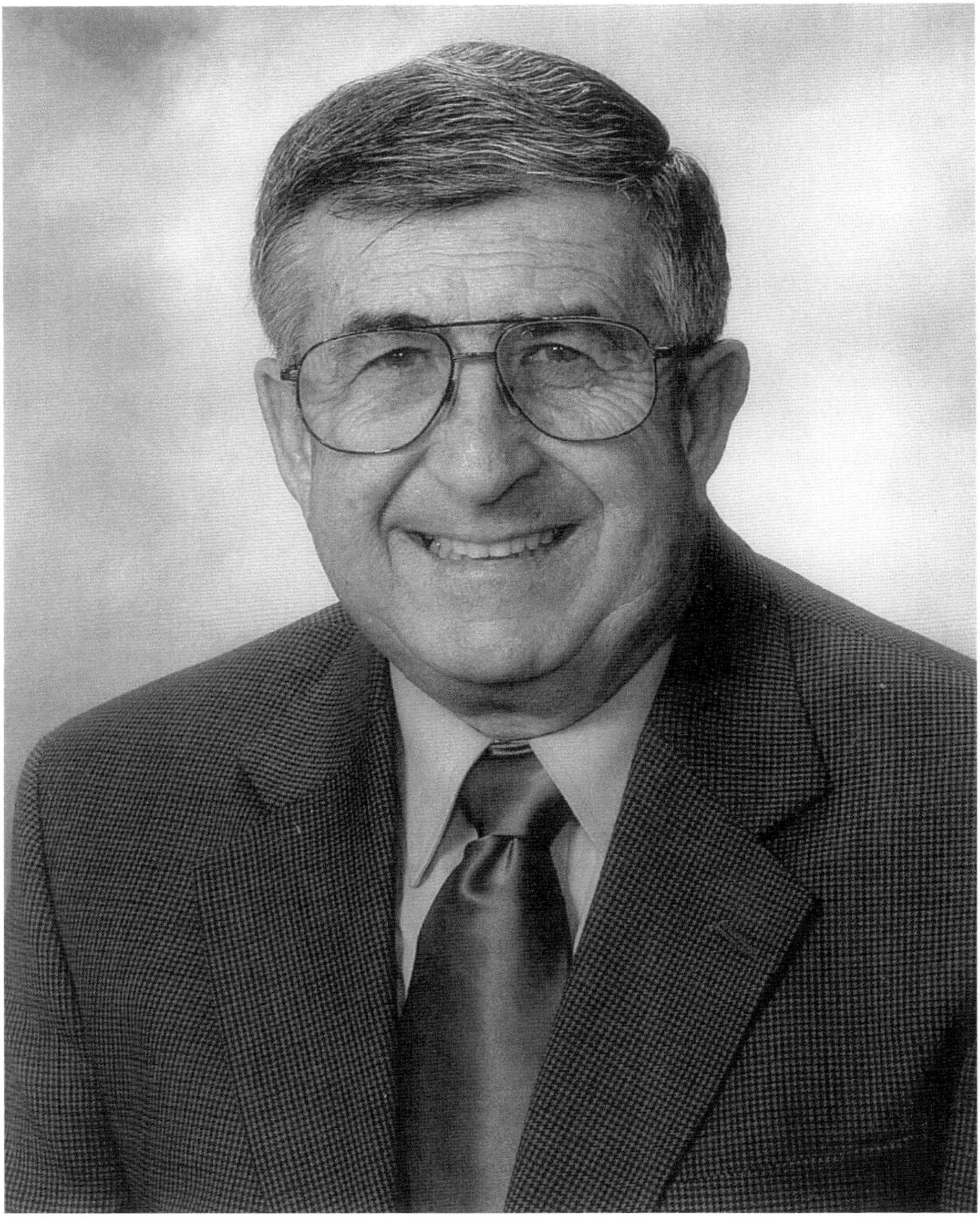

Community Involvement
Harry Francis, a Castro Valley resident, served for 17 years on the Castro Valley Sanitary Board of Directors and 14 years as a commissioner on the East Bay Dischargers Authority Board until his death in 2013. Harry was an Alameda County fire commissioner, a member of the Hayward Area Recreation and Park District Board, Hayward Rotary, and the Young Men's Institute at the Catholic church. He was also a commissioner and player for the Hayward Area Recreation and Park District Senior Baseball League. As a small business owner, Harry served his community for half a century. (Courtesy of Maryann Francis.)

CHAPTER TWO

Hayward

While Don Guillermo Castro owned the entire area that composes the towns of Castro Valley, San Lorenzo, and Hayward, the city where his home was actually located is not named for him. The city of Hayward is named for William Hayward, a gold miner who squatted on Guillermo's land, befriended the landowner, and eventually purchased prime real estate from him, which would become downtown Hayward. On that land, William built a hotel, a city landmark for decades, around which the city grew. He picked a good spot because Hayward sat at a transportation crossroads with a good climate and fertile land.

Others saw the opportunities in Hayward, too. Immigrants from Portugal, Germany, Denmark, and East Coast states began settling in Hayward. They each found their niche. John Johnson, from Germany, noticed that salt accumulated naturally on the Hayward shoreline, so he established a salt-harvesting operation. The demand for salt in metropolitan San Francisco brought him huge profits. The Oliver family, whose patriarch came from Sweden, followed in the footsteps of Johnson and perfected solar salt harvesting along the shoreline. Harvey Rice from New York bought a house in downtown and noticed there was a need for good harvesting equipment. He invented a straw-burning harvester that he manufactured and sold for a short time in town. Portuguese immigrant F.I. Lemos came to Hayward because he knew of other Portuguese people who had settled in town. He learned English working for a Hayward attorney and, within a few years of immigrating, passed the bar and began practicing law. He was the most prominent of the city's attorneys in the early days.

The city grew throughout the late 19th and into the early 20th centuries not only because of its location but also because of its productive land. Farmers in the area grew everything from apricots and tomatoes to currants, peas, and sugar beets. The bounty available in the area brought the Hunt brothers to Hayward to establish a cannery. Hunt Brothers Cannery employed Hayward area residents and bought local produce for over 80 years. The smell of cooking tomatoes was as much a part of Hayward at one time as Hayward's Hotel.

Hayward was a place where individuality and hard work were admired. Artists such as Otto Emerson, a trained impressionist painter and photographer, established his home here. Otto's passion for art was equaled by his interest in the natural environment and birds, which he often incorporated into his art. He built a reputation as an amateur ornithologist. Other people found success in Hayward by working hard. One such individual was William Fletcher, one of a very few African Americans to operate a successful business in Hayward from the late 1930s through the 1950s. In the face of discrimination and economic trials, William established a solid reputation for himself as one of the best mechanics in the area.

Probably the most unique individual to find a safe haven in Hayward was Agapius Honcharenko, a political exile and an Orthodox priest from the Ukraine. He built a modest home in the Hayward hills and raised a small amount of produce to sell. He used a cave near his home for the occasional mass. His life experience coupled with his political views made him an interesting person to know, and many Hayward residents befriended him.

Hayward has benefited greatly from the work of businessmen, politicians, and educators alike. Each individual has worked to make Hayward a better place to live. Businessmen like E. Guy Warren helped persuade the state university system to establish a state college in Hayward, and contractor Resti Zaballos helped in building many municipal buildings around the city, including schools. Politicians such as longtime city councilman Matt Jimenez and current mayor Michael Sweeney—both products of the local school systems—worked tirelessly to improve Hayward because they loved the city and its people. Educators such as Anthony Ochoa, the son of Mexican immigrants, and Nels Nelson, a Norwegian immigrant, taught in Hayward high schools before becoming administrators. Thousands of Hayward students received splendid educations under both men's leadership.

There are countless individuals and organizations that work in many different ways to help the city and its residents. Organizations such as the 100-year-old Hill and Valley Club raise money for scholarships and community projects. Individuals like Banning Fenton and John Sandoval devoted their retirement to educating people about the history of Hayward, showing residents where we have been to better understand where we are today. Some people might help a smaller group of people but have no less of an impact, such as David Kolm, who preserves photographs for senior citizens.

Hayward's legendary locals are an inspiring group of people who helped and continue to help make Hayward the vibrant community it is today.

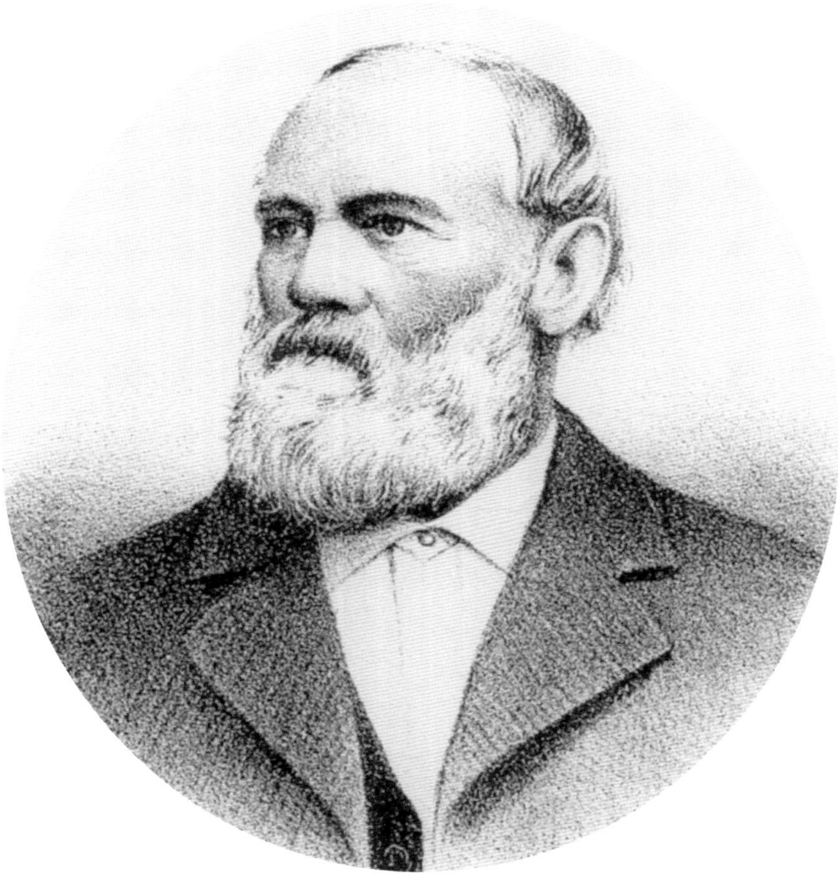

Hayward's, Haywood, Haywards, Hayward

William Hayward, born in Hopkinton, Massachusetts, in 1815, lived on the family farm until 1836, when he moved to Georgetown, Massachusetts, and became a mill-hand in a shoe factory. He married, and soon after his daughter was born, his first wife died. Nine years later, news of the California gold rush reached the east. William left his daughter with relatives and sailed to San Francisco in 1849. Not successful finding gold in the Sacramento area, he worked harvesting hay and tried to homestead on Guillermo Castro's land. After working and saving money, he purchased land from Castro in the area that is now Main and A Streets in downtown Hayward and set up a tent store in 1852. As his business prospered, he built a hotel-tavern that became very popular and was known as Hayward's Hotel. In 1866, William married Rachel Bedford, who had one daughter. He sent for his daughter from Massachusetts to live with them. The Haywards had one son. William was active in community affairs, church, military companies, and the fire department. He was an Alameda County supervisor from Eden Township and was elected justice of the peace. So why was the city named after him? In 1856, William was appointed the town's first postmaster. The mailbags were delivered to "Hayward's place" and the community became informally known as Hayward's. The US Postal Department did not permit a post office named after a living person, so community leaders suggested the name be changed to Haywood, which remained for almost 10 years. In 1876, when the California legislature chartered the town, the US Postal Department approved the name of Haywards without the apostrophe. In 1911, the town officially became Hayward. William died in 1891 at the age of 76 and his wife in 1917. Hayward's Hotel burned down in 1923, leaving only the entire city itself as a lasting tribute to its first American settler.

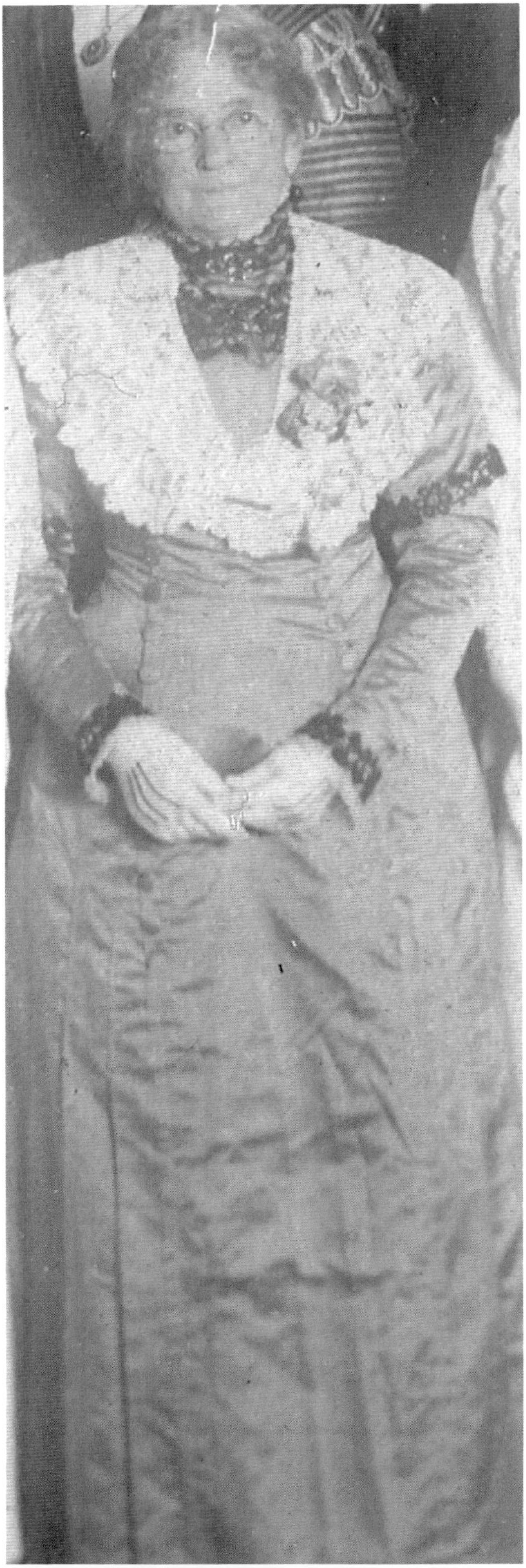

The Mother of Hayward

As the wife of William Hayward, Rachel was referred to as the "Mother of Hayward" for her work in the growing town. She ran Hayward's Hotel, the main attraction in town, from the time of her marriage in 1866 until her retirement. The hotel had great accommodations and food. It was the destination for many community celebrations. Under Rachel's management, the hotel shaped the perception of Hayward as a resort town. Rachel was also a member of local organizations, such as the Rebekah Lodge, Hill and Valley Club, and Farm Bureau. She was well known by the people of Hayward and held in high regard. When Rachel died in 1917, a local newspaper editor said, "To have known Mrs. Hayward was a rare privilege, and many there are who came in touch with her charming personality."

"Hayward Is Good Enough for Me" (OPPOSITE PAGE)

This line is from a poem about the area written by Harvey Rice. He was one of Hayward's pioneers who came to California from New York in 1852 when he was 20 years old. In 1853, he worked on a farm and later bought land from William Hayward to build his home and workshop. Harvey invented a type of steam engine that ran on burning straw to drive a thresher. When he acquired a patent in 1874, he moved the manufacturing to a larger location in San Francisco. In 1864, he was appointed one of Hayward's first school trustees. He was also on the founding board that established Lone Tree Cemetery, where he is buried. His cemetery deed was No. 1.

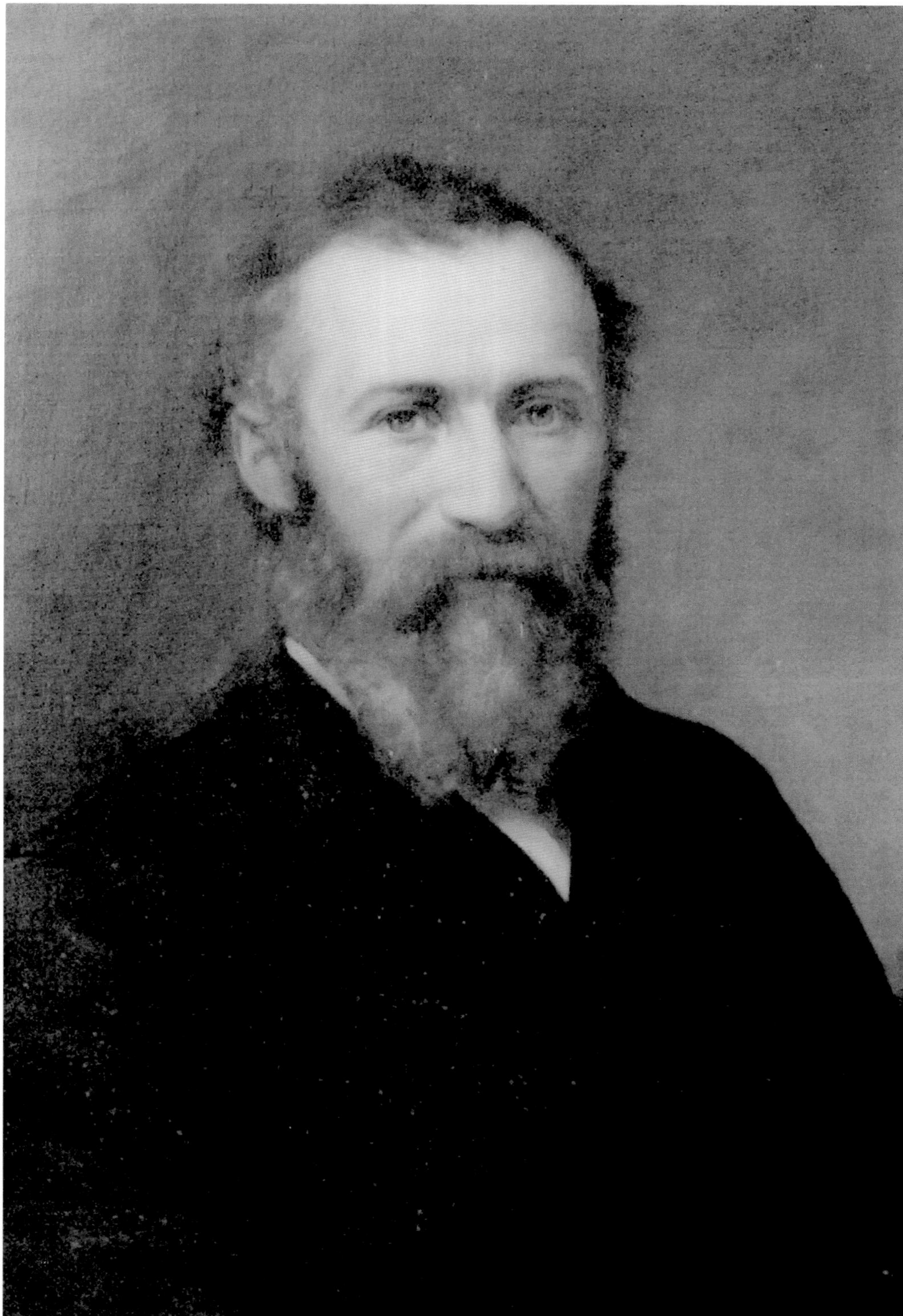

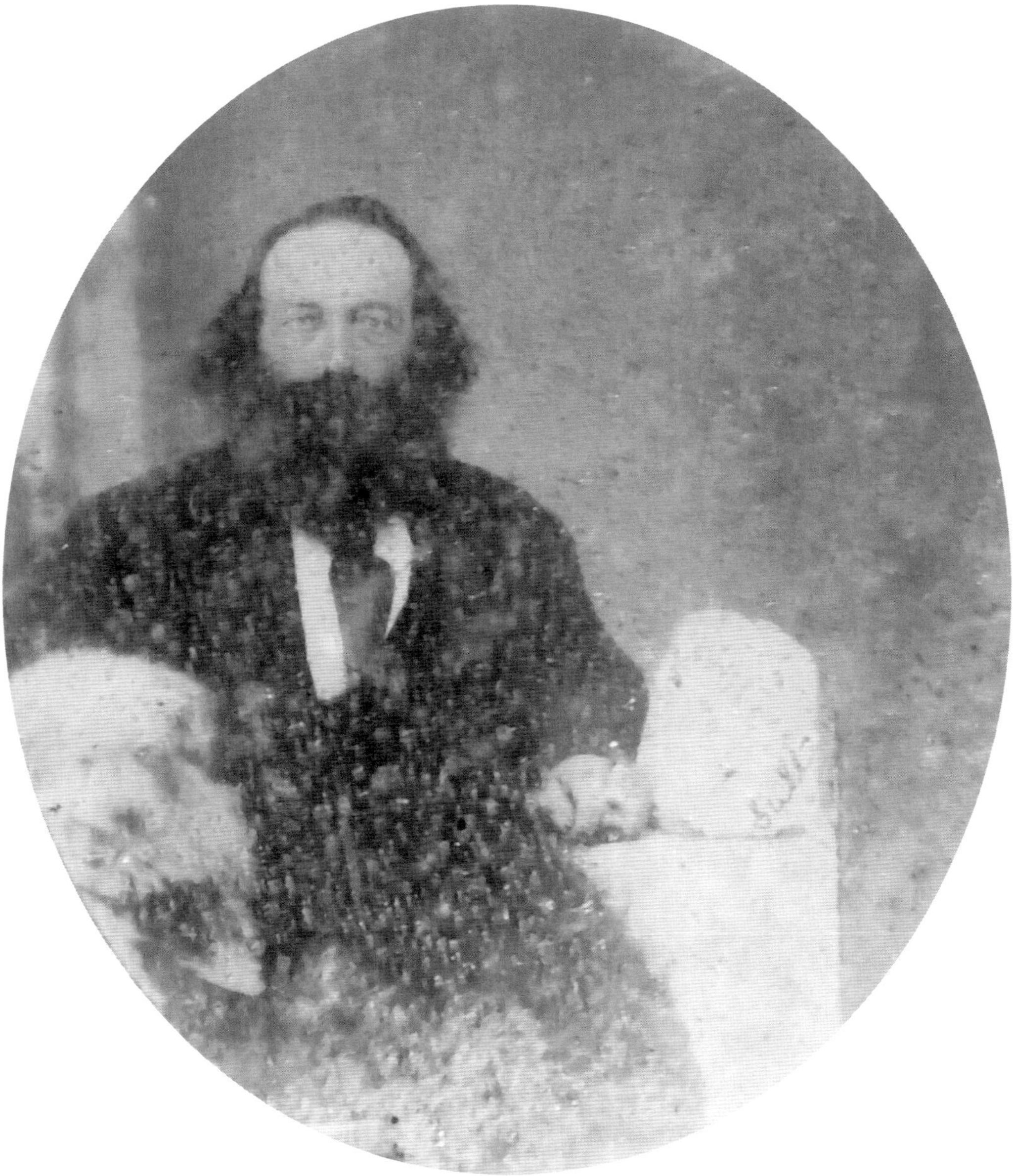

Salt Pioneer
In 1852, a German immigrant named John Johnson took the first step toward commercial salt harvesting along the East Bay shoreline. He built a series of dikes and levees that collected the salty water into manageable ponds. As the sun evaporated the water, it left behind what John had been after—salt, and lots of it. His first commercial harvests in 1854 yielded 25 tons. The salt was shipped from a wharf known as Johnson's Landing. John shipped not only salt but also other farm products from the landing, which was located less than a mile north of where the San Mateo Bridge stands today. John's method of solar evaporation proved a success, and soon, others would follow John's lead and begin commercial salt harvesting along the Hayward shoreline. This photograph shows Johnson with his pet dog and a block of salt.

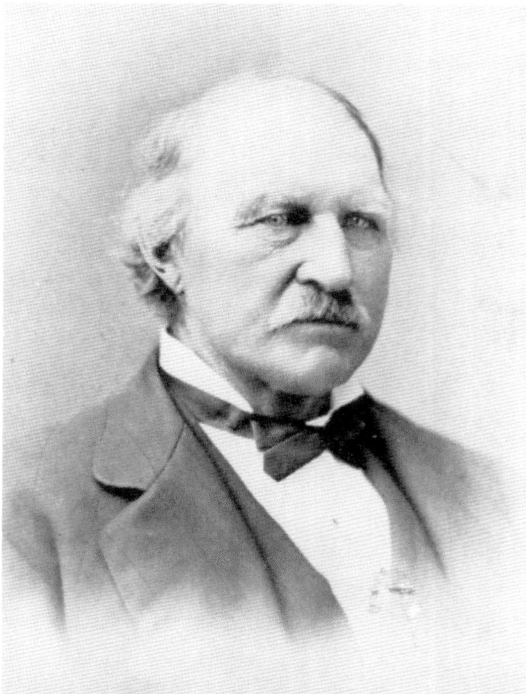

Mohr Estate

Cornelius Mohr, seen at left, came to San Francisco in 1852 aboard a whaling vessel. By 1856, he had acquired enough money to purchase his own land in the Mount Eden area. He raised wheat, barley, horses, and cattle. In 1876, he built a grand home for his family on Hesperian Boulevard, pictured below. His youngest son, William, inherited the family home and surrounding 230 acres. William had many interests including hybridizing flowers, especially iris. Several varieties of iris are named after him. He and his wife, Alfreda, were killed in a tragic accident in 1923, leaving behind their only child Marian. Marian attended the University of California, Berkeley, and married Jeryl Fry in 1935. Jeryl took over management of the farm. In 1961, Chabot College acquired 271 acres of the Mohr property to build the college. Nine acres are all that remain around the historic Mohr Estate today.

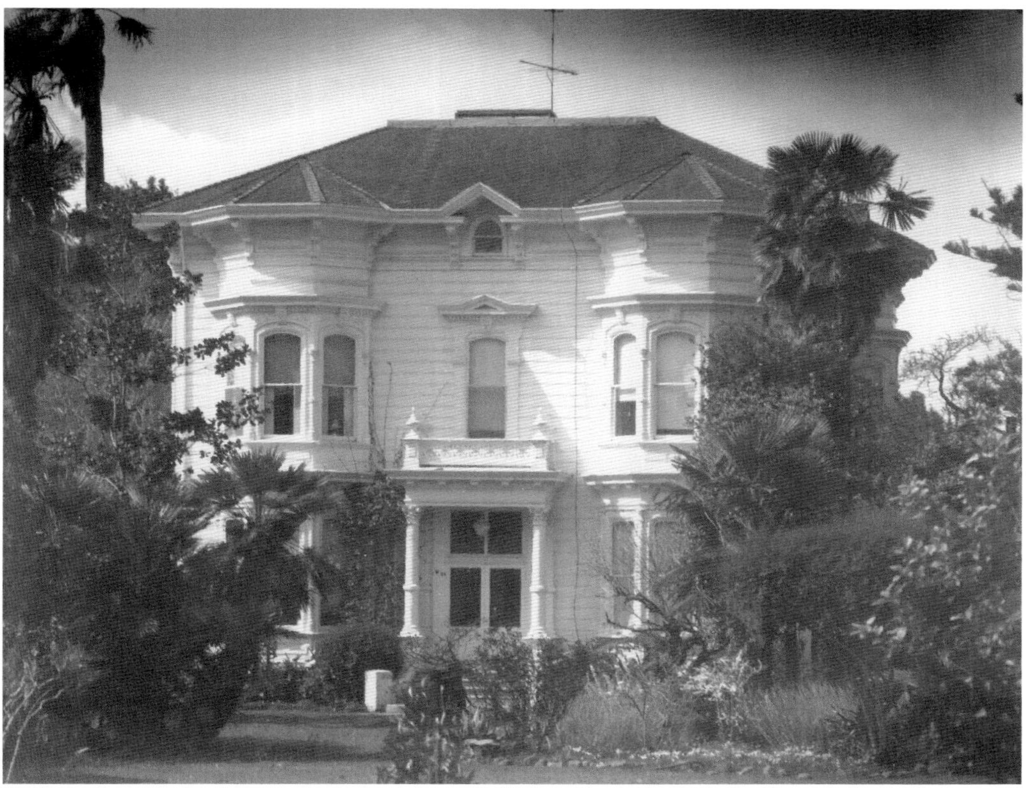

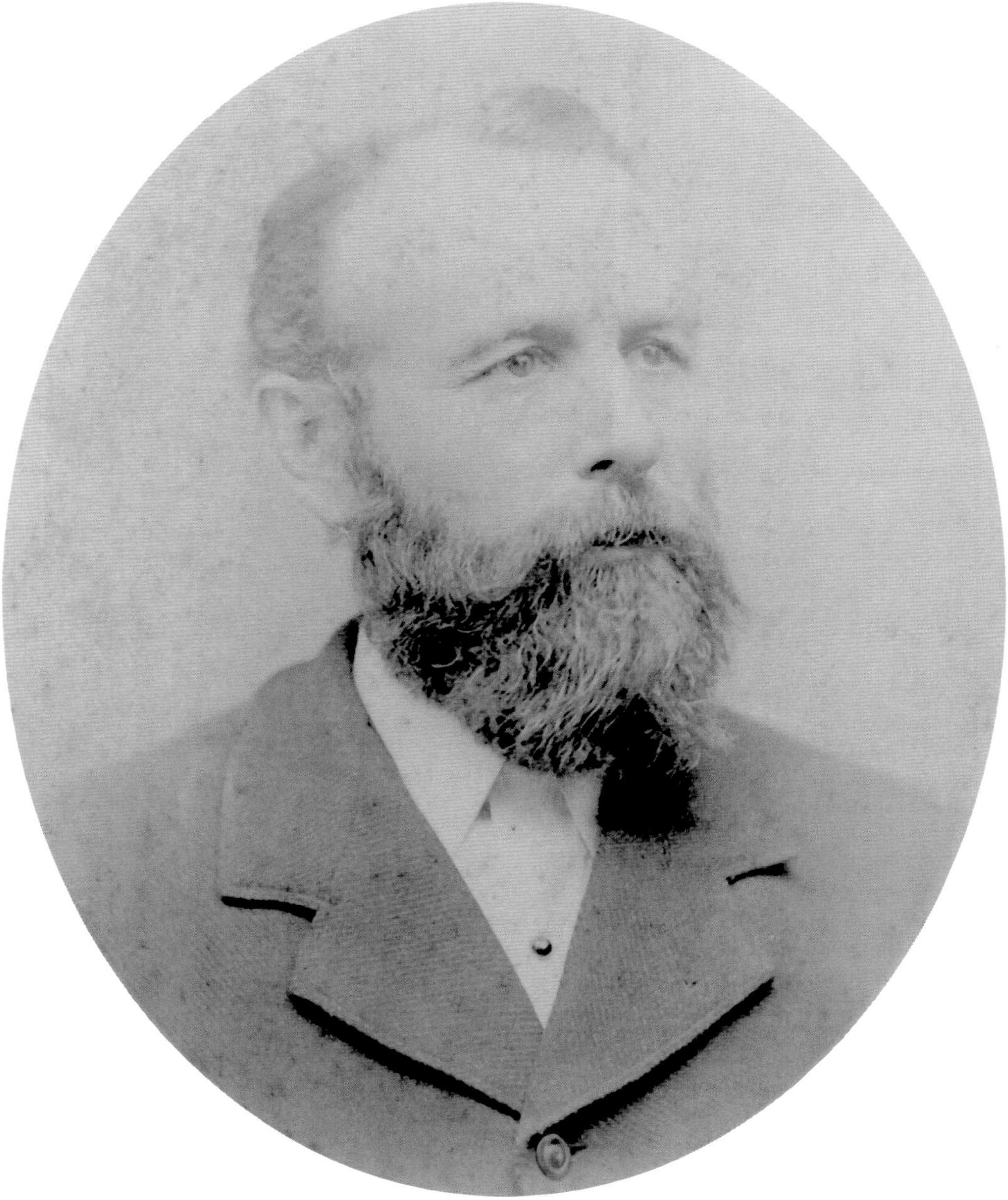

Early Mayor

Leander Linekin was born in Maine in 1833, but his family dates back to the Mayflower. Leander himself settled in Hayward in 1865 after trying his hand at mining. Once settled, he purchased a butcher shop, sold it, and went into partnership with his brother in a hardware store on Main Street. He was also active in political life. He ran for the board of trustees in 1878 and served as its president for several years. This makes Leander one of the earliest mayors of the small town. He made street lighting and road grading his top priorities. In that way, Leander literally shaped the young town, which had only incorporated in 1876. He built a home befitting of his standing in the community. Built in 1893, the Linekin house still stands on Main Street as a law office.

Temperance Supporter

An early pioneer settler in Hayward was Joel Russell. Born in Waterford, Maine, in 1822, he left the family farm to become a teacher. Joel and some friends formed a "California or Bust" mining company in 1849 and sailed for California's gold mines. Having no luck in mining, he spent about a year in Stockton. In 1853, Joel arrived in the Hayward area just as Alameda County was formed and was elected justice of the peace for Eden Township in 1854. He also purchased land and farmed like most of the area's early settlers. Joel was a self-educated lawyer and politically active. He served as one of Hayward's first city attorneys. A temperance supporter, he was nominated by the Prohibition Party to run for governor of California in 1866. He lost but remained active in progressive politics until his death in 1888.

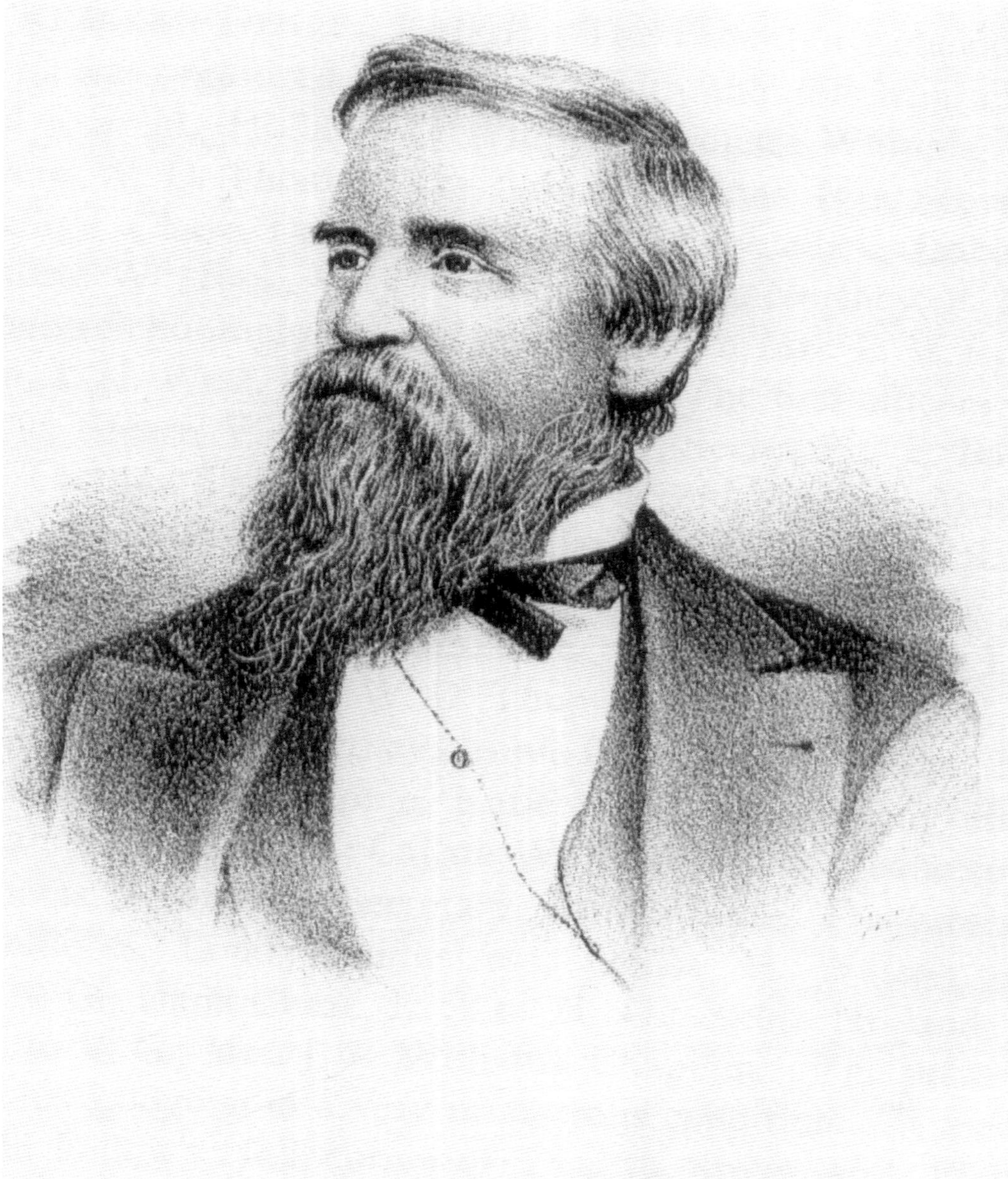

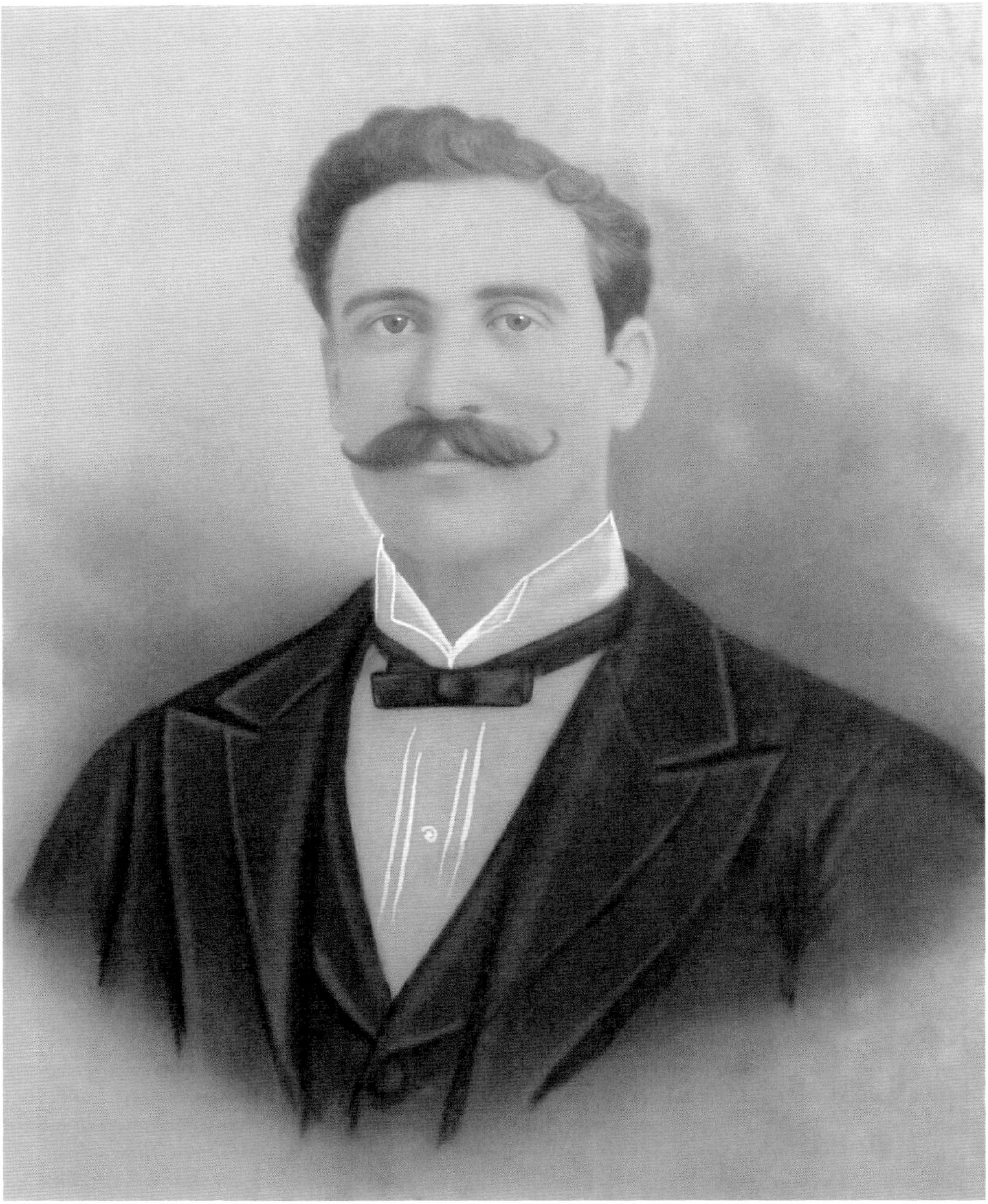

Portuguese Leader

Like many early Hayward residents, Frank "F.I." Lemos came to California from the Azores Islands. He settled in Hayward in 1889 and quickly established himself. Lemos befriended the lawyer G.S. Lagan. Working with Lagan, Frank not only improved his English but also learned the finer points of law. After only five years of study, he was accepted to the Alameda County bar and began practicing law. By 1903, he had his own law firm. Eventually, Frank would become the president and legal consul for the Bank of Haywards. He was not only active in the Portuguese community but served the broader community as a member of the school board.

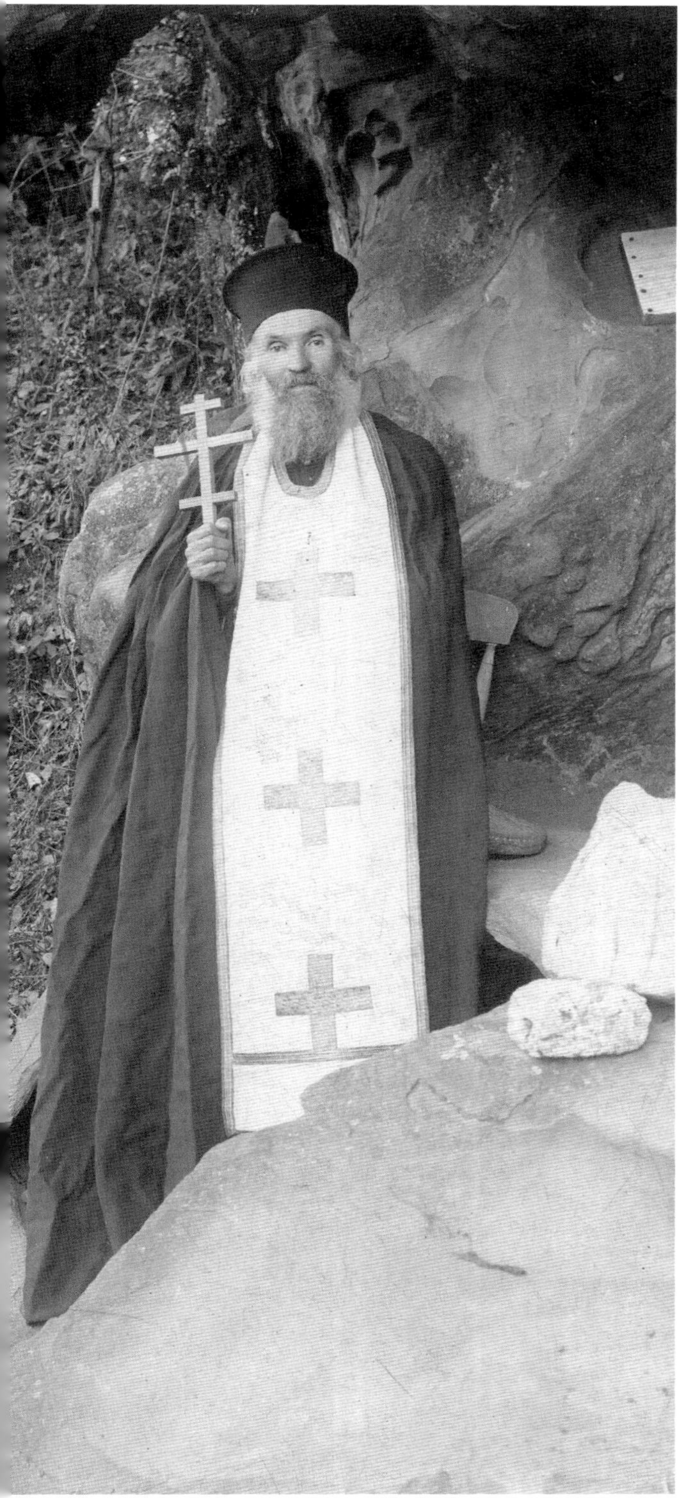

Ukrainian Exile

Agapius Honcharenko was born in Kiev, Ukraine, in 1832. At age 25, he was ordained as a priest in the Russian Orthodox Church. While working in Greece, he was exposed to revolutionary ideas and he soon began publishing articles critical of the Russian czar and calling for greater freedom for peasants in his country. The czar's secret police were soon after Honcharenko, and he was arrested. With the help of friends, he escaped to England where he continued his revolutionary writings. Under constant threat, he was forced to make his way to the United States where he found sanctuary in Philadelphia with a friend. While there, he worked as a translator, helped organize a reformed Russian church, stayed two-steps ahead of assassins, and courted and married his wife, Albina. In the late 1860s, he and his wife moved to San Francisco, where he began publishing a newspaper, the *Alaska Herald*. Alaska had just been purchased by the United States from Russia, and Honcharenko wrote for his fellow countrymen living in Alaska, promoting the ideals of American freedom. He soon began receiving death threats again from Russian sympathizers. Fearing for his life, Honcharenko and Albina moved to the Hayward hills in 1873. There, they built a small cabin and began a modest farm that they named "Ukraina." Honcharenko conducted Orthodox church services in a cave located near the couple's home while Albina held outdoor classes for local children. He had many friends in the community who helped care for him in his old age. Honcharenko died in 1916 and was buried next to his wife under a tree near their home.

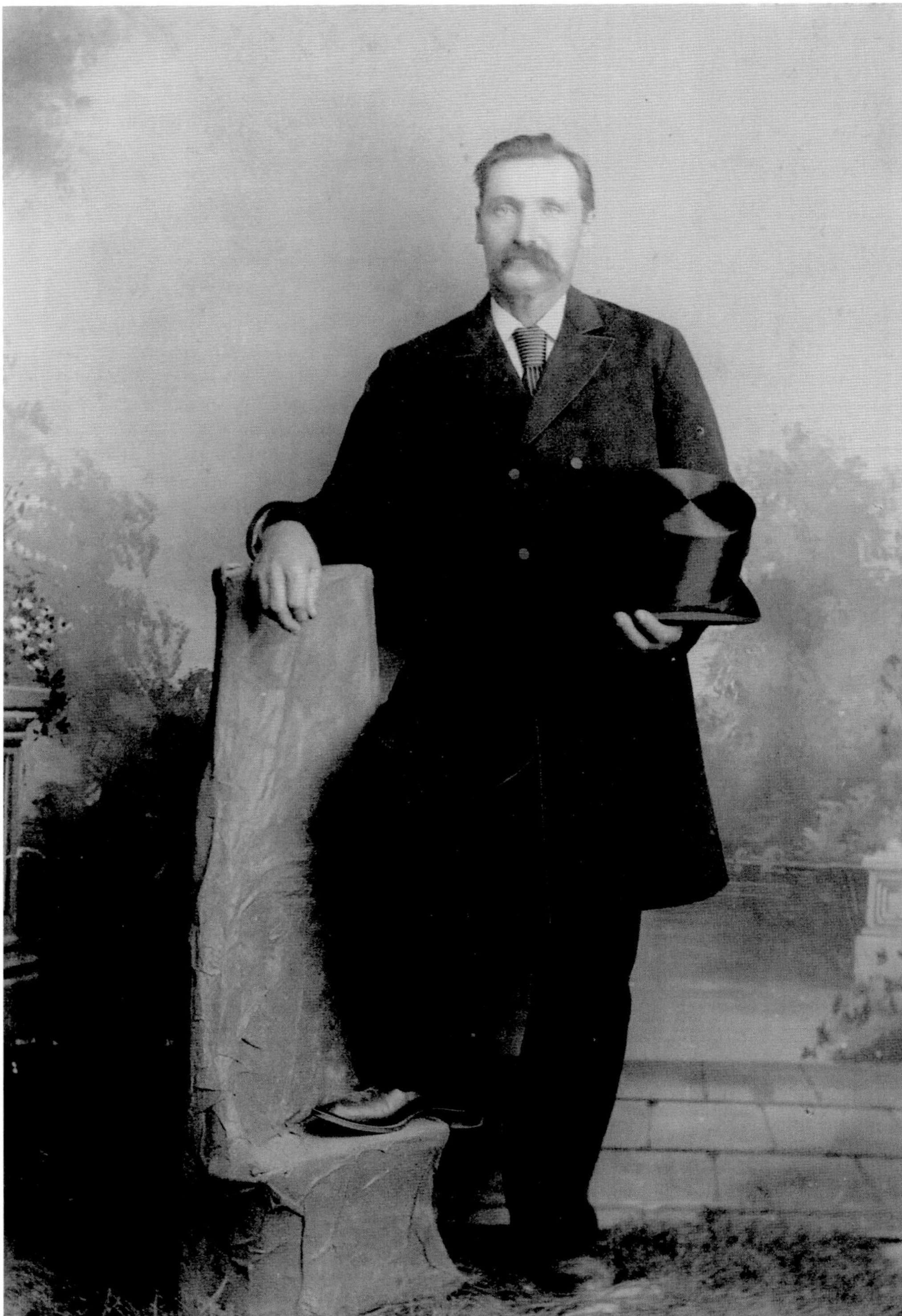

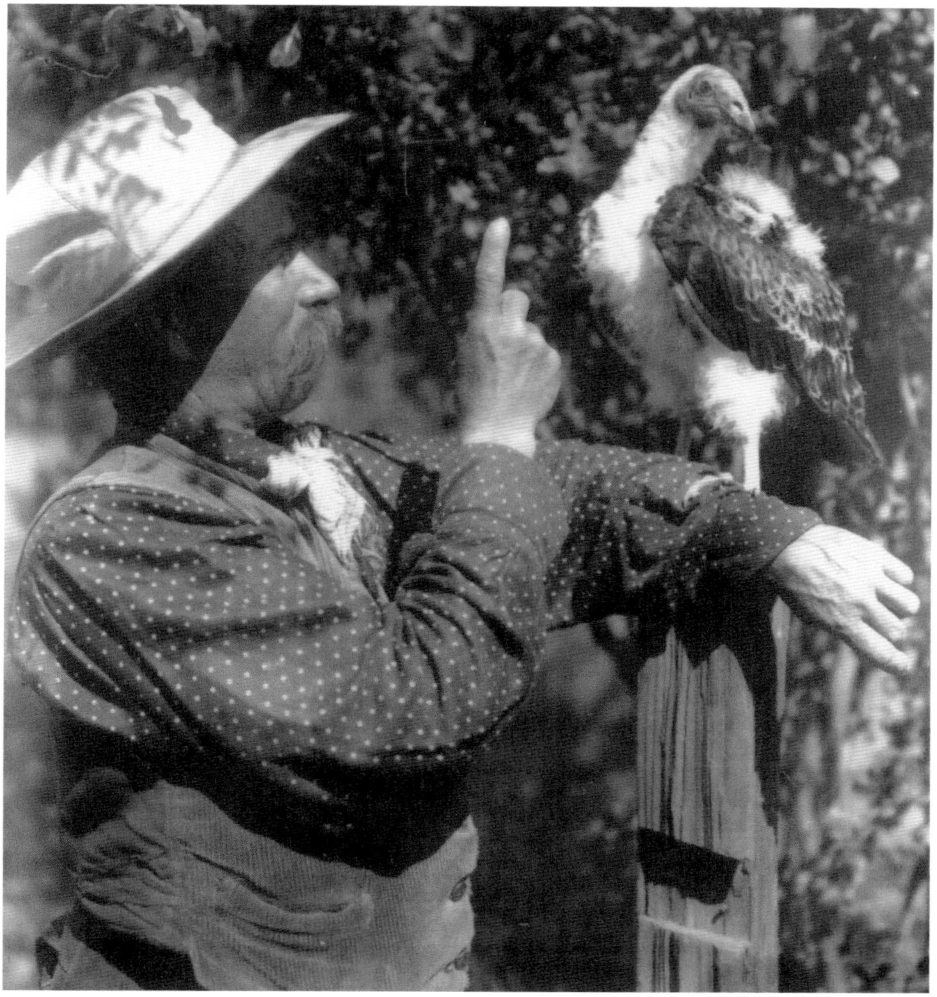

Artist and Naturalist

W. Otto Emerson was a resident of Hayward who became famous for his art and interest in ornithology. His study of birds and depictions of the natural environment were incorporated into his art. As a child, he developed an illness that affected his legs, which resulted in a painful walking disability, but it did not stop him. Once he walked from Hayward to Yosemite to see the sights. Although Otto is known for his fine art, he was also well known for his ornithology and even worked with the California Academy of Sciences and the Smithsonian Department of Ornithology. He was also a photographer, teacher, collector, mentor, Boy Scout leader, and scientist. More than 150 years after his birth, his paintings, photographs, bird studies, and written words can be found in various institutions.

Civil War Veteran and Mayor (OPPOSITE PAGE)

Alonzo Bradford was born in Iowa in 1841. During the Civil War, he served in the Union army under Ulysses S. Grant for four years. After the war, he farmed in Iowa and Missouri, where he married. They came by railroad to California in 1873 and settled in Hayward before the community became a city. As a carpenter, he built many homes and tank houses. For many years, Alonzo was Hayward's postmaster. Alonzo was active in public affairs and was the president of the board of trustees from 1887 to 1891. After 1930, the title was changed to mayor.

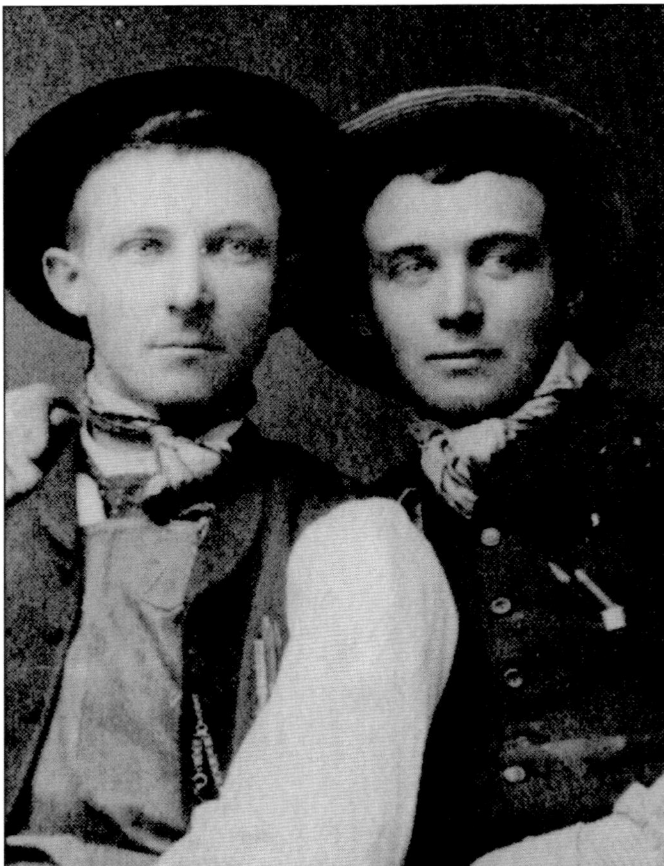

Canning Business

In 1887, brothers Joseph and William Hunt began a fruit- and vegetable-packing firm in the North Bay region. Incorporated as the Hunt Brothers Company, they were encouraged to move closer to the source of the fruits and vegetables and moved to Hayward in 1896. William died that year, and Joseph assumed management of the business. The cannery employed more than 1,000 seasonal workers. Joseph grew the business, adding warehouses, employee cottages, and a large pavilion for workers' children to use. In 1917, Joseph retired and sold the company, but the cannery retained the Hunt Brothers' name because of its reputation for quality. The cannery underwent a series of mergers over the years. The last owners changed the name to Hunt-Wesson Foods, Inc., which produced and sold a diversified line of tomato products, oils, shortenings, canned fruits, and vegetables.

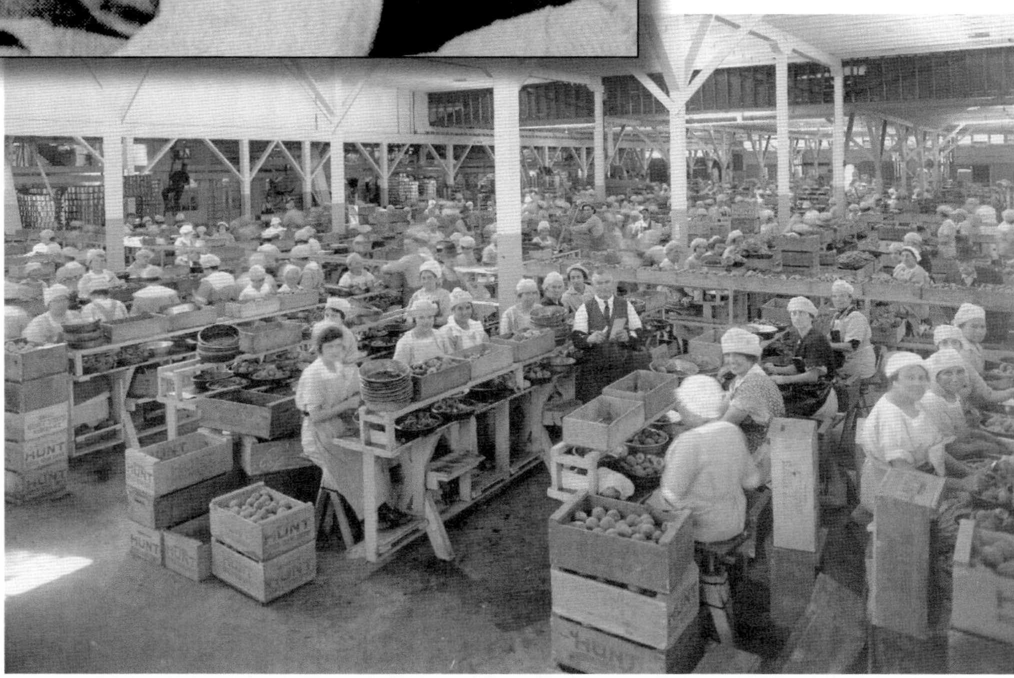

Blacksmith and Wagon Maker

Henry Eggert immigrated to the United States from Germany and settled in Hayward in the 1870s. He was trained as a farrier and found work in a blacksmith shop. He shod the horses of farmers and later bought the shop. Henry's business prospered. In 1878, he purchased more property next to the blacksmith shop on the corner of B and Main Streets for his business and built a wood-framed house for his residence. He married Halwina Pedersen, also from Germany, in 1877. Henry was one of the leading and most reputable wagon-makers and blacksmiths in the region. He used the best materials, and his work was durable. In this photograph Henry is pictured second from the left in the doorway of his shop.

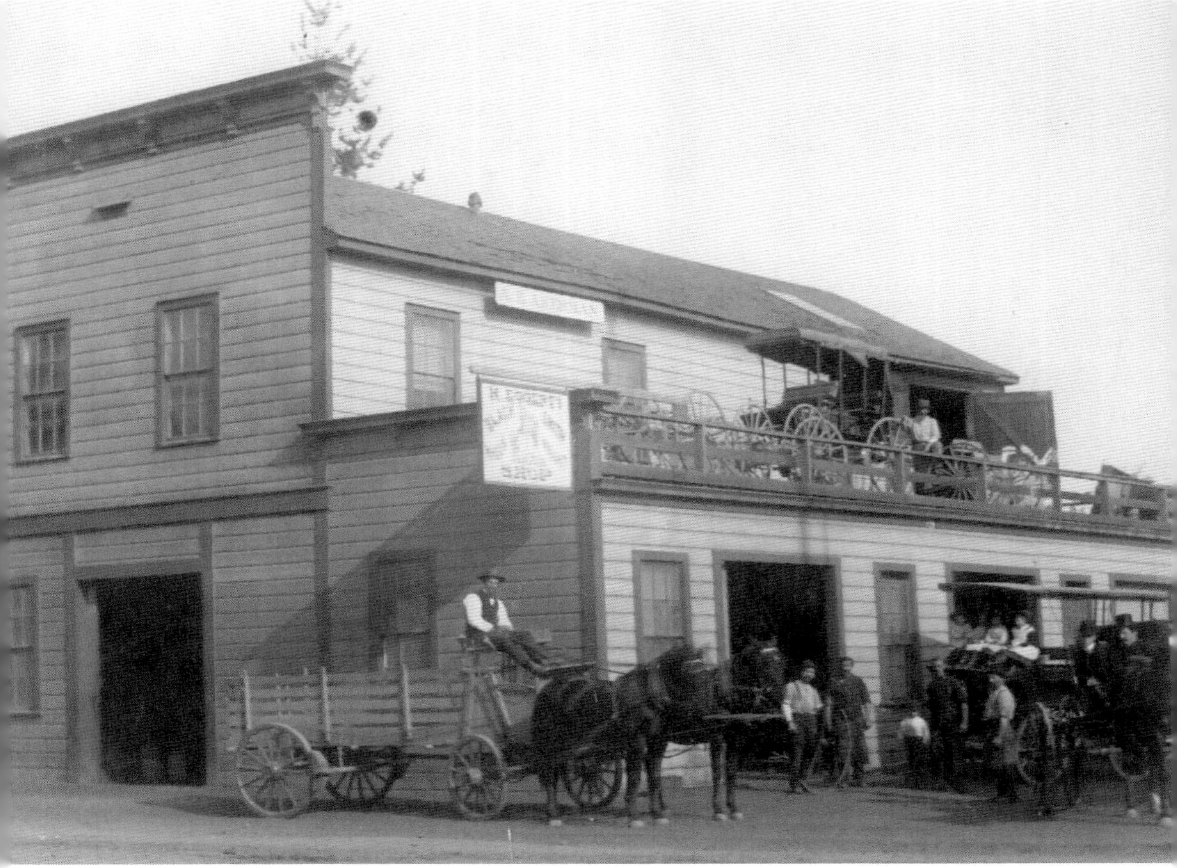

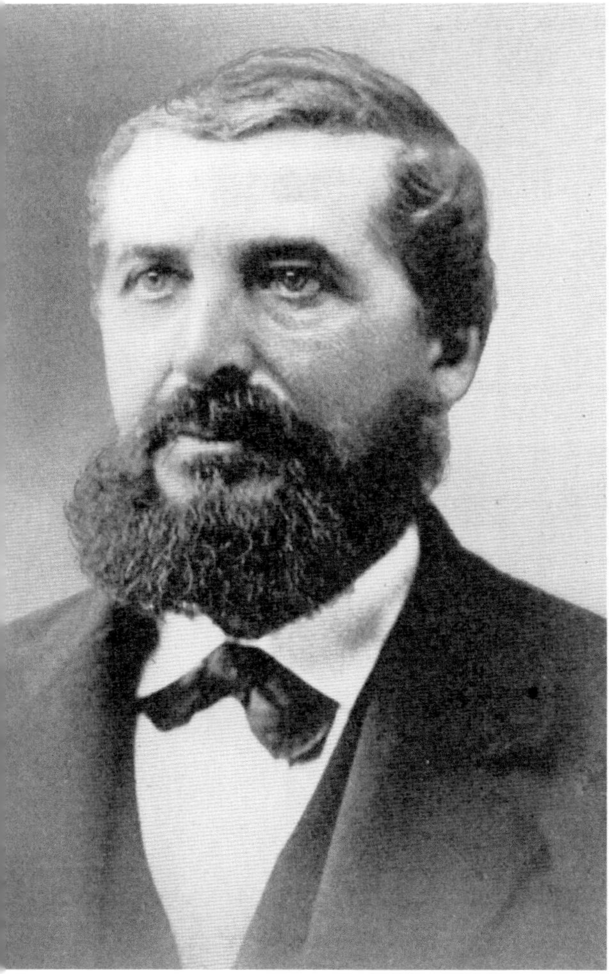

Gading Road
Born in 1835 in Bremen, Germany, Justus H. Gading immigrated with his parents, settling in Mount Eden. Justus, at age 21, went to the goldfields. Eventually, he returned to Mount Eden and bought 299 acres of unimproved land, where he constructed his home. As he prospered, Justus bought 400 more acres. Later, he subdivided and sold his land for houses. A road was named to honor the family.

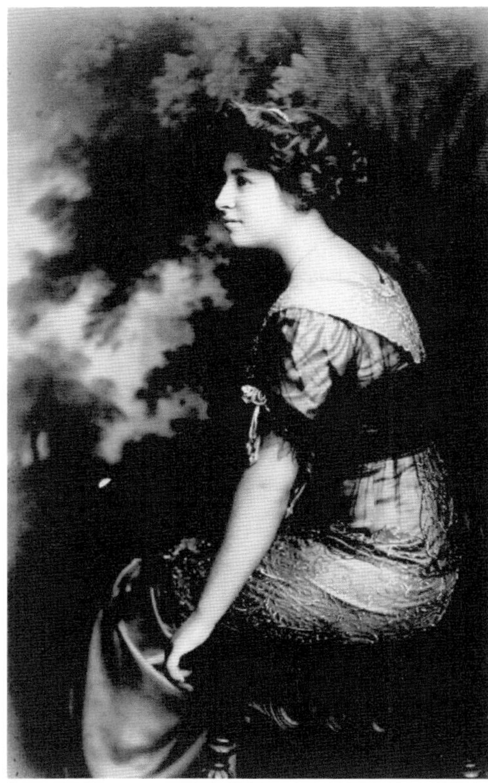

Pioneer Legacy
Alma Eggert was the daughter of Castro Valley pioneer Joseph Brickell. She married Herman Eggert, a Hayward dentist, in 1936. As a daughter of pioneers, Alma had a keen interest in the area's history. She served as the treasurer of the Hayward Area Historical Society. Alma also helped to establish a dental scholarship in honor of her husband. She lived to be 101 years old.

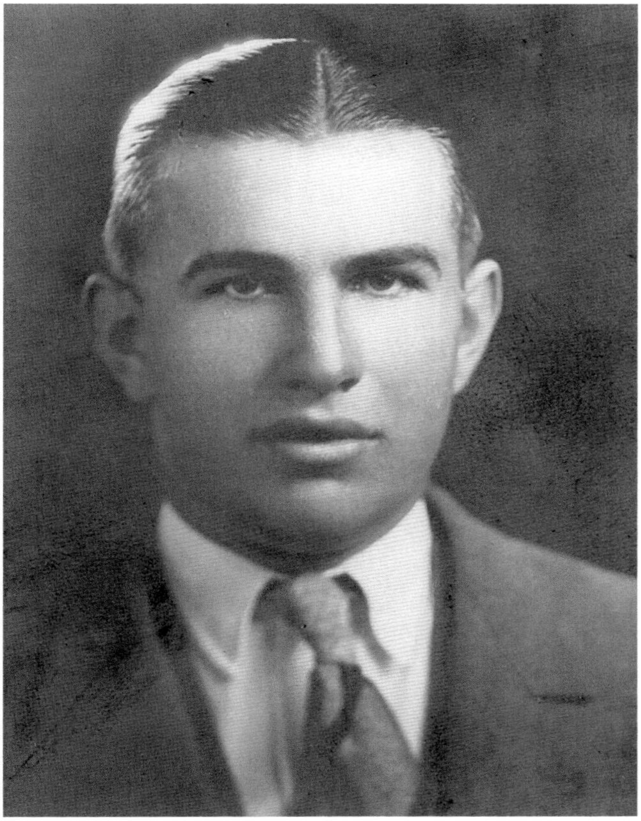

The Salt Ponds

In 1871, Andrew Ohleson, a Swedish immigrant, changed his last name to Oliver and purchased 120 acres of shoreline in Mount Eden and went into the salt-harvesting business. The original Oliver Salt Company (pictured below) was sold in 1927. In 1935, Andrew's grandson Alden (pictured at left) started his own Oliver Brothers Salt Company with his younger sibling Adolph. Alden was very active in the community. He was a member of the Hayward Rotary Club and was a Mount Eden Cemetery trustee. He passed away in April 1987. In his will, Alden created a trust for both the Hayward Area Historical Society and the Eden United Church of Christ. The 25-acre Alden E. Oliver Sports Park was named in his honor. Today, some 155 acres of former salt ponds along the Hayward shoreline have been converted into a wildlife habitat.

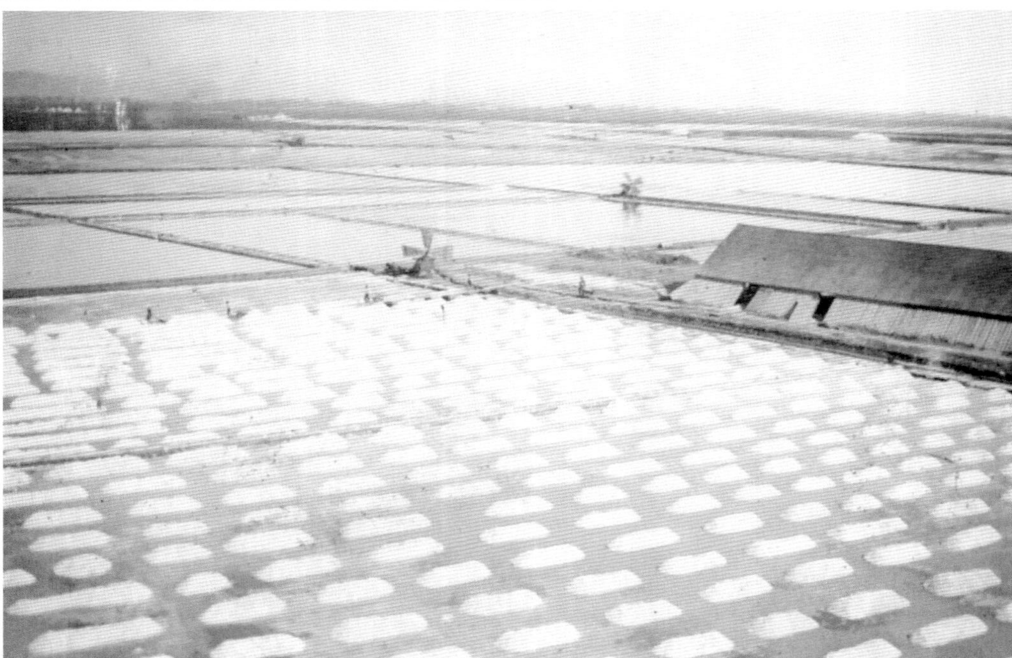

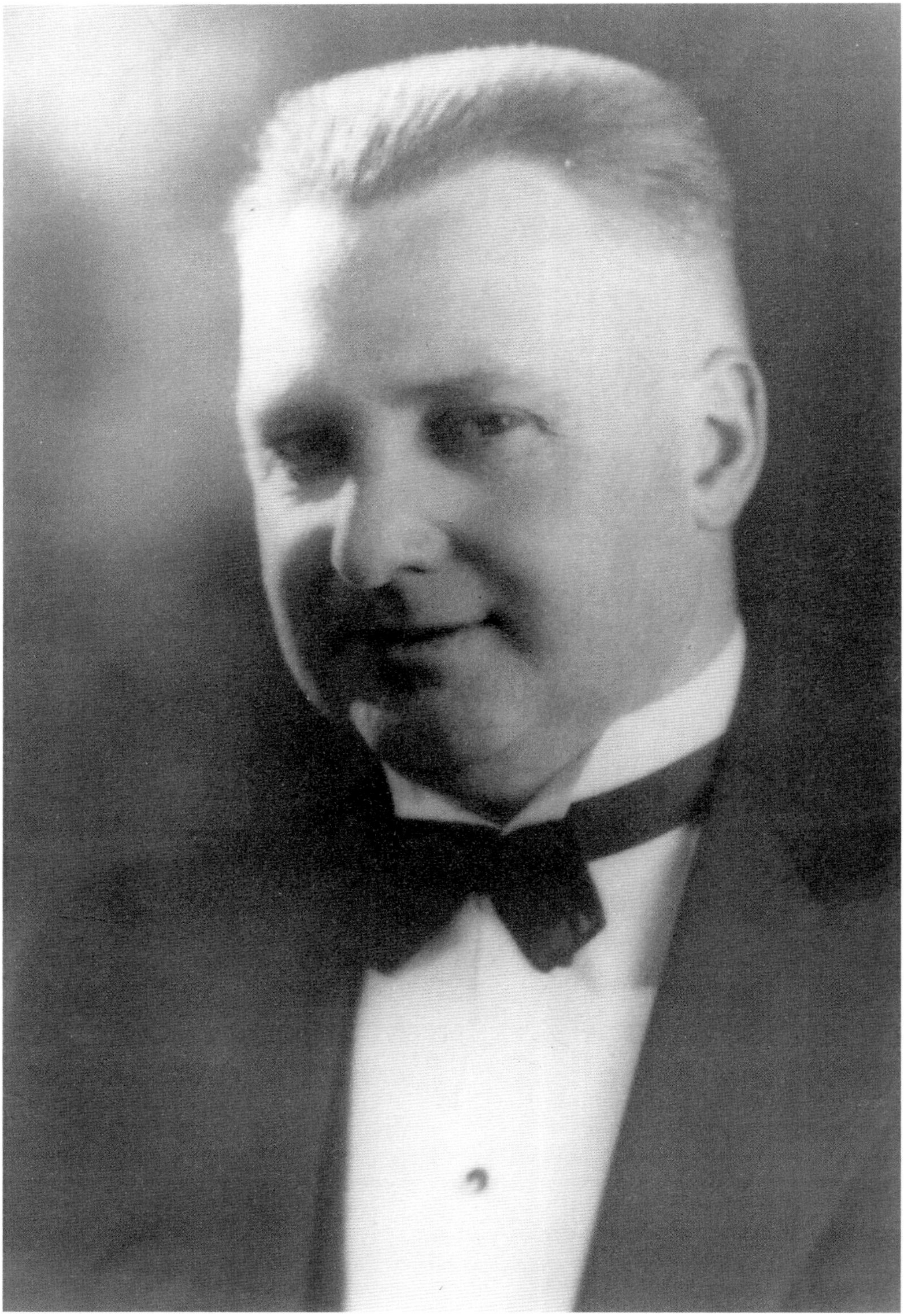

Postmaster and Historian (OPPOSITE PAGE)
Born in Hayward in 1886, Harry Bradford graduated from Hayward Union High School in 1905. He worked with his father as a clerk in the post office until 1909, when he enlisted in the California National Guard. During World War I, he joined the Army Air Corps. After the war, Harry returned to the Hayward Post Office as assistant postmaster until 1922, when President Harding appointed him postmaster. He served under the administrations of Presidents Coolidge and Hoover. When Franklin D. Roosevelt became president, Harry, a Republican, served as a postal clerk until 1948. Harry was appointed city librarian until 1955. His hobby was the histories of Hayward, the Civil War, and California Missions. He gave history presentations to various groups. Harry was also the longtime curator for the Hayward Area Historical Society's museum.

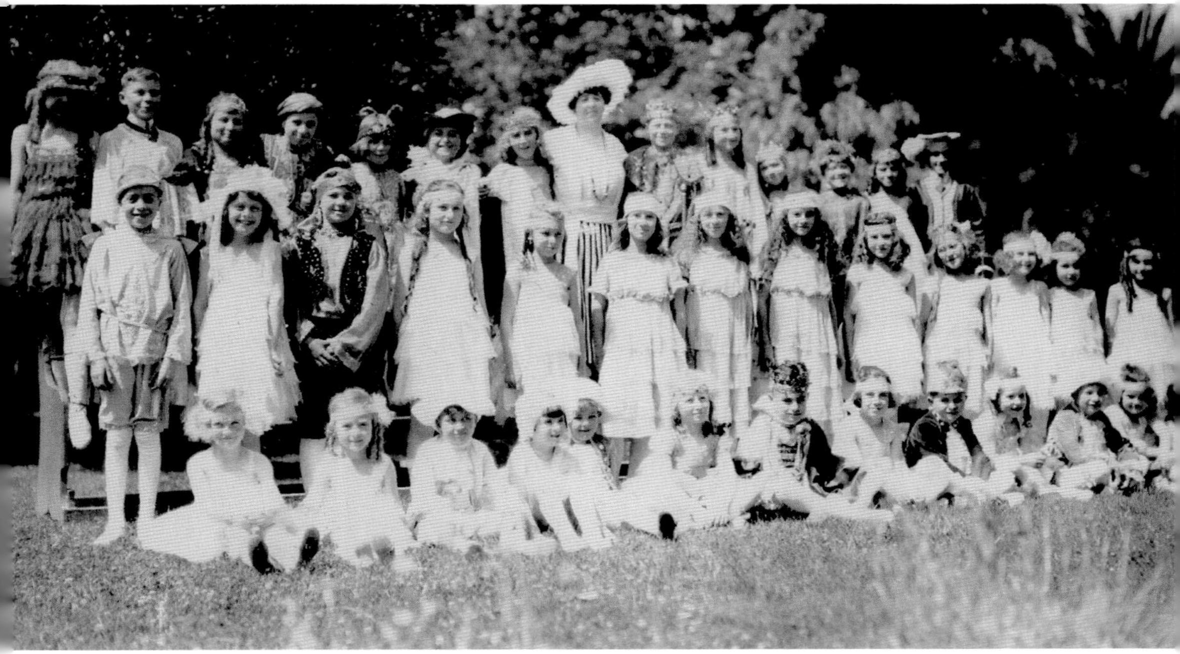

Kelly's Klever Kiddies
Hayward's leading producer of amateur theatricals, Carol B. Kelly always had children in her plays and pageants. She began her free drama school a few months after her marriage in 1906 to Tony Kelly. Carol taught the children singing, acting, and dancing. When the children reached adolescence, she would replace them with a new group of younger children. From the beginning, any play or pageant featuring the "Klever Kiddies" was sold out. The money collected was given to Hayward organizations for worthy causes. Carol wrote all the plays, designed the sets and costumes, and played the piano. Carol loved theater and music. While a student at College of the Holy Names, she learned to play the organ and was organist at All Saints Catholic Church for 50 years. Carol touched many lives with her theatricals. She is shown here with one of her Klever Kiddies troupes.

The Hill and Valley Club

On March 14, 1910, Hill and Valley Club was organized at the home of Edith Park. Ninety-one charter members unanimously elected Park as president. They formed organized departments, which included educational, philanthropic, and civic focuses. The philanthropic work was done through the needlework guild under the direction of Edith. Donations by the guild were given to the poor and needy in the community. The club is a member of the General Federation of Women's Clubs, which began in 1868 by a newspaperwoman because she and other women were not allowed to attend the New York Press Club dinner honoring Charles Dickens. It became the most effective organization of women in the world. The Hill and Valley Club awards high school scholarships and participates in many community projects. Here are the members in 1911 at the Park's home on First Street. Edith Park sits in the first row, sixth from the right. Mr. Park is the lone male in the back row.

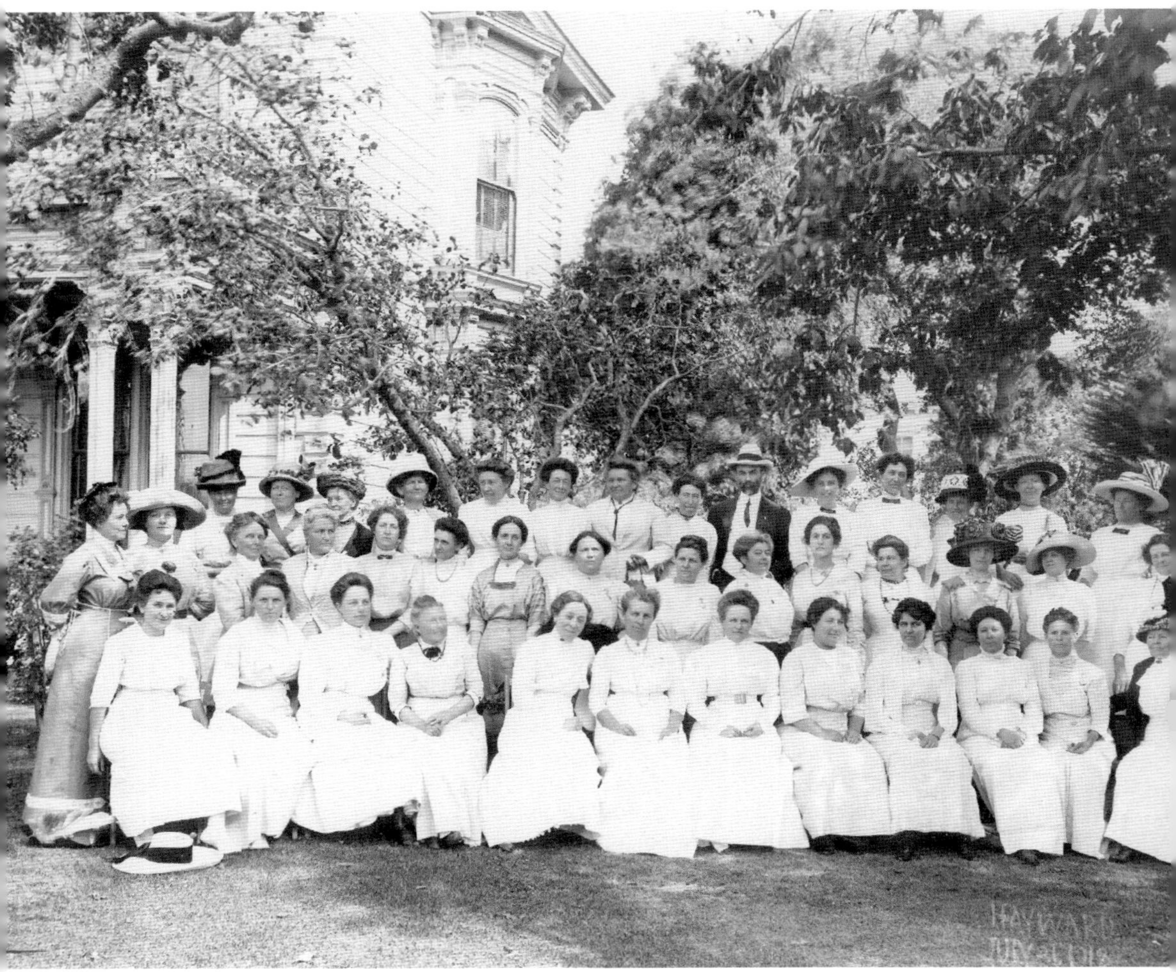

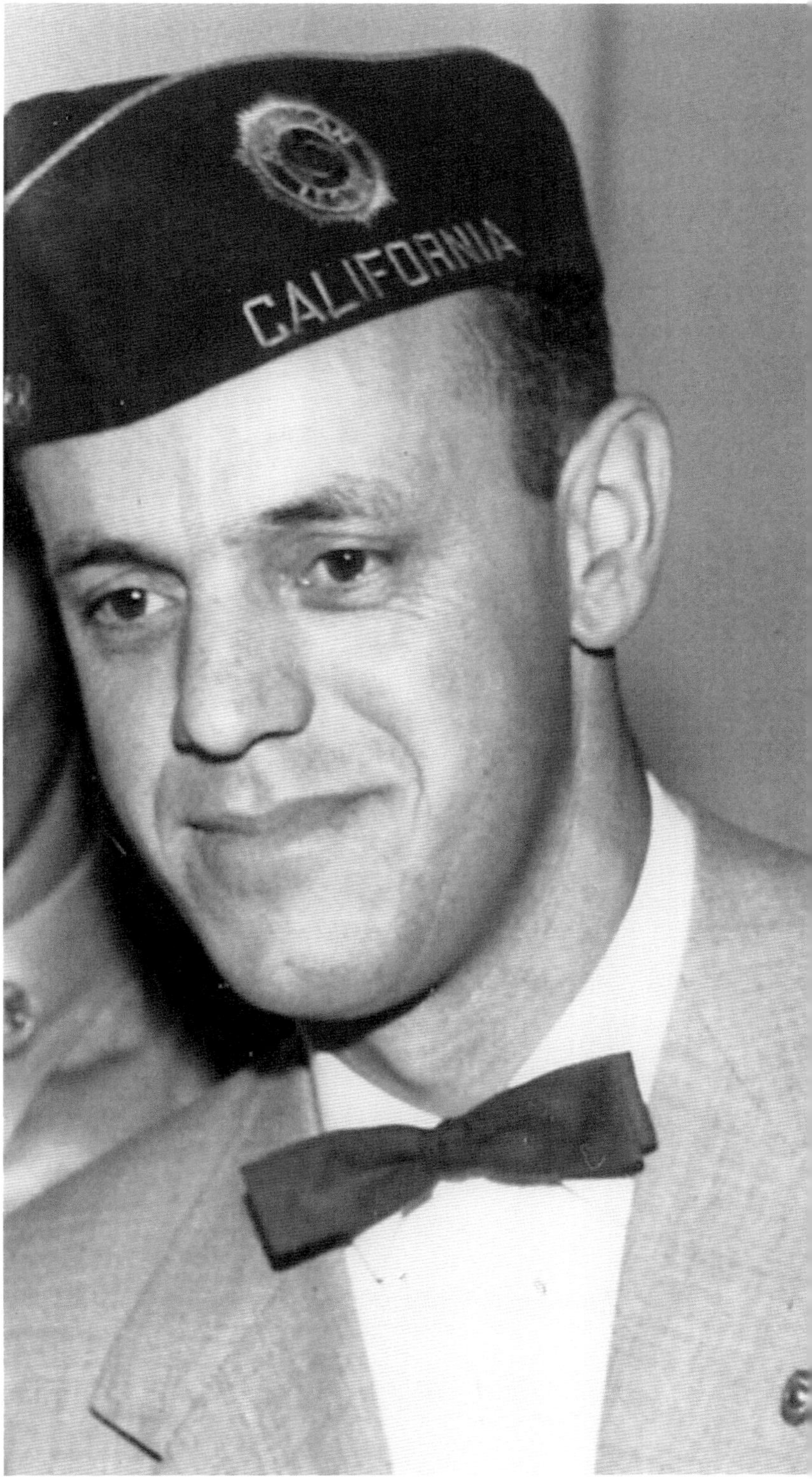

Serving Others
Allen F. Strutz was a resident of Hayward for over 85 years. He helped others through his community service, especially in veterans' affairs. Allen was chaplain of the Hayward American Legion for over 20 years and chairman of the Alameda County Veterans Parade and Memorial Day services for 53 years. He oversaw the restoration of veterans' plots at Lone Tree Cemetery and was a veteran of World War II. For his patriotism and volunteer service for veterans, Alameda County in 2000 rededicated the Hayward Memorial Building as the Allen F. Strutz Veterans Memorial Building. Allen also volunteered for the USO, American Cancer Society, Veterans Affairs Commission, Veterans Hospital of Livermore, and Hayward Chamber of Commerce. As one of the founders of the Hayward Area Historical Society, he was board president from 1957 to 1961.

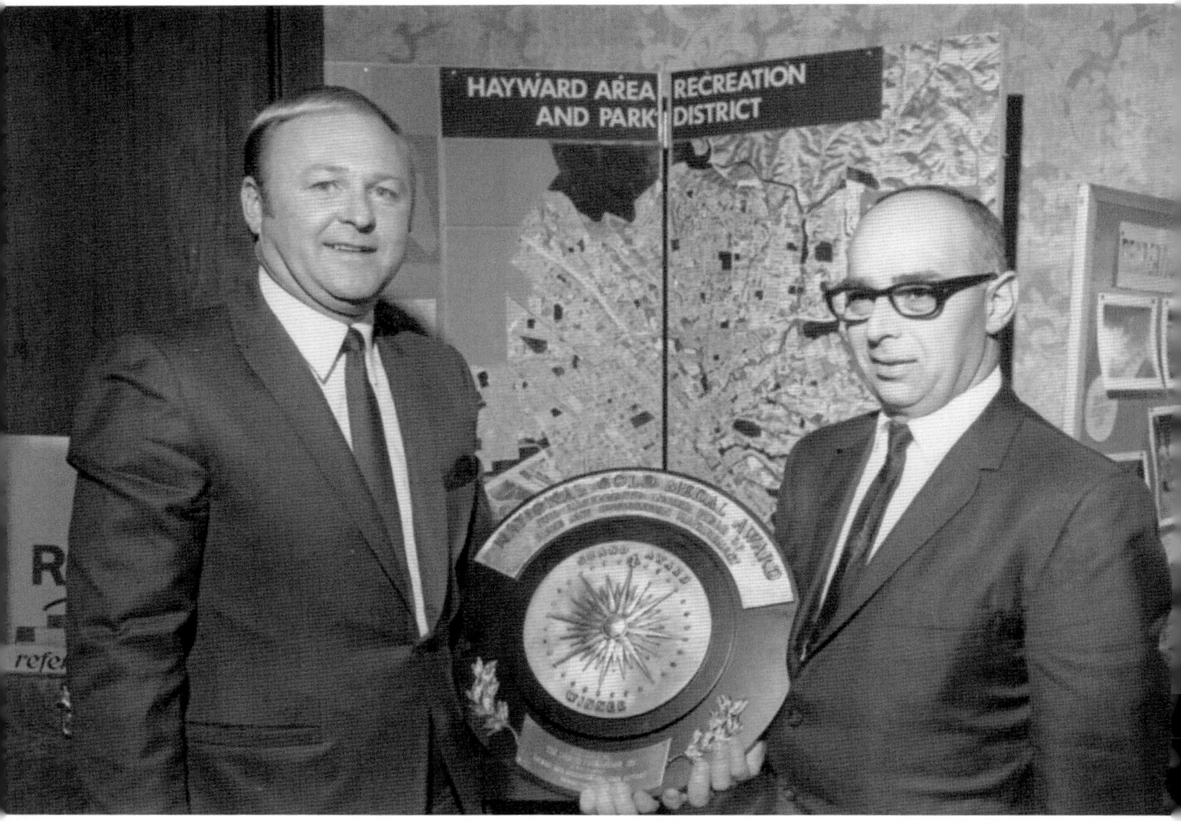

Recreation

Bud Critzer began working for the Hayward Area Recreation and Park District (HARD), which was established in 1944, as a recreation supervisor in 1959. He became superintendent of recreation in 1963 and retired as the sixth general manager. Although retired, he continues working on legislation with the California Association of Recreation and Park Districts. HARD is an award-winning, nationally recognized park and recreation district that operates more than 100 facilities. They include historic estates, golf courses, a little theater, senior centers, nature center, aquatic facilities, Japanese Garden, tennis courts, and the Rowell Ranch Rodeo Park, which Bud helped to acquire in 1977. The Skywest Golf Course Clubhouse is named for Bud Critzer. Bud is pictured, left, with Hayward City councilman Julio Bras, right, receiving a National Gold Medal award for the park district.

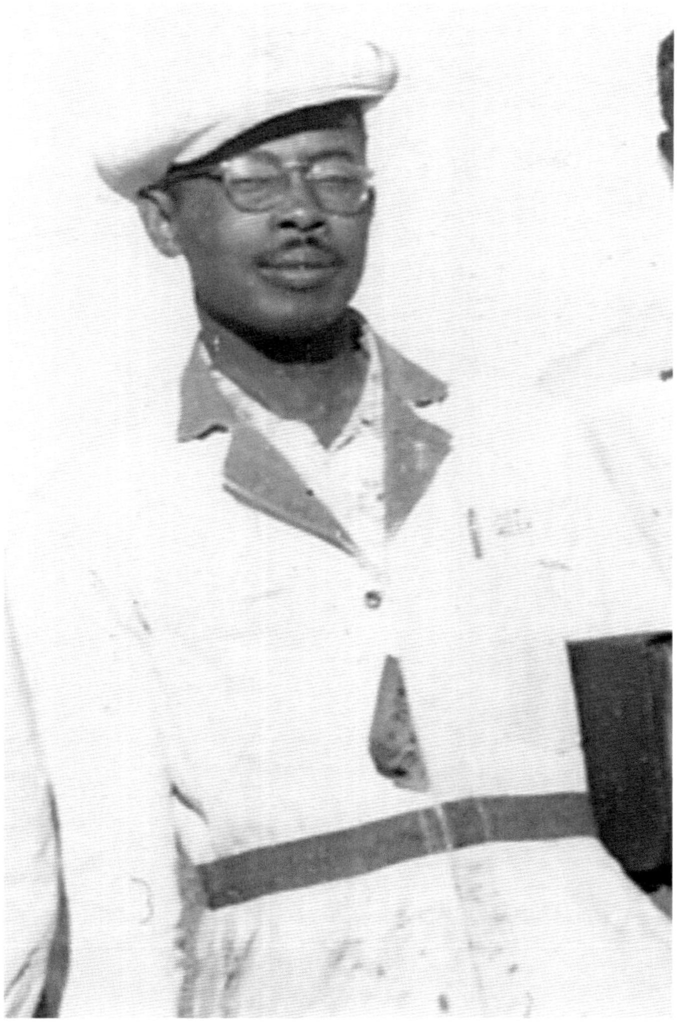

Black Pioneer

William Fletcher was one of five African Americans living and working in Hayward in the 1930s and 1940s. He was born in Stockton and became fascinated with cars at an early age. He saved his money from his sidewalk business to buy a $2 manual on auto repairs, which he carried under his arm all the time. At age 11, his family moved to East Oakland. A few years later, his father was killed in a work-related accident, so he dropped out of school to find work. William had a variety of jobs during his teen years but never lost his passion for cars. Working as a janitor at an Oakland car dealership, William continued to learn about auto repair whenever he had a chance. In 1936, he came to Hayward and took a job in an auto repair shop. By 1939, he had earned the reputation as one of Hayward's best mechanics. He decided to buy his own property and bid on a Foothill Boulevard location. The deal did not go through. Fletcher and others believed it was a case of discrimination. Although William was disappointed, he decided to rent the Foothill Boulevard property until 1955. With the help of friends, he purchased a building and operated another shop on Smalley Drive until 1975, when he retired. Not only did William have his own business but he also worked with some friends building and racing cars at the local speedway. William's cars were always the fastest, and the team won many races. Even in the face of discrimination, William built a successful life in Hayward.

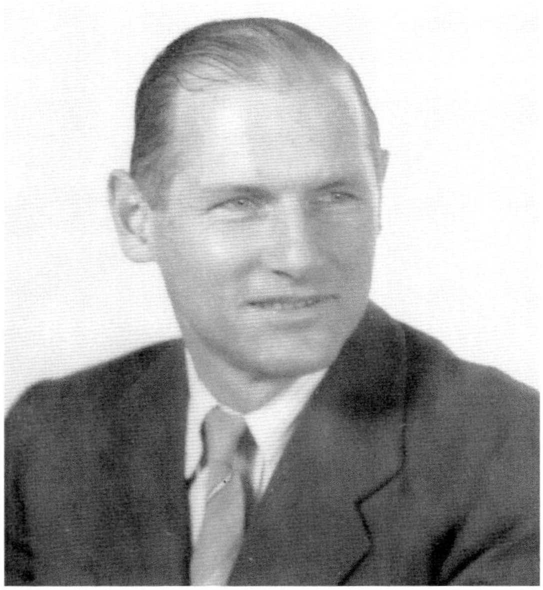

Fourth Generation

Born and raised on the family farm in 1902, E. Guy Warren was the fourth-generation Warren to live in Hayward. He began a trucking business in 1930 and also had a farm equipment company, pictured below. By 1940, he was president of the Hayward Rotary Club and the Hayward Chamber of Commerce. For 25 years, Guy was also a Hayward Union High School trustee. California governor Pat Brown appointed Guy to the Board of Trustees of the state college system after he helped select the location of California State University in Hayward. In 1938, Guy purchased a cattle ranch in Castro Valley's Crow Canyon. Still, Guy found time to serve on committees, ranging from the prevention of juvenile crime to the Board of Bay Area Pollution Control, and ran for the state senate. Guy passed away in 1971.

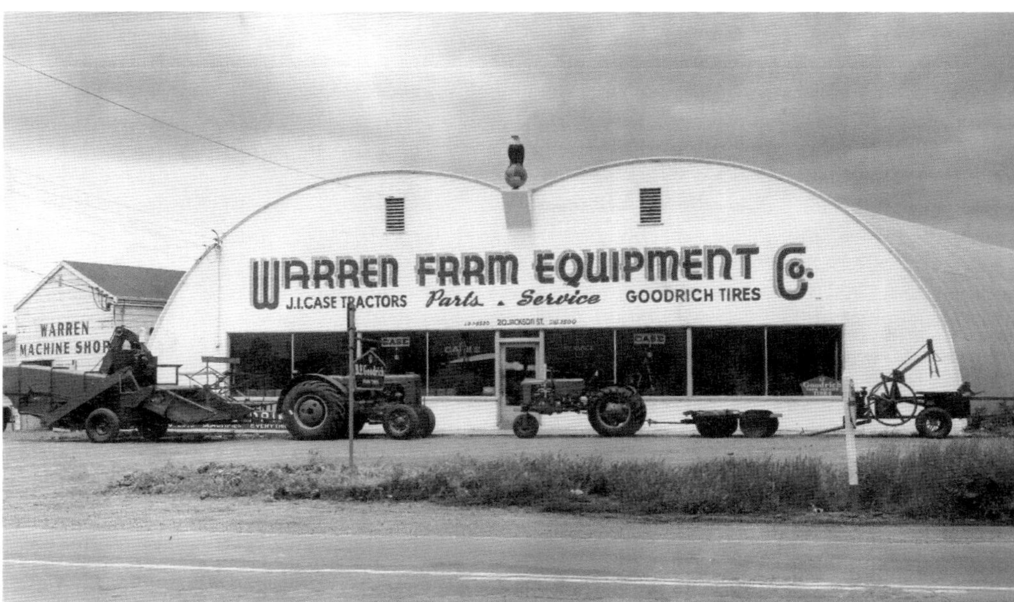

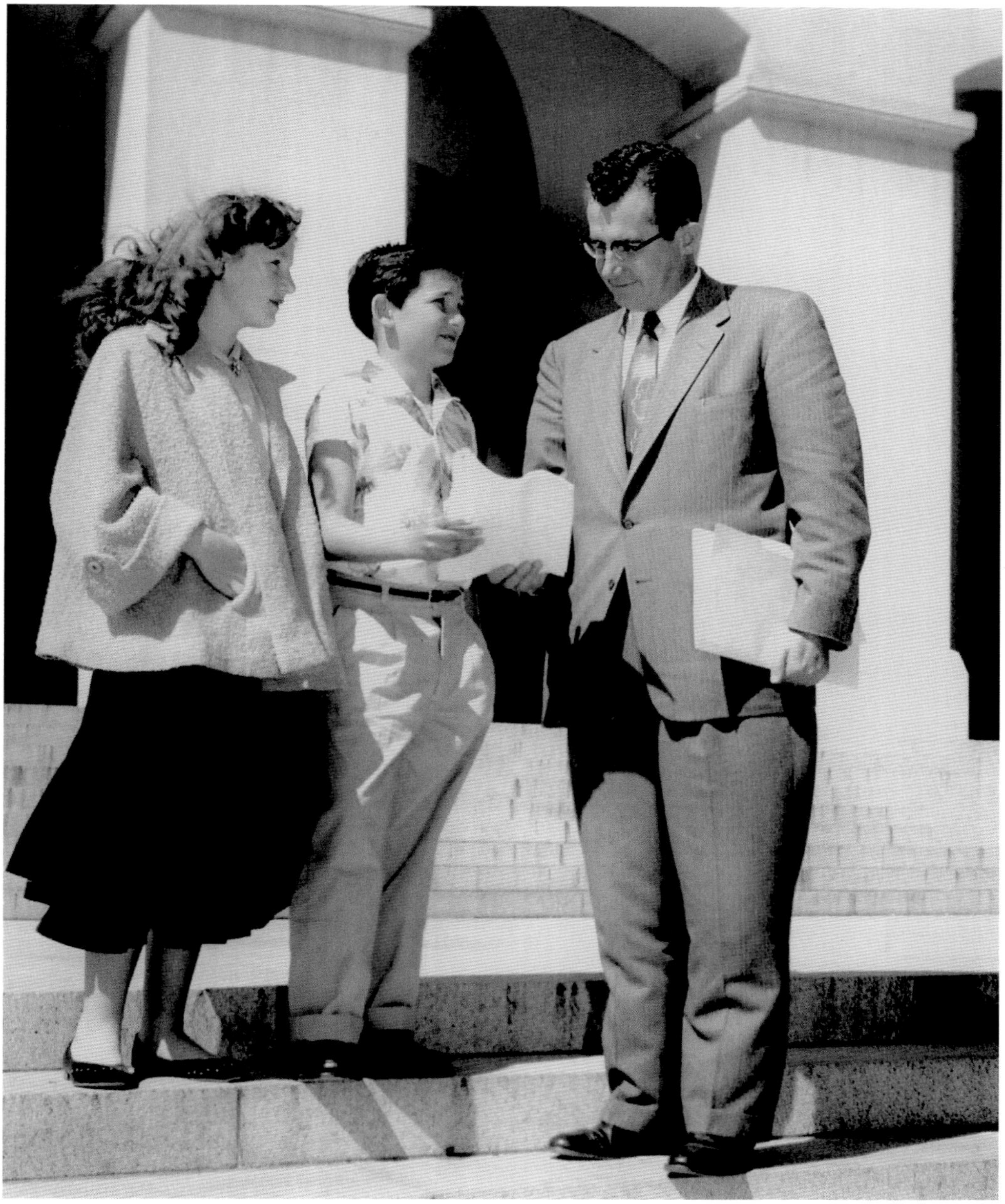

Public Service

Born in Berkeley, Carlos Bee graduated from the University of California, Santa Barbara, in 1940. After serving in World War II, he completed graduate work and began teaching at Hayward Union High School. In 1949, he was elected to the Hayward City Council, served as mayor of Hayward in 1950, and was elected to the California State Assembly in 1954. In this 1955 photograph, he visits with Hayward students in Sacramento. Assemblyman Bee introduced a bill in the state legislature in 1957 that established a college in Southern Alameda County. Carlos Bee was presented a plaque in 1964 and honored as the "father" of California State College at Hayward.

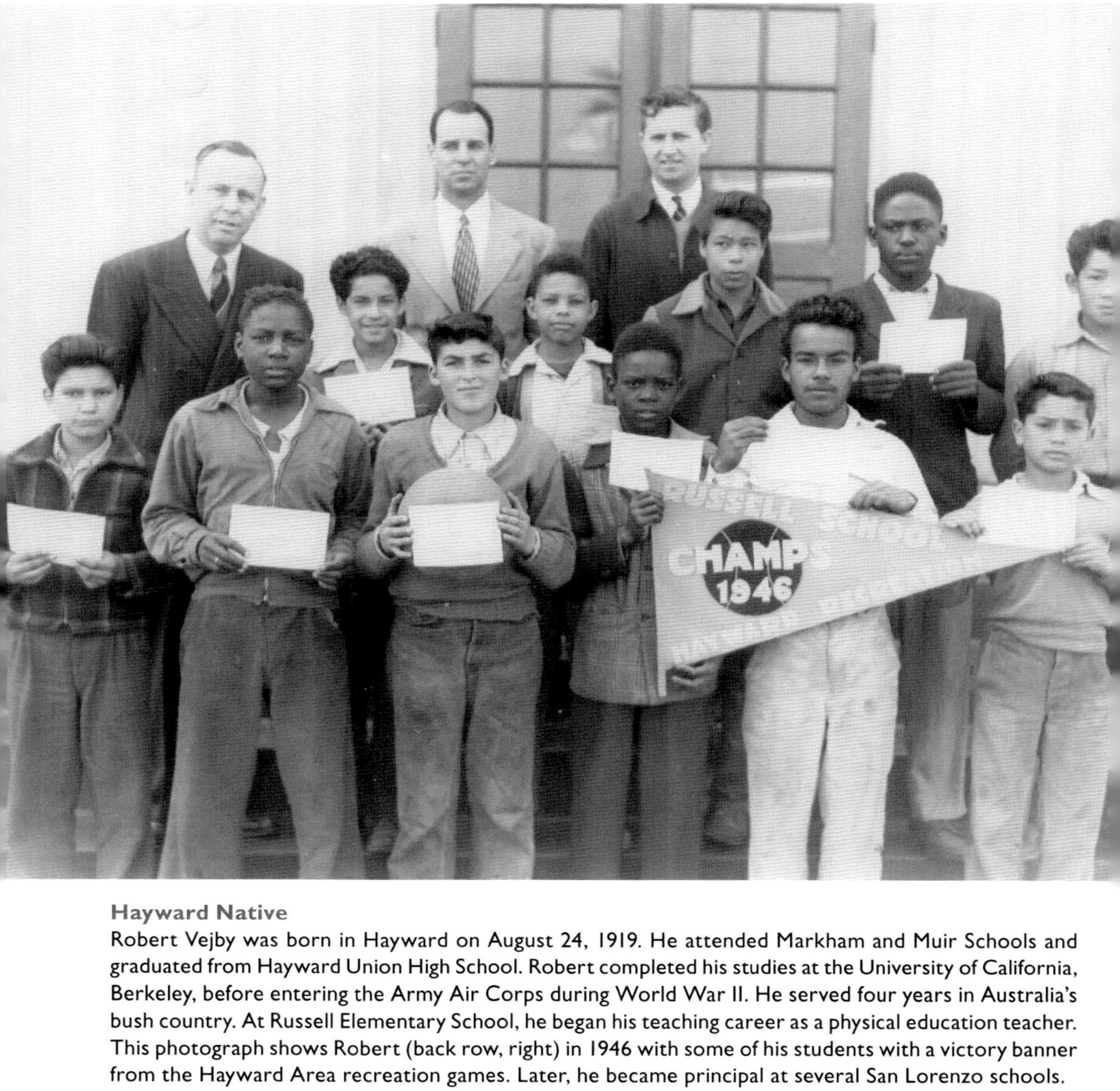

Hayward Native

Robert Vejby was born in Hayward on August 24, 1919. He attended Markham and Muir Schools and graduated from Hayward Union High School. Robert completed his studies at the University of California, Berkeley, before entering the Army Air Corps during World War II. He served four years in Australia's bush country. At Russell Elementary School, he began his teaching career as a physical education teacher. This photograph shows Robert (back row, right) in 1946 with some of his students with a victory banner from the Hayward Area recreation games. Later, he became principal at several San Lorenzo schools.

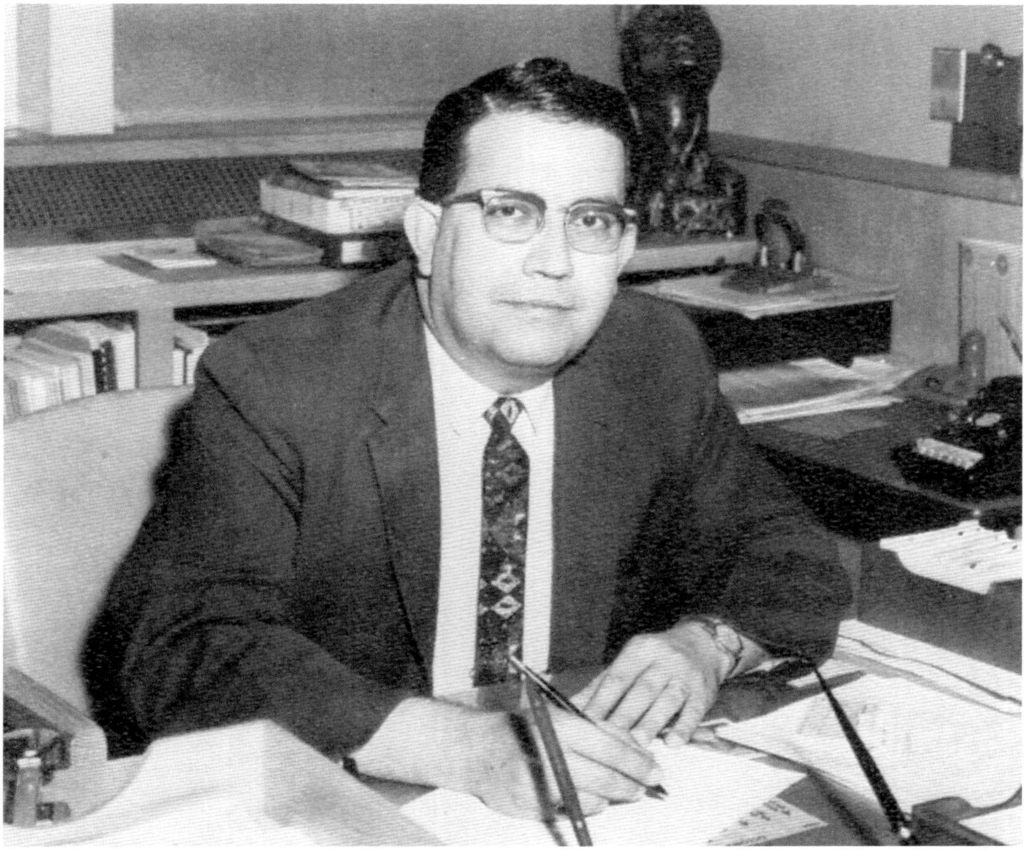

Champion of Education
As an educator and public school advocate for more than 35 years, Anthony W. Ochoa served the parents and students of Hayward as a teacher and school board member. Education was important to Anthony because he viewed it as a means to improve people's lives. A native of San Francisco, he received his teaching and administration degrees at the University of California, Berkeley, and began his teaching career in San Francisco. In 1950, Anthony married Christine Valtierra of Stockton, and they lived in Oakland, then San Lorenzo, and finally Hayward, where he taught at Hayward Union High School beginning in 1958. In 1969, he moved his family to South America, where he served as a consultant to the Colombian Ministry of Education. Upon their return to the United States, he spent 17 years as professor and chairperson of Mexican American studies at California State University, Hayward. Later, he became a professor of teacher education. In 1979, he was elected to the Hayward School Board, where he served until his death in 1988. Because Anthony believed that public education was the cornerstone of a community and he practiced those beliefs, a Hayward middle school was renamed in his honor.

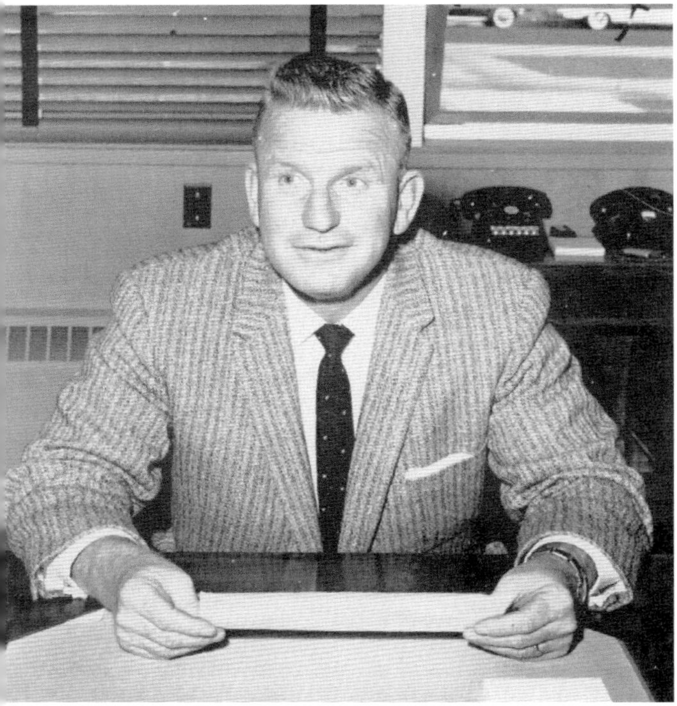

Dedicated Educator

George Weekes Jr., born in Michigan in 1916, moved to California as a child. He attended Oakland schools and earned a bachelor's degree from the University of San Francisco and a bachelor of arts degree from San Francisco State. In 1946, he began as a physical education instructor and director of intramural activities at the University of Pittsburgh, where he completed his master's degree. Returning to Santa Rosa, California, in 1947, he taught history. From 1952 to 1955, as superintendent of schools in Middletown, he attended Stanford to complete his doctoral degree. Hired by the Hayward School District in 1957, he became the first principal of Tennyson High School and then Mount Eden High School when it opened in 1960. As a dedicated educator, Dr. Weekes devoted himself to the Hayward schools and community. For this dedication, a park was named in his honor, pictured below.

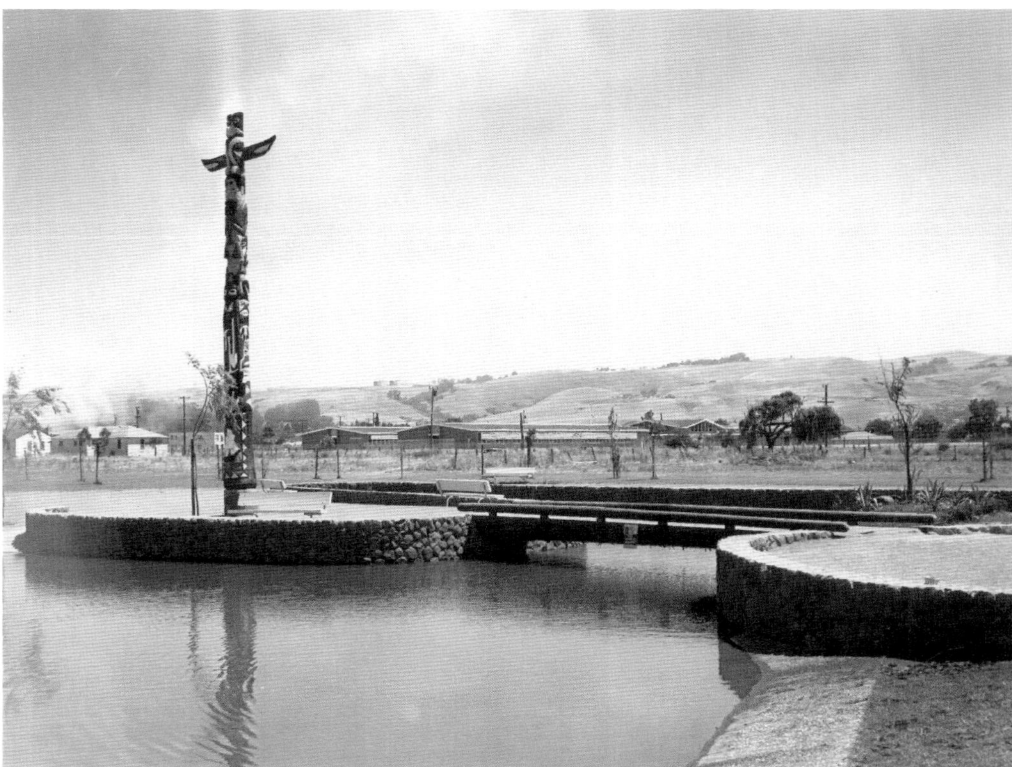

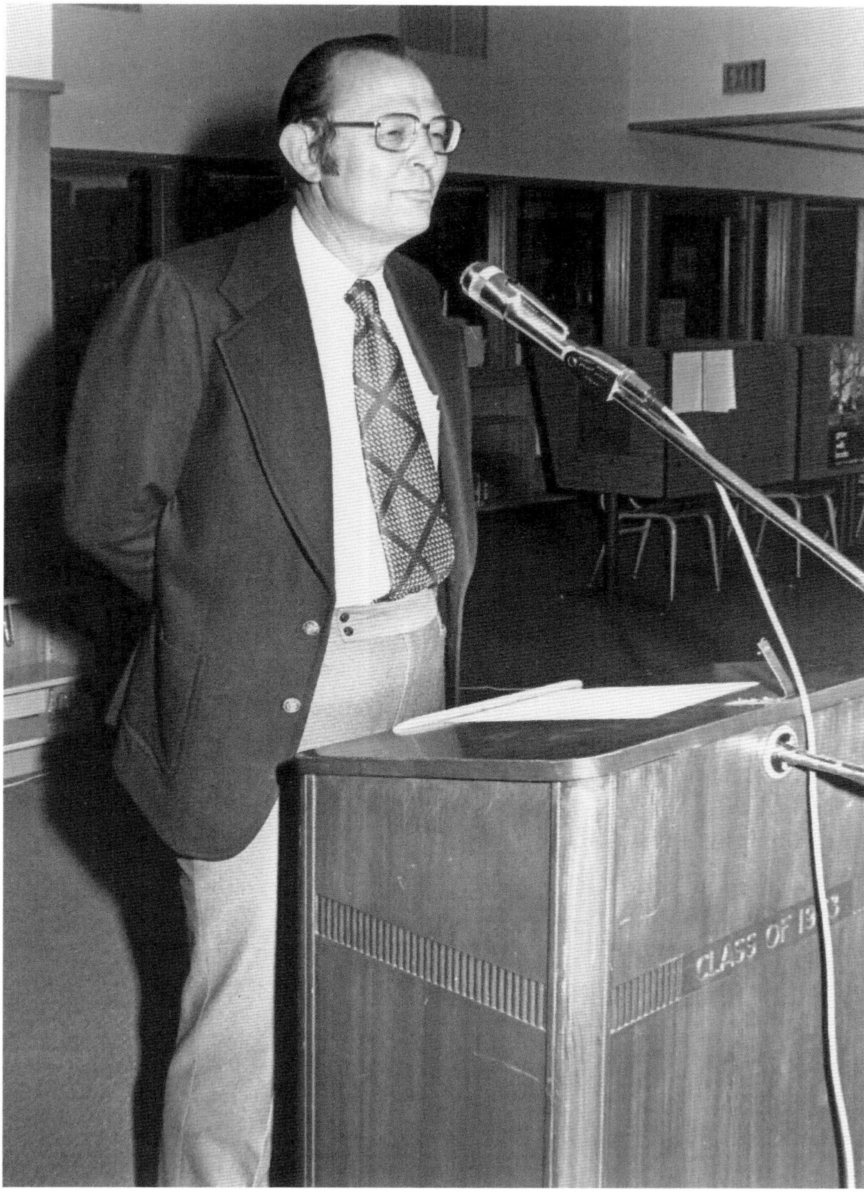

Active Educator

Nels Nelson was born in Norway in 1919. He came to Petaluma, California, in 1930 and later lived in Berkeley, where he attended the University of California. He received history and political science degrees and a doctorate in educational administration. He moved to Hayward in 1948 to begin teaching at Hayward Union High School. He left to become principal at San Lorenzo High School in 1952. In the mid-1960s, he was principal at Sunset High. Nels founded the Hayward Education Foundation and Hayward Scholarship, Inc., which nominated him for the Hayward Volunteer Award in 2011. In addition, Nels received the Hayward Area Historical Society's John Sandoval Award for contributions to local history and served on the society's board. Although retired, he remains very active in many organizations and enjoys writing short stories and attending the opera and the Shakespeare Festival in Oregon with his wife.

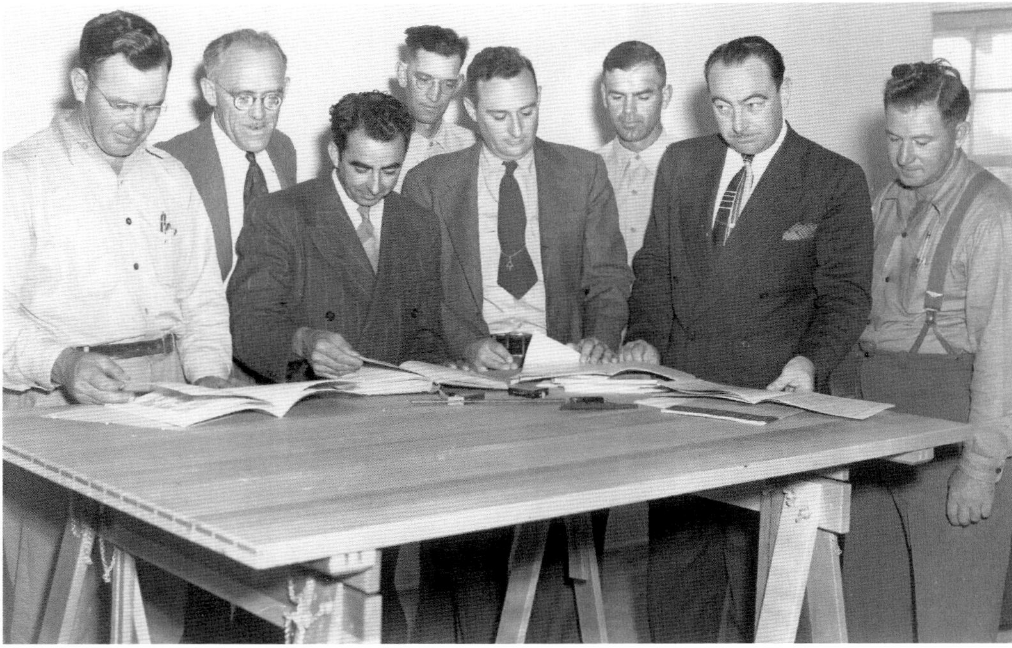

Hayward Builder
Restituto Zaballos, better known as Resti, emigrated from Salamanca, Spain, to Mount Eden via Hawaii in 1913 at age seven, with his family. His father worked at the salt ponds, and the children earned money picking fruit and vegetables in the summer. Later, his father rented a small ranch. Resti helped on the farm and dropped out of high school to be a carpenter. He helped build the Veterans Memorial Building, which was dedicated in 1931. At age 25, Resti and his brother Henry formed a general contracting partnership. They bought land to build and sell houses. They constructed seven schools, a bowling alley, and a hospital during Hayward's postwar building boom. After his brother retired, Resti continued the business with his sons, forming Zaballos and Sons Construction. He helped with many community projects and is remembered as the "Hayward Builder." Resti is pictured, third from the left.

A Wonderful Life (OPPOSITE PAGE)
Enjoying exciting, sometimes stressful, adventurous careers was Matt Jimenez's life. His Spanish family arrived in Hayward in 1920. Matt was born in 1922. He graduated from Markham Elementary, Bret Harte Junior High, and Hayward Union High School. Joining the Navy during World War II, he was stationed at Treasure Island and other California bases. He began his boxing career, becoming the Navy's Pacific Coast heavyweight champion in 1944. When Matt was discharged from the Navy, he married and joined the Hayward Fire Department. In 1950, he became captain and the city's fire chief in 1952. During his tenure, the Hayward Fire Department grew into the modern firefighting unit it is today. He retired in 1977. In 1982, Matt was elected to the Hayward City Council and reelected for his seventh term in 2006, which he never began because of his death. Matt helped establish the Hayward Boys & Girls Club in 1962. Its new building was named in his honor. He was known around town as "Mr. Hayward" because of his love and devotion to the city of his birth.

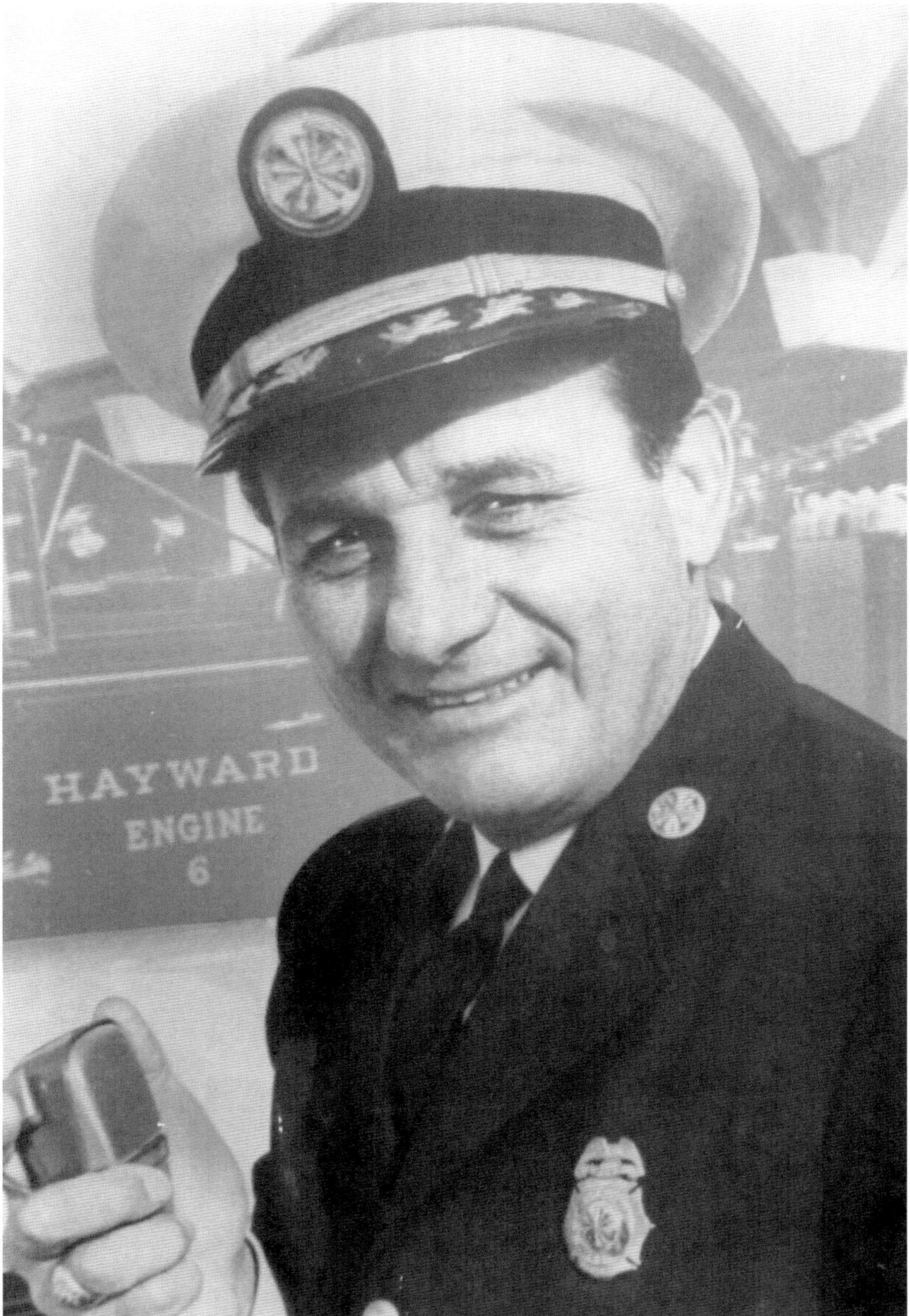
HAYWARD
ENGINE
6

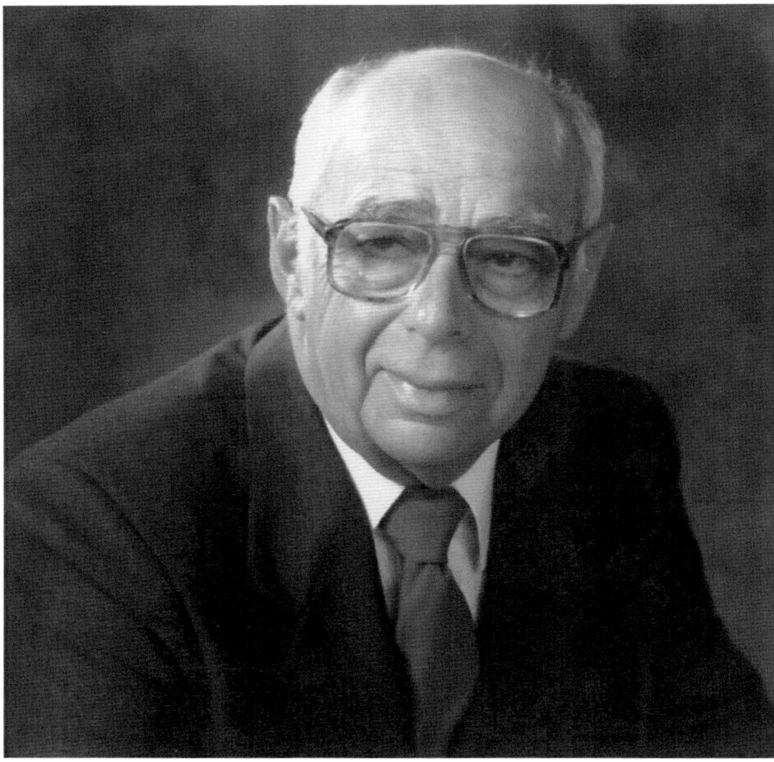

Name Changed

Julio Gomes was born in Petaluma in 1925; his name was changed to Julio Bras in 1935. His father from Sao Bras, Portugal, spoke limited English. On Immigration Day, he went before a judge. The judge said, "Antonio Gomes from Sao Bras," and Antonio said, "Si." The judge thought that was his previous name not the town he was from. So when Antonio said "Si," the judge changed his name to Antonio Bras. Julio's father, a stonemason, rode the ferry from San Francisco where the family lived to Oakland. There he carved grave markers at a monument shop. Purchasing the business and moving it to Hayward in 1935, Julio began working with his father at age 14. He graduated from Hayward Union High School and the California College of Engineering Sciences in drafting. In 1954, Julio bought the monument business from his father. Proud of his Portuguese ancestry, he brought expert tile workers from Portugal to his home to build the Portuguese Centennial Park in Hayward. Julio was very active in his community. He served four terms as an elected member of the Hayward Area Recreation and Park District Board of Directors and was president of the Bay Area Park and Recreation Commissioner's Council, which represents nine counties. In addition, he was a member of the Hayward Citizens' Advisory Committee, Hayward Park Commission, and the board of zoning adjustments, and he was elected a Hayward City Council member. Active in service and fraternal organizations, Julio was affiliated with the South Hayward Lions Club; VFW Post No. 1882; American Legion; Hayward Eagles; and various Portugese and Catholic organizations. He was interested and active in youth programs, such as the Hayward Boys Club, Little League softball, Boy Scouts of American, and other youth organizations. Julio lived by the following motto: "Find a need and fill it. It is not what the community can do for me; it's what I can do for the community." Using his time, humor, business, and financial support if necessary, he was well known throughout the community. In 1961, Julio received the Distinguished Service Award from the Junior Chamber of Commerce as Man of the Year, he was chosen the 1970 Citizen of the Year by the *Hayward Journal* newspaper, and in 1996, he received the City of Hayward Volunteer Award. (Courtesy of Beverley Bras Ford.)

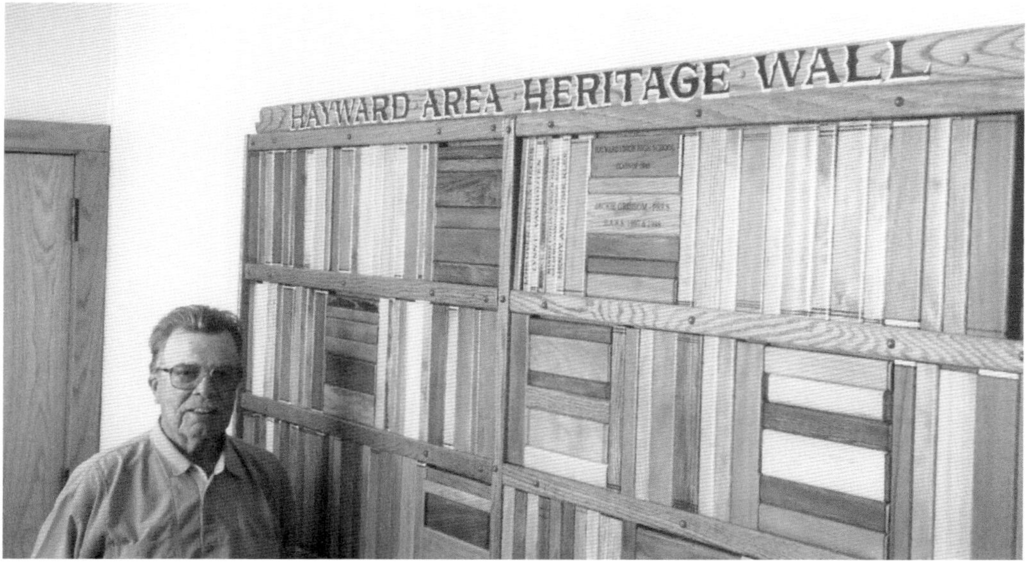

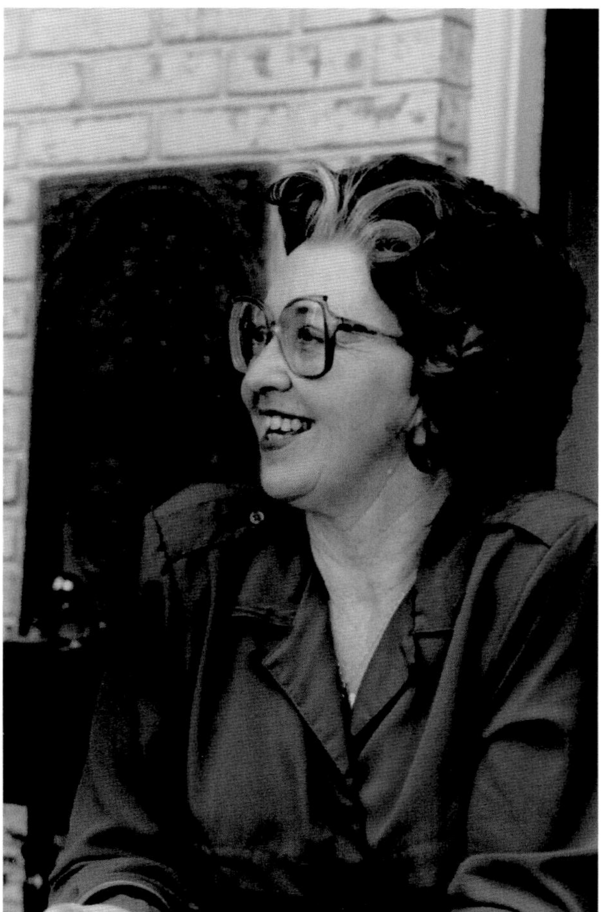

The Heritage Wall

Willard "Will" Hendrickson was involved in many community organizations. As a longtime volunteer of the Hayward Area Historical Society, he took it upon himself to design and build the unique "Heritage Wall" for the historical society. The wall provides a place for people to memorialize groups and individuals. Not only a fundraiser for the historical society, the wall has become a permanent reminder of the individuals who helped build the organization.

Passion for History

Lois Over's passion for history was unmatched. Lois actively worked to preserve the McConaghy House, tirelessly researching the history of the McConaghy family and the area. She worked as the assistant curator and director of promotions for the Hayward Area Historical Society for several years and was the first woman to serve as the society's president. In 2005, a rose garden at the McConaghy House was dedicated in her honor.

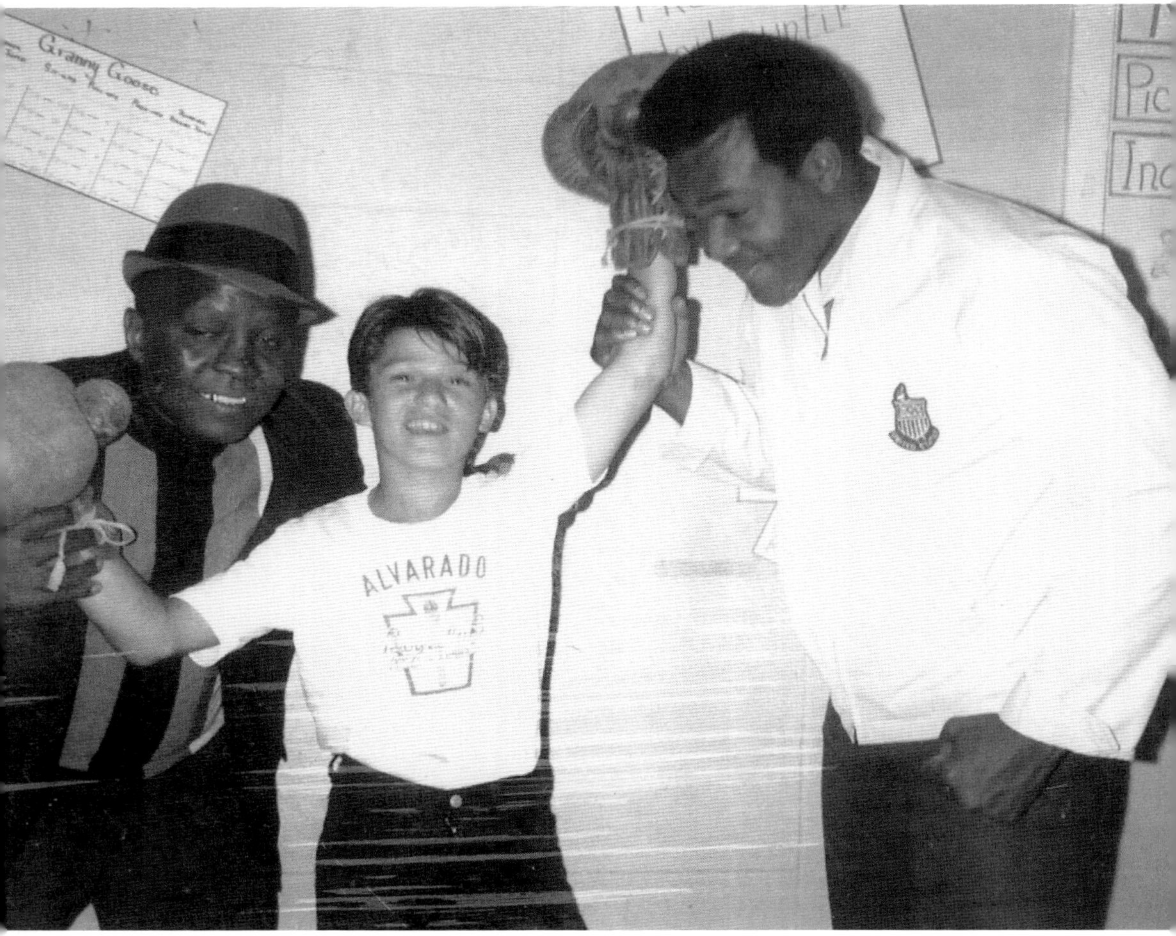

In Their Corner

Originally from Ohio, Dick Sadler came to Hayward in 1939 as an undistinguished lightweight boxer. In Hayward, Sadler would make his reputation training other fighters, most notably George Foreman, whom he trained at the Hayward Boys Club. Pictured are, from left to right, Dick, a Boys Club participant, and George Foreman. Sadler's commitment to area youth was unrivaled. Sadler supported numerous charities for mentally disabled youth as well as the Boys & Girls Club. Alameda County presented Sadler with a certificate of appreciation in 1959 and has had two "Dick Sadler" days declared in his honor by the Hayward City Council in 1969 and 1974. He was also named both honorary police and fire chief of the city. In a 1990 interview, as his health began to fail, Sadler said, "I'd rather be sick here in Hayward than the Mayor of New York City." Sadler died in 2003.

Little Theater

Douglas Morrisson, a native of South Dakota, was a Marine Corps World War II veteran. He graduated from San Jose State College with a teaching degree and moved to Hayward with his wife, Maggie. As a drama teacher at Hayward High School for 30 years, he also managed the high school auditorium. After retiring in 1977, Douglas continued his second career as a booking agent and special events director for the Alameda County Fair. He was the force behind the construction and financing of the Hayward Little Theater, the city's performing arts center. A longtime resident dedicated to the community, he was on the Hayward Area Recreation and Park District (HARD) Board of Directors for 45 years. In 2003, the HARD directors renamed the performing arts theater in his honor. (Courtesy of the Hayward Area Recreation and Park District.)

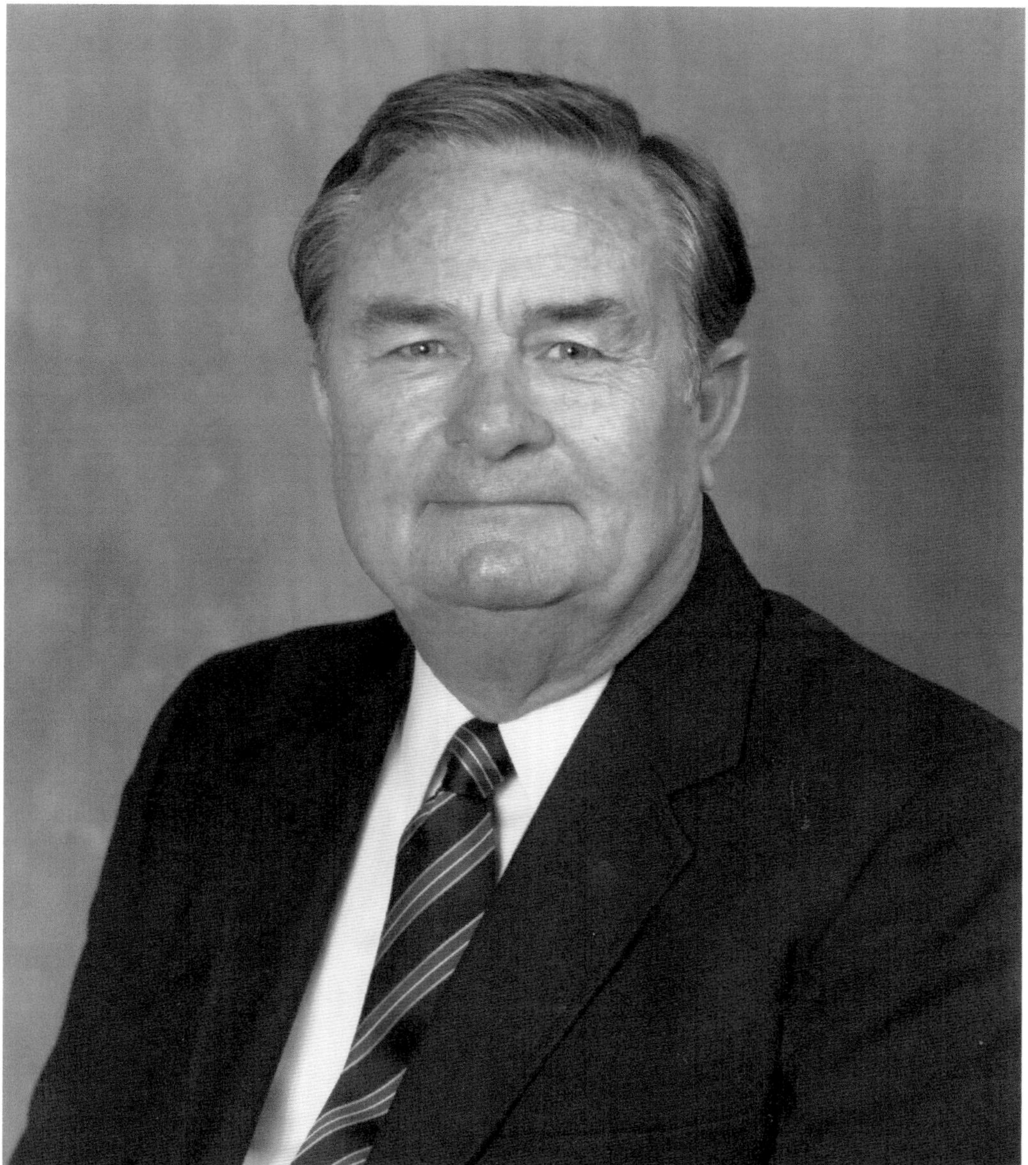

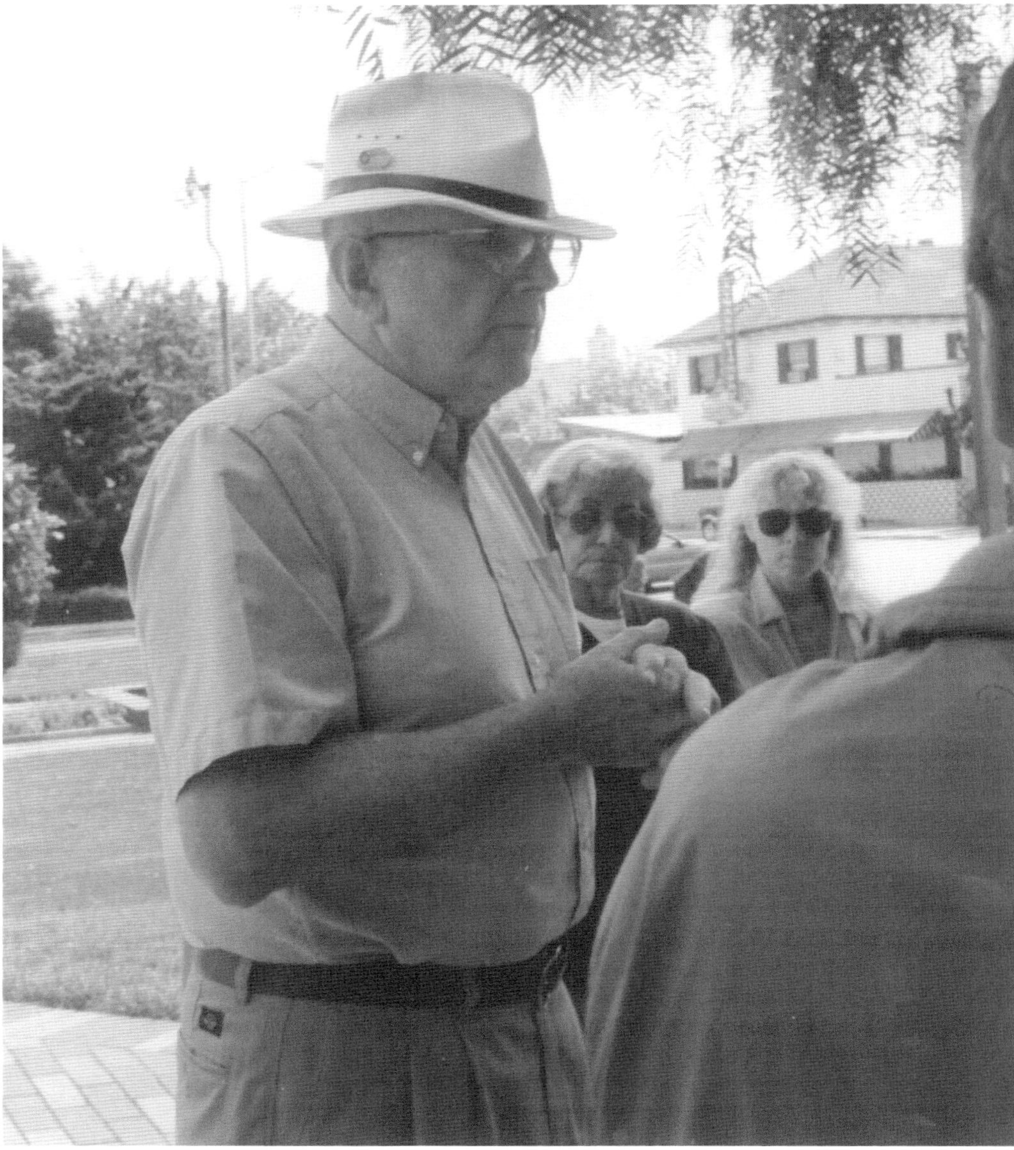

Award-Winning Volunteer
Banning Fenton, a teacher and administrator for the Hayward School District from 1949 to 1981, received many awards for his volunteer work. The city of Hayward gave him a lifetime achievement award for serving as a volunteer guide and teacher for the Hayward Area Historical Society and chairing the city's 125th anniversary celebration. Banning led historical walking tours (pictured) in downtown Hayward. He taught a Hayward history class for senior citizens and wrote the book *Hayward: Heart of the Bay.* Leading tours to help elderly people learn how to use the Bay Area Rapid Transit District train to San Francisco resulted in Banning and his wife, Alwine, receiving a "Senior Award." The historical society also gave Banning the John Sandoval Award for promoting and preserving Hayward's history. He loved to share his passion of history with others.

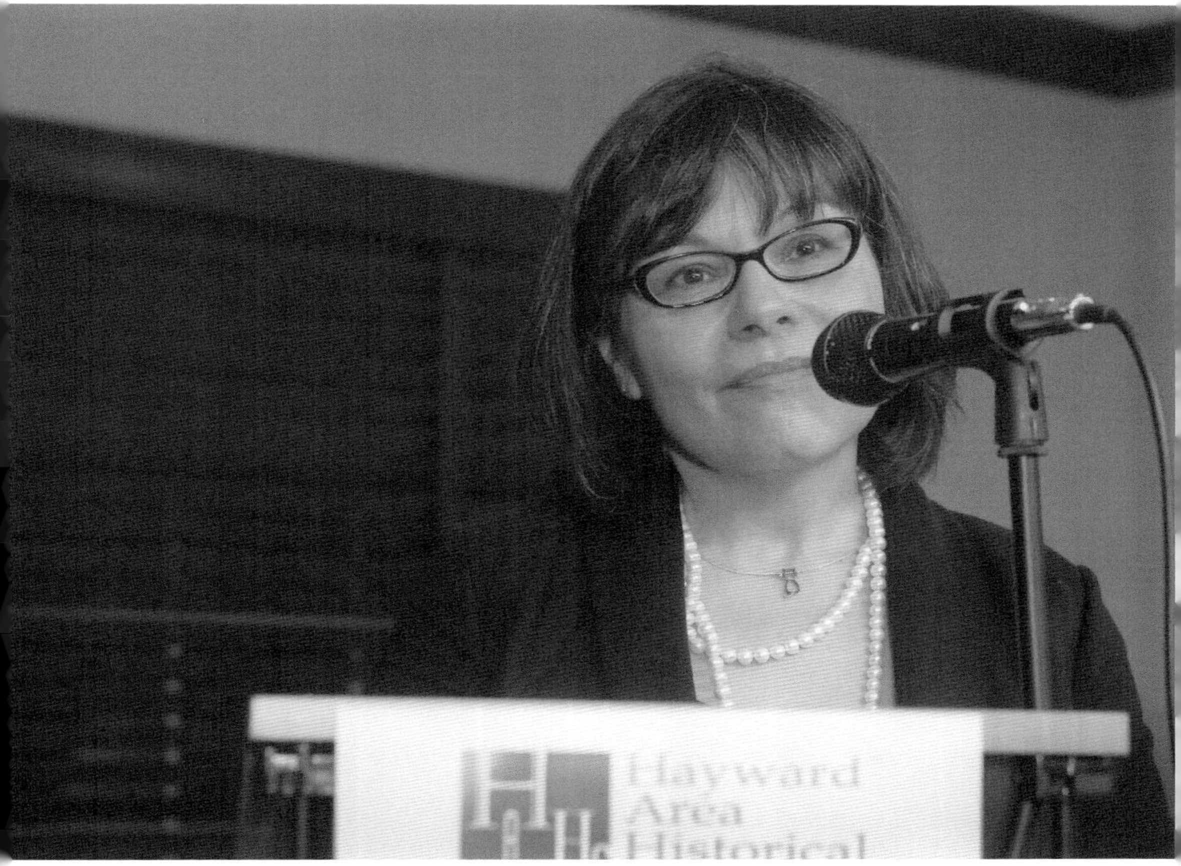

Writing is Her Life Force

Maria Ochoa contributes to the community in many ways. She served as the first Chicana member of the Alameda County Commission on the Status of Women and was chairperson in 1977–1978. Maria was in the first group of Puente Project mentors begun at Chabot College in 1981. Lieutenant Governor McCarty appointed her in 1986 to a Task Force on the Feminization of Poverty, where she assisted in the development of 25 pieces of legislation, 10 of which became law. Maria began writing at an early age. Her first book was *The History of San Lorenzo,* which she wrote in the fourth grade as a student at Hesperian Elementary. As an adult, she has written the books *Russell City, Creative Collectives: Chicana Painters Working in Community,* and *Shout Out: Women of Color Respond to Violence. Adventures of a Brown Biscuit* is her memoir, in which she tells stories about how reading and writing changed her life. She graduated from Mount Eden High School in 1968 and received her doctorate in 1995 from the University of California, Santa Cruz. She has taught at Stanford University and San José State University. In addition to her work as a writer and professor, she has worked in electoral politics, including the campaigns of her husband, Hayward mayor Mike Sweeney. Maria lives in Hayward with her husband and four felines. In 2009, she received the John Sandoval Award from the Hayward Area Historical Society for her work on documenting the history of Russell City.

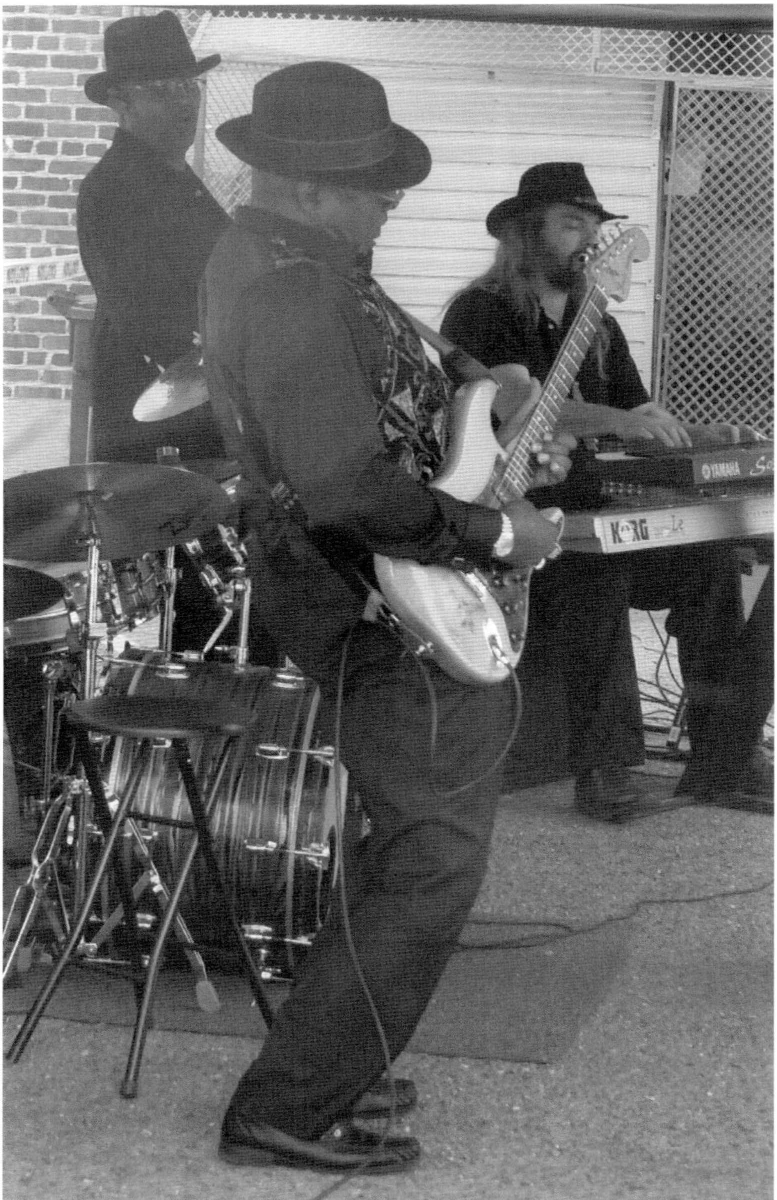

Blues Festival
Organizer Ronnie Stewart of the Bay Area Blues Society began the Hayward-Russell City Blues Festival in 1996. Ronnie is seen here playing guitar in 2011. Ronnie wanted to revive the music tradition once heard in the dirt-floor nightclubs of the former Hayward shoreline community of Russell City. The community of small farms and modest houses was known for musicians playing a style of Delta blues. Artists such as Jimmy Witherspoon, Big Joe Turner, Big Mama Thornton, L.C. "Good Rocking" Robinson, Johnny Hartman, Lowell Fulson and other big-name blues stars all played there. Russell City is now a landmark on the map that contributed to world culture reflecting the unique African American musical sound that is still heard at the annual festival.

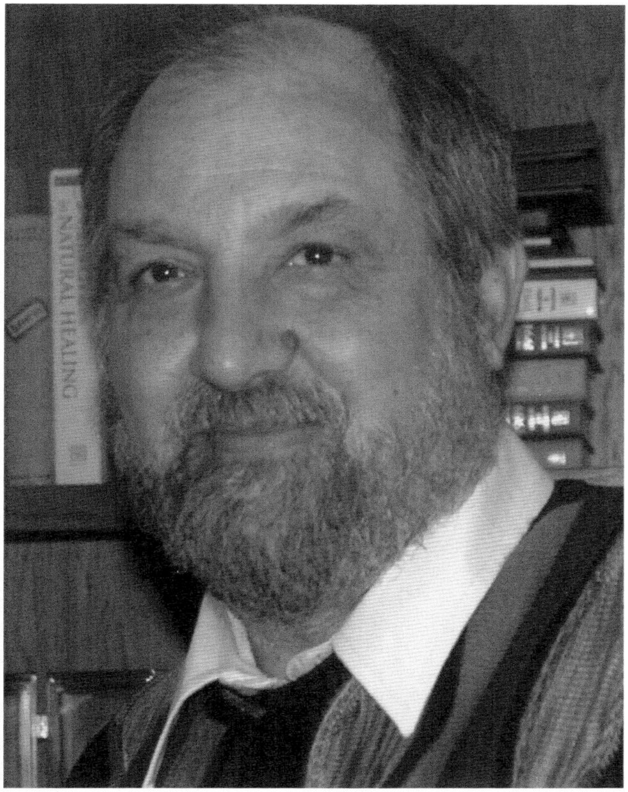

Historic Preservation

A resident of Hayward since 1956, Frank Goulart arrived at age seven when his father was transferred to the former Parks Air Force Base in Dublin. He attended Hayward schools, graduating from Tennyson High School in 1967. Frank also attended Chabot College, the University of California, Berkeley, and graduated from Armstrong School of Law in 1981. During this time, he had a band, The Gates of Eden, married, and had two sons. He began his law practice in downtown Hayward. In 1994, Frank, his wife, Julie, and her parents purchased the historic Linekin Building for his office. He was the construction manager and house tour guide for the renovation project. The Victorian farmhouse was built in 1893 for one of Hayward's original city trustees, Leander Linekin. It was researched by Frank and then added to Hayward's list of significant buildings. In 2005, Frank self-published his handwritten research in the Linekin book, titled "Notes and Selective Index to Haywards Weekly Journal 1877–1903." The Lyndall House was purchased by Frank and Julie in 2006 for their residence restoration. He was construction manager on the renovation of this notable 1920 Craftsman Shingle house. Many historic buildings have been saved because of Frank's leadership and research. He helped form the Friends of Historic City Hall to save the first city hall. He worked to have Judge Harder's house moved to another location and stopped the sale of the Hayward Odd Fellows Hall. In response to pressure, the City of Hayward began a process to inventory the historic structures. For Hayward's 125th birthday, the Friends group (now called Friends of Hayward), headed by Frank, conducted the Hayward Historic Building Tour by bus. From 2006 to 2008, he was a Hayward Area Historical Society Board director and volunteered in the library helping the public with research questions while working on the Hayward history walks that he conducts during the summer. Membership on the Hayward Area Shoreline Planning Agency Citizen Advisory Committee from 1982 into the 1990s found Frank helping to establish the Bay Trail to save the historic shoreline and wildlife. Frank continues to work on retaining the memory of local history, saving local historic buildings, and improving the community in the city of Hayward. (Courtesy of Frank Goulart.)

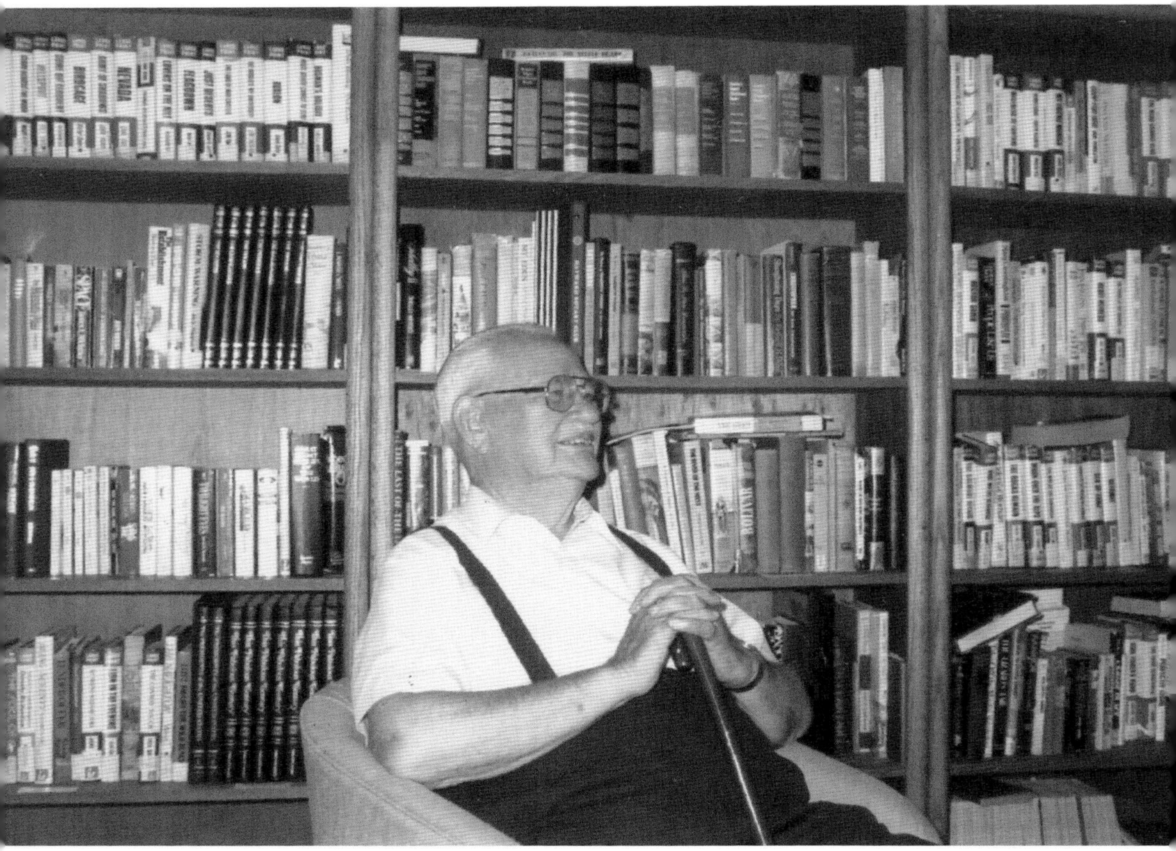

Hayward Historian

John Sandoval was born in Sonora in 1906 and graduated from the University of California, Berkeley, in 1927. For most of his career, he was a factory representative for the Sunbeam Corporation, but his avocation was the study of California history with the emphasis on Southern Alameda County. As a Hayward resident, John became a columnist for the *Daily Review* newspaper. He wrote more than 100 articles on the history of Hayward, California, and Alameda County as well as several local history books and historical pageants. In 1971, John was president of the Hayward Area Historical Society Board and received the Distinguished Citizen of Hayward award in 1975. Due to John's unwavering interest in history, the historical society named an annual award after him, given to an individual or group for extraordinary service in support or promotion of Hayward area history.

Service to Community (OPPOSITE PAGE)

Known for her involvement in education, art, and community is Doris Rodriquez. Returning to college after raising a family, she received an associate's of arts degree at Chabot College and a bachelor's of arts degree in art history at California State University, Hayward. Doris, who grew up in Oakland, has lived in Hayward over 40 years. She was a computer technician at Mervyn's Business Office and served the City of Hayward in many capacities. For 15 years, Doris was a member of the city council and spent many years on commissions. She was a member of the Chicano Student Union at Chabot College and a board member of the Hayward Area Historical Society. Active in the Hayward Arts Council, Southgate Area Homeowners Association, Chabot College Foundation, and St. Rose Hospital Foundation Board, she is making her community better for everyone.

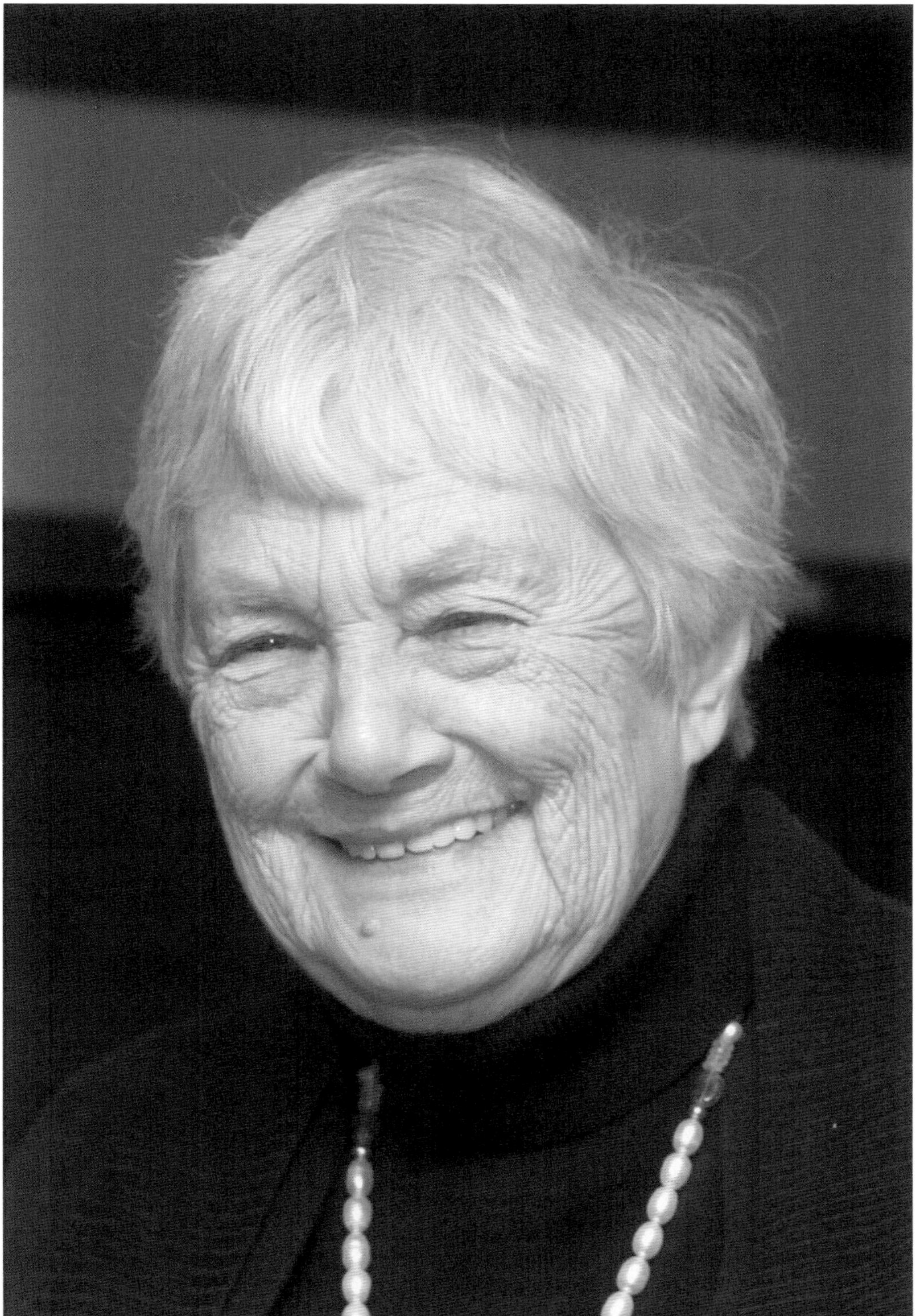

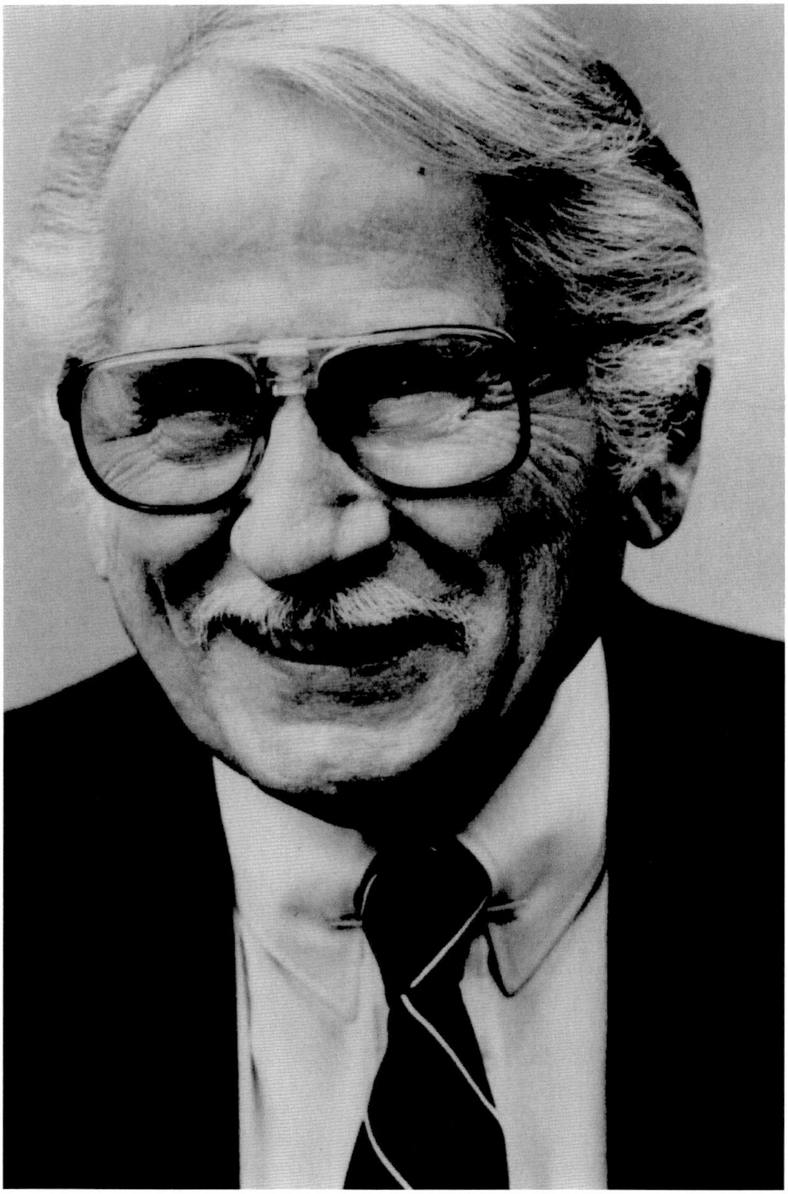

Politician

The son of a Greek immigrant, John Pappas moved to Hayward in 1950. John was a longtime member of the Democratic Party and was active in the affairs of the Southern Alameda County branch. His political career began on the Mount Eden school board. In the 1950s, John also served on the city's planning commission at a time when Hayward was expanding rapidly. In 1960, he ran for and won a seat on the Hayward City Council. He would hold that position until 1976 and serve as the last council appointed mayor between 1964 and 1965. John used his position to improve the relationship between the city and Hayward residents by encouraging volunteerism. In recognition of his efforts, the John N. Pappas Award is presented by the city of Hayward every year to community volunteers. Pappas passed away in 1999.

Product of Hayward

Early in life, Michael P. Sweeney learned that politics impacts people's lives. Politics were always a part of his family house. His father Daniel was president of the local postal workers union and was involved in city, state, and national elections. Michael has lived in the Hayward area all of his life. In 1968, he graduated from San Lorenzo High School and then earned his bachelor's and master's degrees in political science from California State University, Hayward. While in college, he worked at the Hunt Brothers Cannery, where Michael witnessed firsthand the issues facing Hayward's laborers. After college, he taught government and history at the Hayward Adult School. Michael's youthful, genuine enthusiasm for his hometown led him to enter city politics. In 1982, at the age of 32, Michael was elected to the city council and he became the second youngest person ever elected to that body. He was reelected in 1986 and won a tough mayoral race in 1990 with 70 percent of the vote, winning all 57 Hayward precincts—defeating a respected and admired incumbent. Michael resonated with voters over matters ranging from development issues to rent control and the environment. He distinguished himself as a slow-growth advocate, working to scale back development on Walpert Ridge, the Pleasanton Ridge, and along the Hayward shoreline. After a single term as mayor, he was elected to the California Assembly's 18th District, serving two terms starting in 1994. Gov. Gray Davis appointed him in 1999 to the position of undersecretary for the California Resources Agency. In 2004, Michael became the director of Spectrum Services, a nonprofit providing essential services to low-income seniors, and he continues as its director today. In 2006, he was once again elected mayor and then reelected in 2010, again building a broad base of support and taking up issues that concerned residents most. His most recent success was the establishment of the popular Keep Hayward Clean and Green Task Force. Michael's adaptability has continued to serve him. What started with youth and excitement has matured into a wisdom that could only come from living in the same town most of one's life.

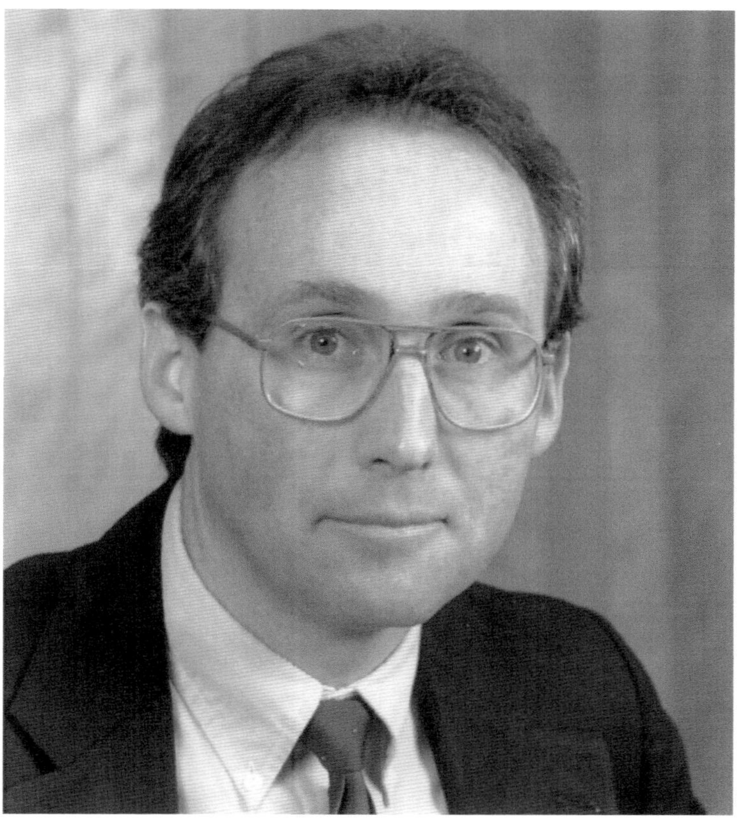

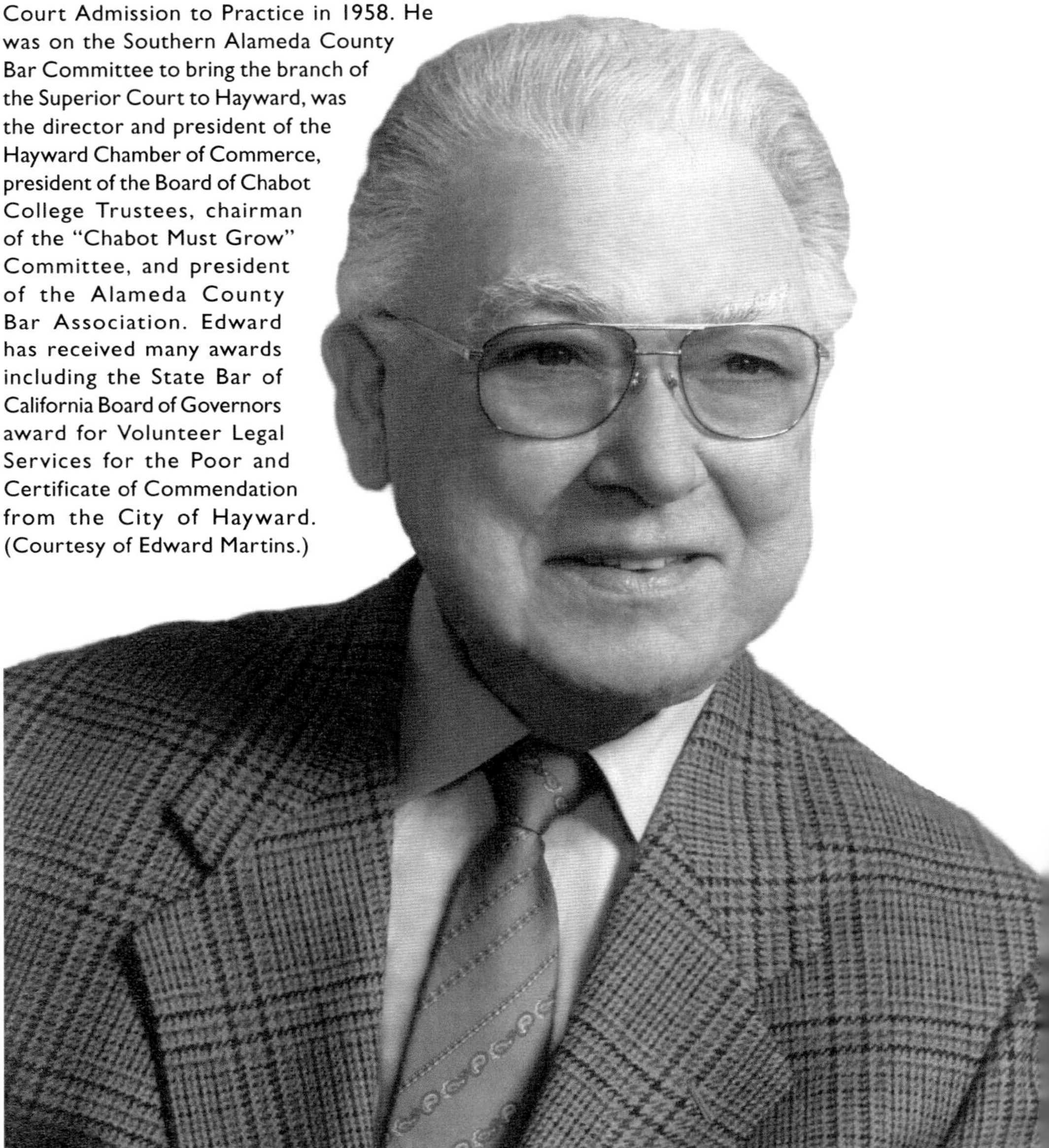

Hayward Attorney

Edward Martins has been a Hayward attorney since 1952. He attended high school in Patterson, California, and graduated in 1949 from the University of California, Berkeley, with a bachelor's of science degree in business administration. He received his law degrees in 1952 at the University of San Francisco and the US Supreme Court Admission to Practice in 1958. He was on the Southern Alameda County Bar Committee to bring the branch of the Superior Court to Hayward, was the director and president of the Hayward Chamber of Commerce, president of the Board of Chabot College Trustees, chairman of the "Chabot Must Grow" Committee, and president of the Alameda County Bar Association. Edward has received many awards including the State Bar of California Board of Governors award for Volunteer Legal Services for the Poor and Certificate of Commendation from the City of Hayward. (Courtesy of Edward Martins.)

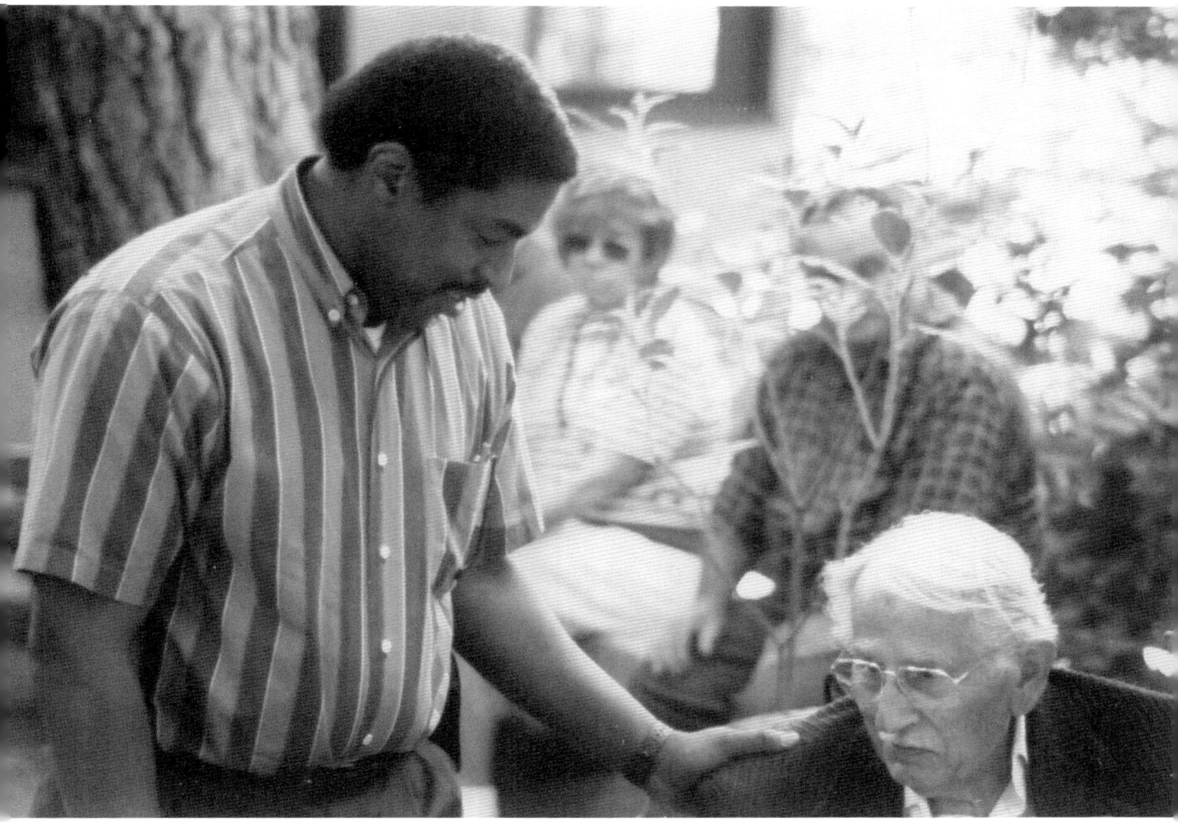

Public Servant

A self-employed computer programmer with a master's degree in physics does not sound like the makings of a career public servant—Olden Henson is an exception. Olden served on the Hayward City Council between 1994 and 2012. He is one of the longest-serving African Americans on the council. Olden was originally appointed to the council but was elected in his own right in 1996. He is shown here with former city councilman John Pappas. He went to work encouraging development of housing and recreation in the city. Before his election, Olden served on the citizens advisory commission in 1987 and then on the planning commission in 1991. In his 20-plus years as a public servant, Olden said, "I wanted nothing more than to see this city do well."

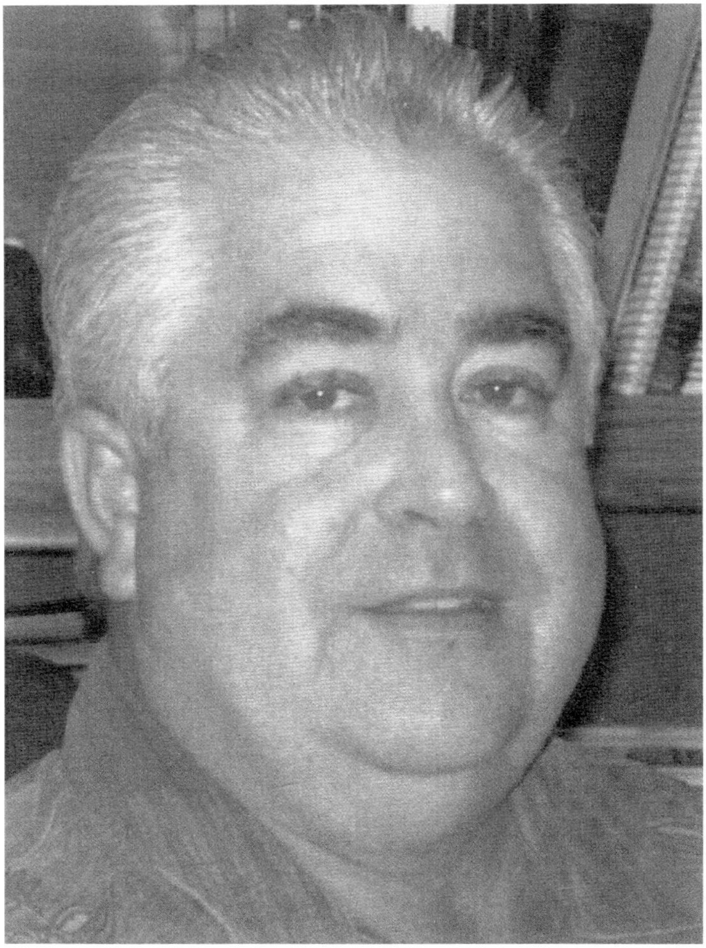

Community Involvement
Born and raised in Hayward, George Pacheco Jr. attended local schools. After graduating from Chabot College for business administration, George went to the University of California, Davis, for horticultural studies. He and his brother established the Pacheco Brothers Gardening business in Hayward. George donates to the community his time, talents, and business resources for many projects and organizations. He also leads the annual "Let's Go Fishing" for developmentally disabled children and has coached and managed Little League teams. The Hayward and Castro Valley Chambers of Commerce have named George as Business Person of the Year. In 1999, he received the City of Hayward Mayor's Award and in 2010 the John N. Pappas Award for his participation in community organizations and projects.

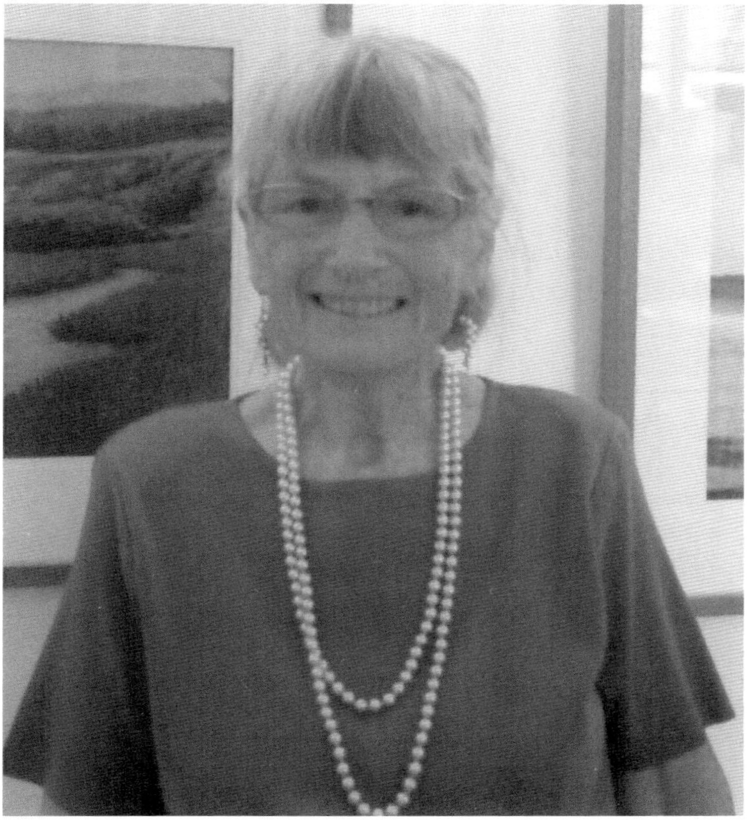

Children's Issues and Health

Gail Steele has made the Hayward area a better place to live for almost 50 years as a Hayward City Council member for eight years, as founder and executive director of the Eden Youth Center, and as an Alameda County supervisor representing Hayward for 18 years. Gail grew up in Guerneville, California. She received her bachelor's of art degree in sociology from the University of California, Berkeley, and master's degree in public administration of nonprofit from the University of San Francisco. Gail is a supporter of children's issues and health services meeting behavioral and health needs of children, youth, and adults. As an advocate for children's mental health services, she was the liaison between the Mental Health Advisory Board of Alameda County and the Alameda County Board of Supervisors. In 1986, Gail joined the St. Rose Hospital Foundation Board and worked to improve community access to health care in the Hayward area. In 2008, she was nominated by St. Rose Hospital to receive the City of Hayward Volunteer Award for her foundation work. For her many years of devotion and commitment to the wellness and recovery of those suffering from mental health issues, a new behavioral health building was dedicated the Gail Steele Wellness and Recovery Center in 2012.

In 1994, Gail began the Children's Memorial and ceremony to raise awareness and honor the children under 18 from Alameda County who lost their lives to violence. It is located at the Children's Memorial Grove where a grove of oak trees leads into a large stone octagon structure on a ridge overlooking the Bay Area at the border of Castro Valley and San Leandro. The parents impacted by the loss of their children formed a Children's Memorial Committee. They and Gail selected a flag design from 164 schoolchildren entries to make the Children's Memorial Flag. The Child Welfare League of America took the flag project from the county to the state and national level. In 1997, the California assembly declared the fourth Friday in April as a statewide annual observance to fly the flag. The US Congress passed the same resolution in 2001. (Author's collection.)

Senior Family Album

David Kolm of Hayward created the "Senior Family Album" website in 1998 as a personal site for his photographs. As a senior citizen and retired furniture store owner, David knew other seniors might have photographs and be interested in getting them online. It gives people a chance to see and share a lifetime of events and to bring back memories that have been forgotten. David believes it is better than keeping memories stashed away in a box. Seniors use the site to post up to 30 photographs for free. David scans and uploads them at home. (Courtesy of David Kolm.)

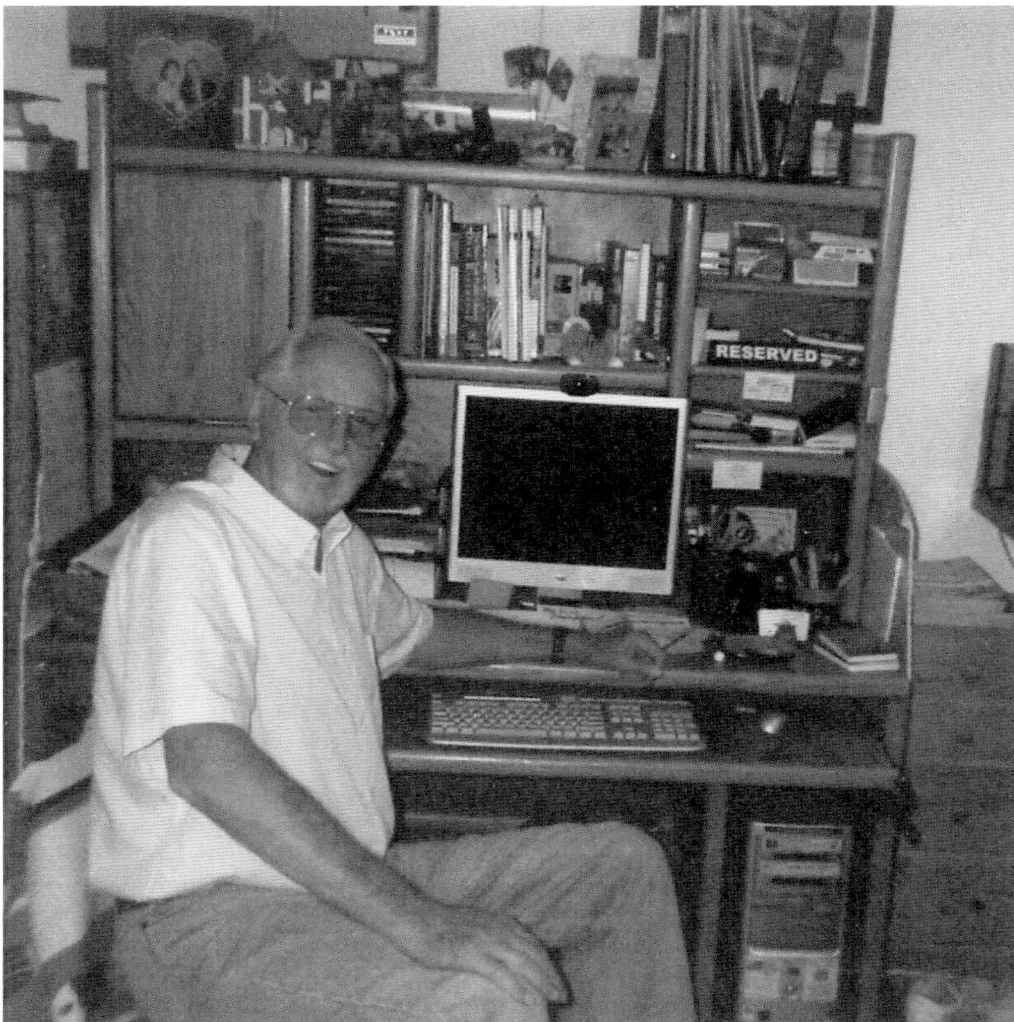

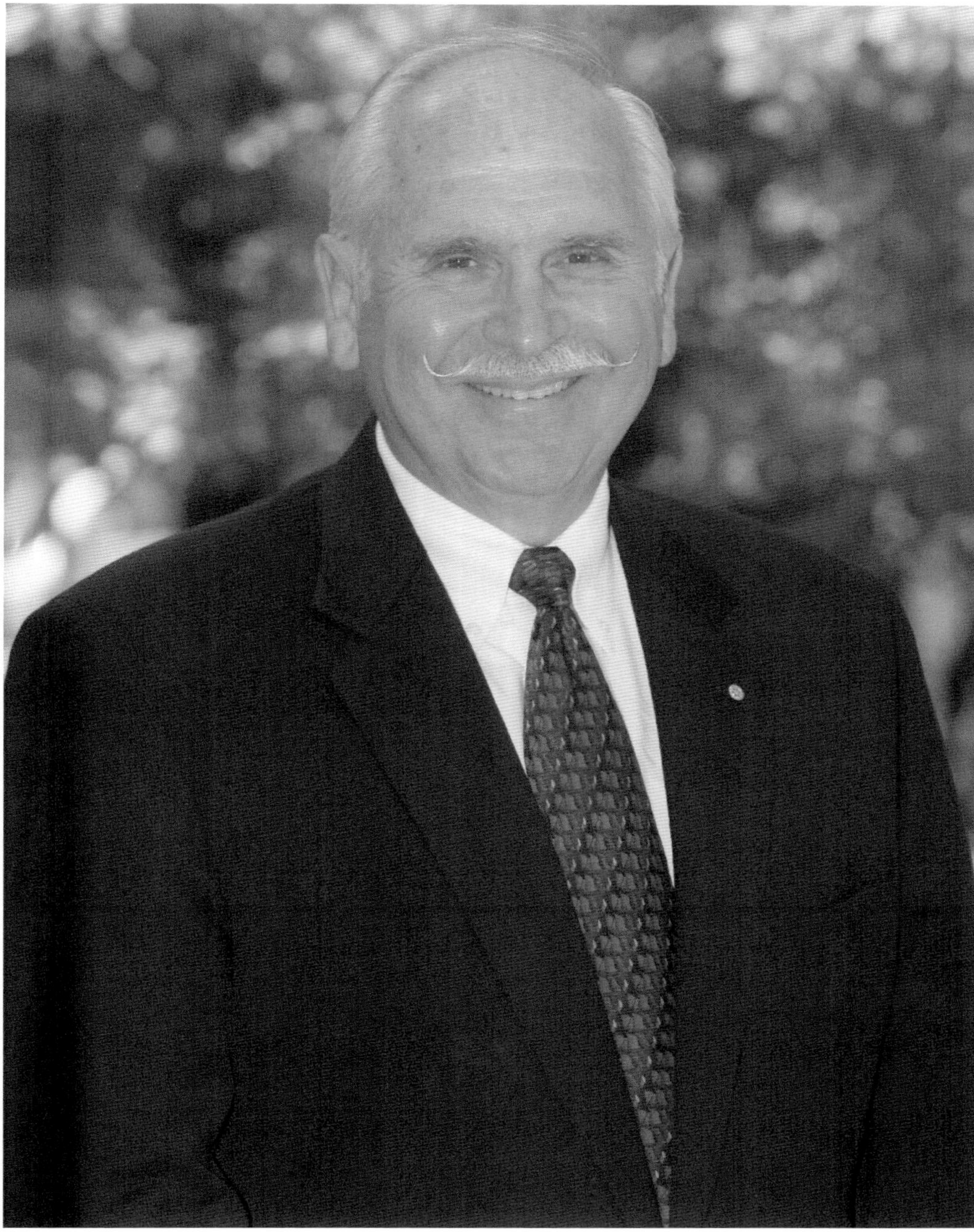

Community and School Involvement
Working for the betterment of Hayward as a part of numerous boards and commissions was two-term city council member Larry Ratto. Larry was dedicated to the students of the community. He was a high school teacher, counselor, and principal at all four Hayward high schools for 36 years. Continuing to contribute to the community as a member of the Alameda County Planning Commission, St. Rose Hospital Foundation Board, Hayward Chamber of Commerce, and the Hayward Rotary Club, Larry received the Mayor's Award for his dedication and service to others in 2012.

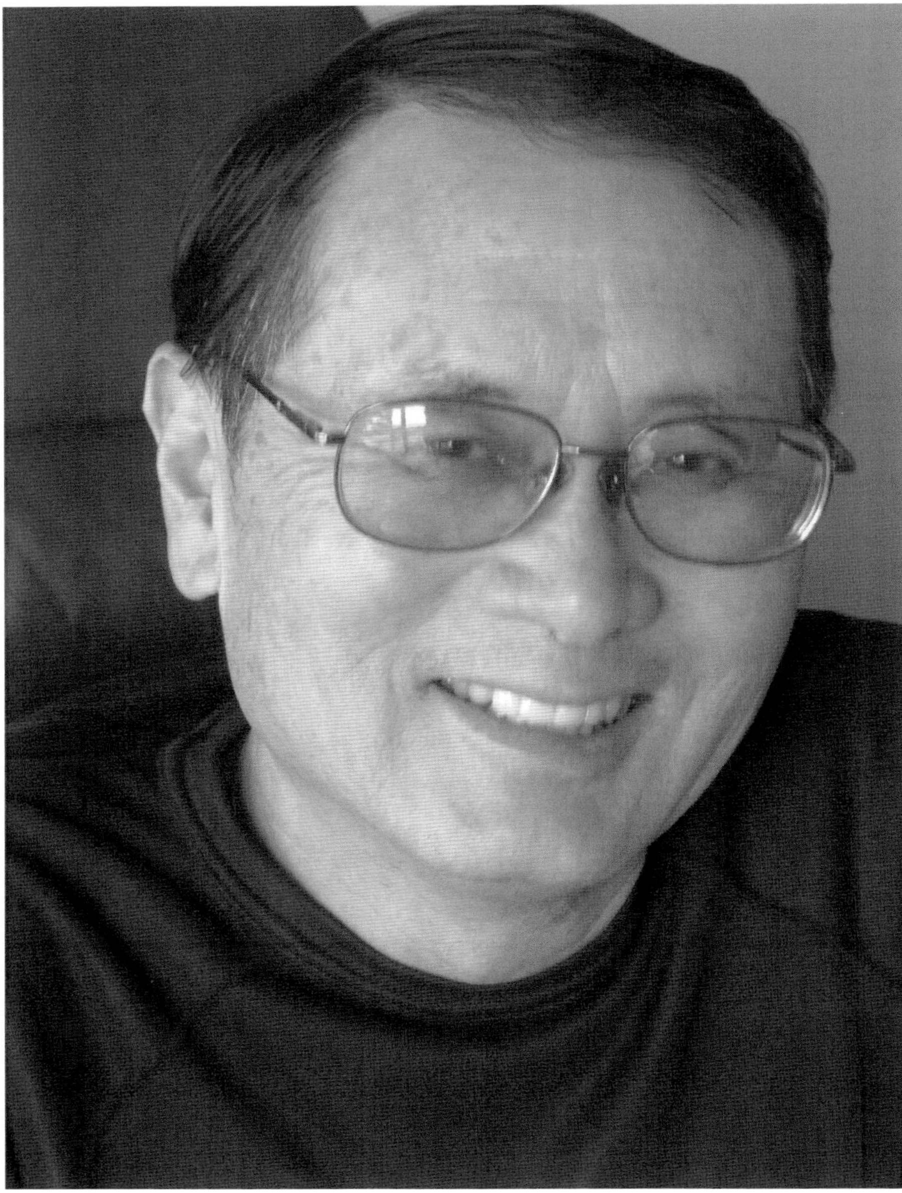

Devotion to Community

Robert "Bob" Sakai was born in Richmond, California, in 1945. His parents came to Hayward in 1948 to establish a nursery. It was a branch of the first Sakai nursery in Richmond begun by his grandparents. Bob was one of nine brothers and sisters. They were raised to be a part of the business and community of Hayward. After graduating from Tennyson High School, he went to the University of California, Berkeley, and graduated in 1967. He later graduated from Hastings College of Law in 1974. Bob practiced law with Haley, Purchio, Sakai & Smith for 33 years before beginning his independent law practice. Well-known for his devotion to the Hayward community as a member of many organizations, he was honored as the Outstanding Hayward Rotarian in 2008—the club's highest accolade—and received the Hayward Chamber of Commerce Business Person of the Year Award in 2011. (Courtesy of Robert Sakai.)

CHAPTER THREE

San Lorenzo

The unincorporated town in Alameda County was formally called "Squatterville" until 1864, when the post office was established. A rich, fertile area with the San Lorenzo Creek and many water springs, the area attracted settlers wishing to raise profitable crops, which resulted in the building of large homes and mansions. One of the first farmers and largest landowners was William Meek. The area surrounding his mansion is now called Meekland or Cherryland for the many cherry trees he grew. Here, Donna McCarty and Maybelle Rasmussen's parents built their homes in the 1920s. William Meek's mansion stands today as a symbol of the long agricultural history in the area. Many volunteers, such as Robert and Erica Campisi, helped save and maintain the mansion. Horticulturalist John Lewelling owned a large estate near his friend William Meek, and both served on community and county organizations. Other early pioneers were Henry Smyth and the Marlin, McConaghy, and Rodrigues families.

The first commercial business in San Lorenzo, located by the San Lorenzo Creek, was a blacksmith shop, established by John Boyle and later purchased by Henry Smyth. Teubert Smith's father built a blacksmith shop east of Telegraph Road along the San Lorenzo Creek, where it remains today.

The town developed around the Four Corners, the intersection of Main Street (now Lewelling Boulevard) and Telegraph Road (now Hesperian Boulevard). Businesses, such as Richard Kraus' parents flower shop, Fred's Flowers, began here. Also near the main section of town were the first church, where John King completed a stained-glass window project in 1993, and the San Lorenzo Pioneer Cemetery, where Jack Marlin became the last member of the cemetery committee.

The town changed dramatically with the establishment of the San Lorenzo Village community that was planned by developer David D. Bohannon during World War II on farmland south of San Lorenzo Creek. The new homes brought a huge population boom to San Lorenzo, causing postmaster Gertrude Mooney to obtain mail delivery for the new village homes and later move the post office with her assistant Mary Videll to the San Lorenzo Village shopping center. The shopping center included a movie theater, the fire department, and stores. Mervin Morris opened his first department store in the San Lorenzo Village shopping center, and Frank Denevi began his photography business there. In 1982, Sung Han Lee opened his dry cleaning business nearby, becoming the leading green dry cleaners in the region. The San Lorenzo Village Homes Association, one of the oldest homeowners associations in the country, continues to oversee further development of the village. Nancy VanHuffel was the first and longest-serving woman administrator of the San Lorenzo Village Homes Association, and Esther Jorgensen was the first female board member.

Some land around the village was saved for many years from being converted to housing. The carnation flower nursery of George Gianelli's parents was one such place. Eventually, the continued demand for housing forced the sale of the nursery and a few other small farms. The memory of those long-standing businesses and landowners lives on with the Spanish street names.

The San Lorenzo Elementary School District, which began with three schools under the leadership of Supt. Claude Lawson, grew along with the population. The second superintendent, Paul Ehret, led the six-school district in 1948 through a period of phenomenal growth and the creation of the San Lorenzo Unified School District, which brought the elementary, junior, and high schools into one district. Evelyn Poston was the superintendent's secretary during this time. In the 1970s, the district had a declining enrollment and closed many schools. In 2007, Dr. Dennis Byas became the seventh superintendent with 16 schools, including one nonpublic charter school. San Lorenzo High School has developed innovative programs such as the Green Academy, taught by Alan Fishman. Tom Longaker founded the San Lorenzo High Sports Hall of Fame. The San Lorenzo Unified School District once contained the Wes Gordon Science Museum and now contains the only Native American Museum in any local school district developed by Deanna Espina.

San Lorenzo residents are now focusing on improving the community and volunteering. Residents like Dorothy Partridge, Tom Vierra, Mary Bossley, and Keith Barros continue to improve San Lorenzo and help others.

The farmland is now occupied with homes and businesses, but the history is preserved through the efforts of Tom and Cathy Clements and third-generation San Lorenzo historian Doris Marciel.

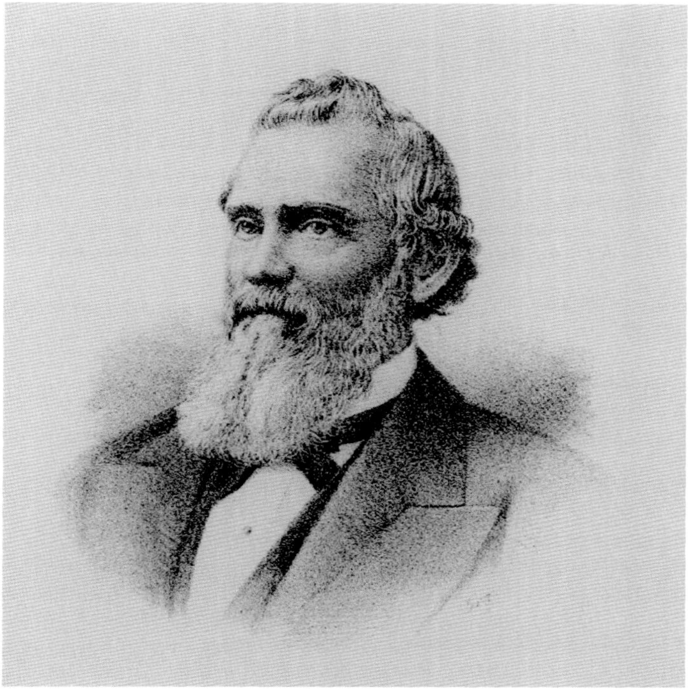

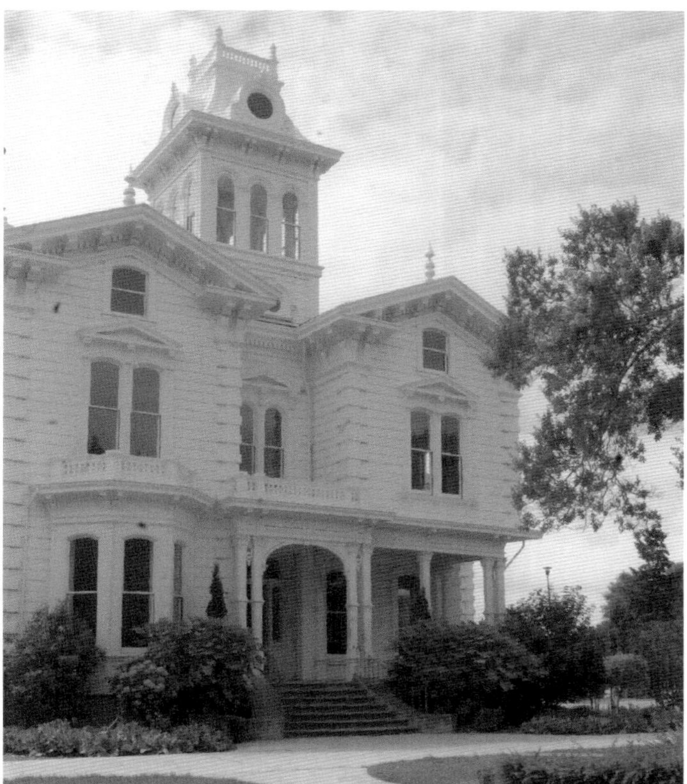

First Farmer

William Meek was born in Ohio in 1816. At age 21, he moved with his family to Iowa. He went overland to Oregon in 1847, formed a partnership with Henderson Lewelling, and opened a successful nursery and mill. In 1859, he moved to San Lorenzo. Ten years later, William owned close to 3,000 acres in the area and built a beautiful mansion, pictured here in 2009. William was known as Alameda County's "first farmer" due to his large landholdings and successful farming practices, like rotating crops and developing a good water supply. He grew a variety of products from grains and corn to sugar beets, almonds, apricots, and cherries. His cherries brought in as much as $10,000 in a single season. William was civic-minded and served with many organizations and government positions. He died on December 27, 1880, at the age of 64.

Horticulturalist

John Lewelling was one of eight children born to a Quaker horticulturalist in 1811. John, along with his brothers, followed their father's example, each becoming adept at grafting fruit trees and operating successful nurseries. John came to California in 1850 with one of his brothers to try their hand at gold mining. In 1853, John returned to Iowa to his family and then brought them to San Francisco and, eventually, to San Lorenzo. He acquired property and set up an orchard and nursery operation. He became involved in politics, serving as an Alameda County Supervisor, and was a founding member of the San Lorenzo Cemetery Association. Due to poor health, John moved to St. Helena in 1864, selling his land in San Lorenzo to his son Eli, who continued to operate the successful orchards for many more decades.

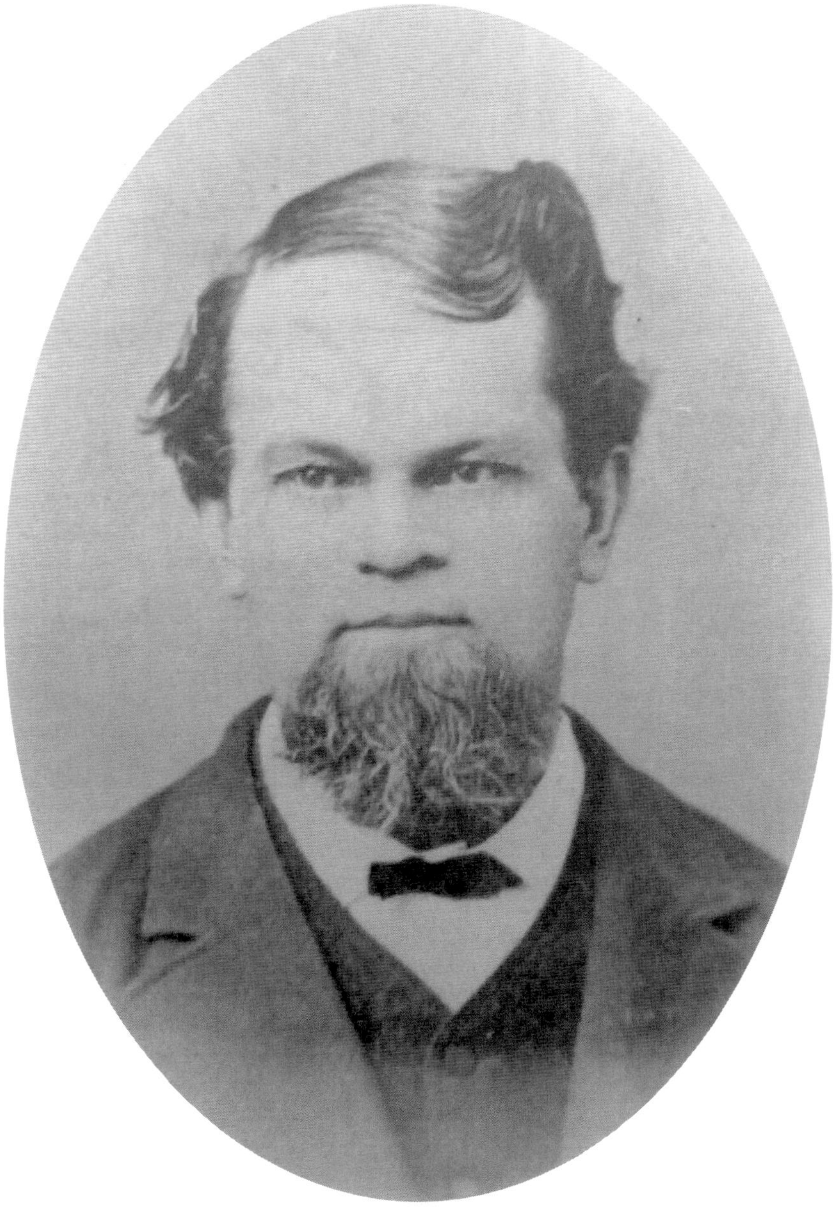

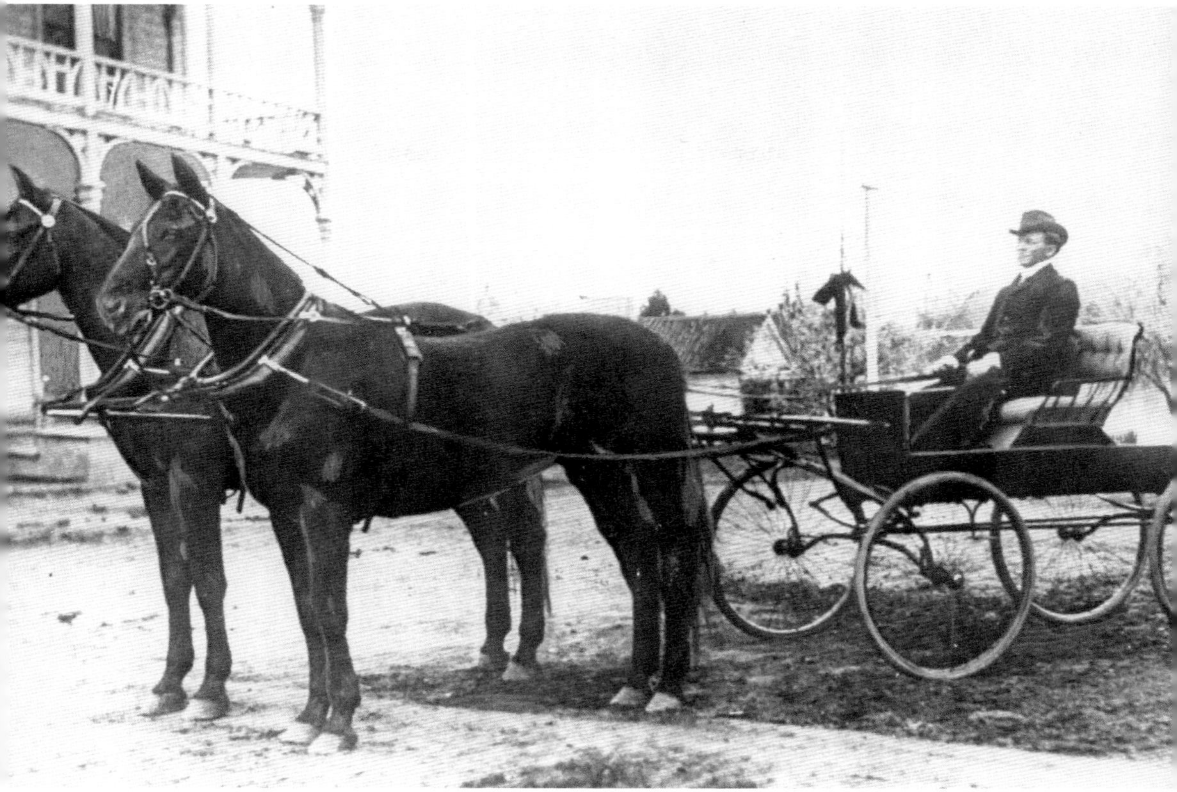

A Century of Living

John McConaghy lived for more than a century. John was born in San Lorenzo to Scottish immigrant parents in 1871. He was their youngest child but became responsible for the family farm, helping raise tomatoes, cucumbers, asparagus, and pears. John lived 86 years in the iconic McConaghy House, which his parents had built in 1886. John was an active traveler, taking many trips with his wife, Florence Smyth, who was also from a pioneer family. John's life spanned the arch of the development of the entire Hayward area. In his lifetime, he saw the sparsely populated farming town transform into a booming suburb. In this photograph, he poses with his matching horses in front of the Hayward's Hotel in about 1900. Even before his death in 1972, John was still adjusting to the changes that had taken place. In a 1960 interview, he observed, "I used to know everybody around. Now I feel lost when I go out."

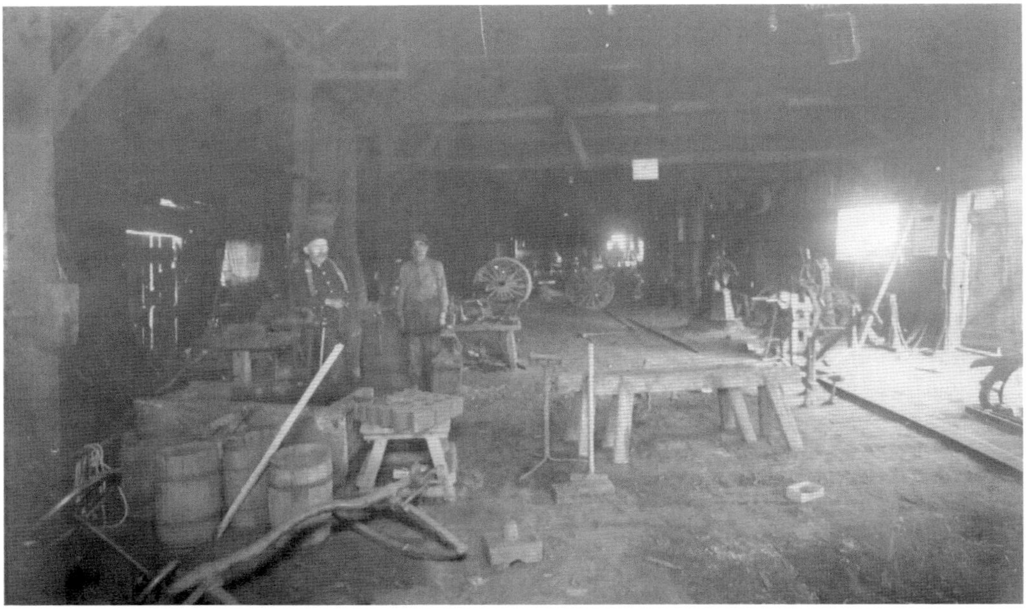

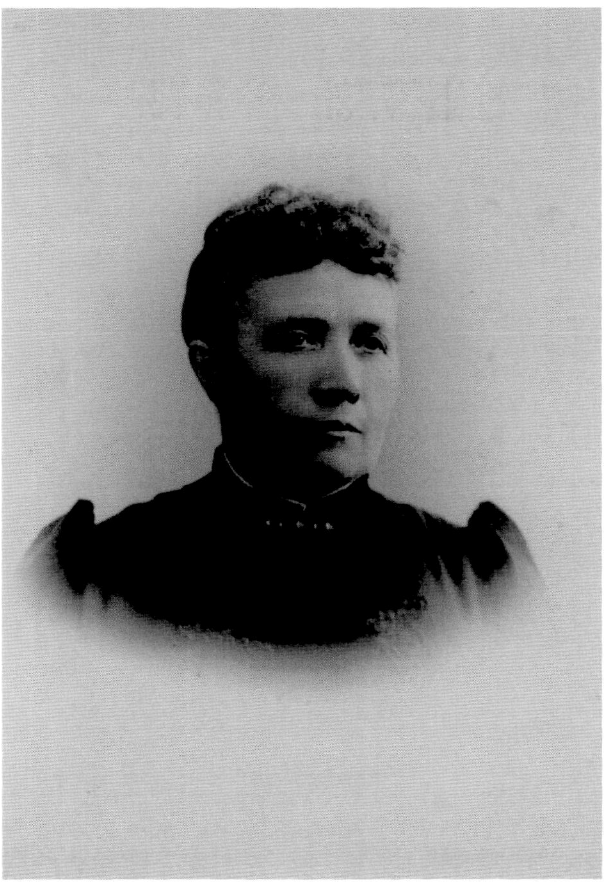

Blacksmith and Farmer
Scottish-born Henry Smyth came to California from Philadelphia in 1850. He soon went to work for John Boyle as a blacksmith. This was the first and chief business in San Lorenzo that repaired wagons, buggies, and farm equipment. In 1854, he purchased the shop and manufactured agricultural implements. Henry invented a riding plow pulled by horses that he used on his vast farm. (Author's collection.)

Amateur Artist
Mary McConaghy was the daughter of San Lorenzo pioneers, Neal and Sarah McConaghy. Born in 1866, Mary spent most of her life living in the family home on Hesperian Boulevard along with her brother John and his wife, Florence. Mary was a talented artist during a period when few women were recognized for their artistic talent. No one but family and friends ever saw her delicate oil paintings and porcelain vases, but many examples of her work still decorate the family home.

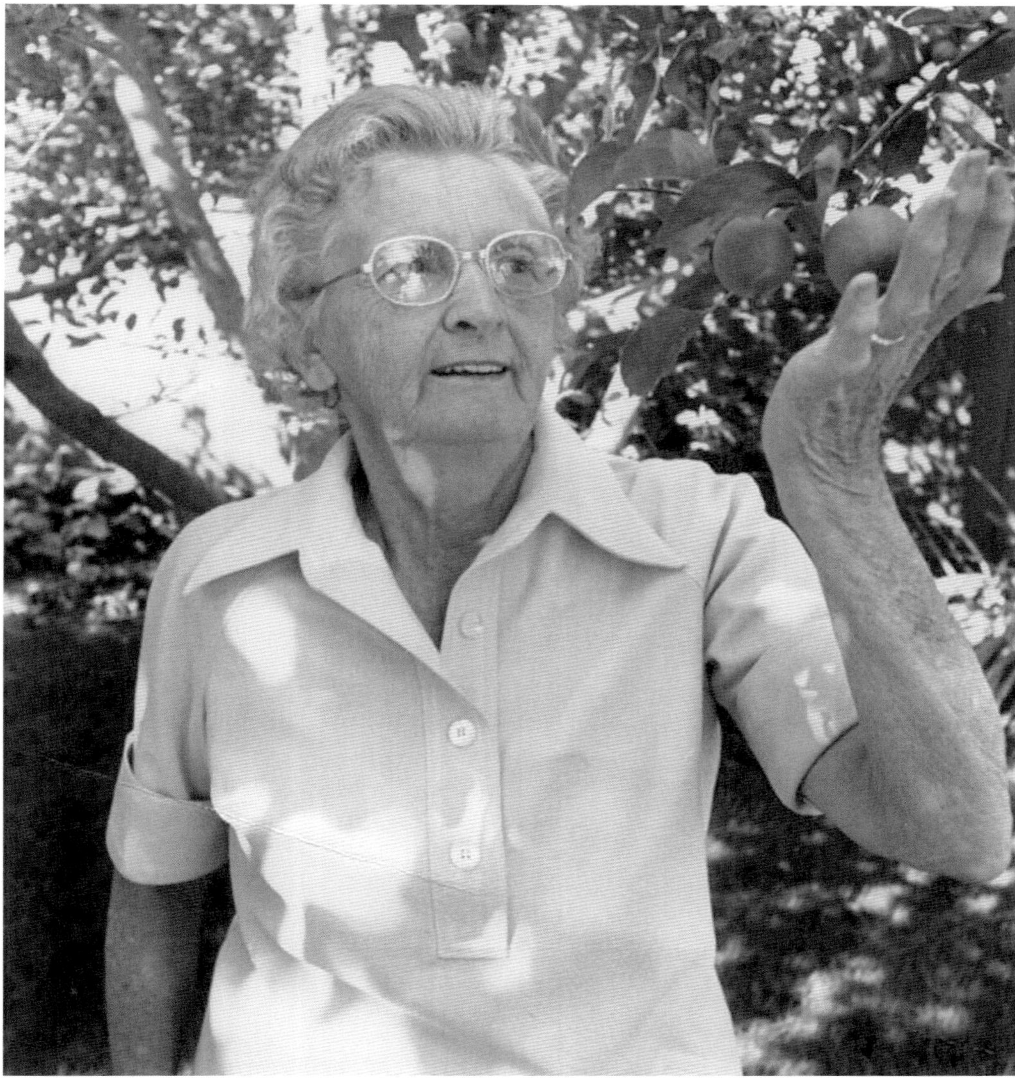

Lifelong Resident

Elvira Therkelson was born in 1908 on a six-acre Grant Avenue farm near the San Lorenzo Creek to Danish and Irish parents. When Elvira's father died in a hunting accident near the creek a few months before her birth, her older brother helped to keep the farm operating. Elvira graduated from Hayward Union High School and received a teaching credential at the University of California, Berkeley. During the Depression, teaching positions were scarce so she was a substitute teacher. She married Elwyn Woodward and lived on the family farm where they raised their two daughters. Elvira was the first president of the San Lorenzo Elementary School Parent-Teacher Association and involved with the formation of the Hayward Area Recreation District. When the farm was vacated to build Grant Elementary School, she and her family purchased a San Lorenzo Village home.

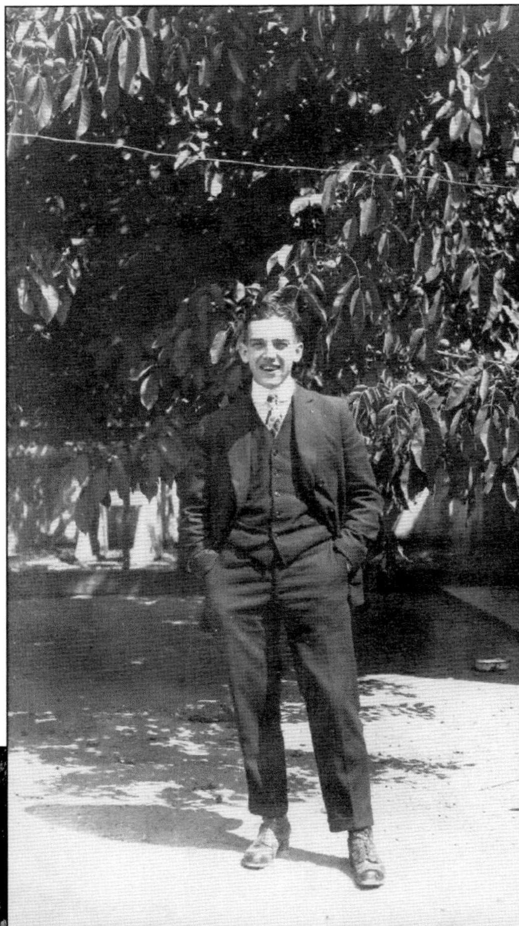

Pioneer Cemetery

John Edward Marlin, better known as Jack (pictured here in 1919), and his wife, Doris, were the last members on the San Lorenzo Pioneer Cemetery Board. Jack's grandfather John Marlin was the president of the group that formed in 1864 to issue deeds to cemetery landowners, lay out the plots, and maintain the grounds. In the late 1950s, the cemetery association realized they needed to find some organization to take over care of the cemetery. Jack approached the Hayward Area Historical Society and Alameda County for assistance. After much discussion and the passage of an assembly bill in the state legislature, in 1964, the county took ownership of the cemetery and dedicated it as the San Lorenzo Pioneer Memorial Cemetery (pictured below). Doris and Jack were buried in the Marlin family plot. (Left, courtesy of Lucille Lorge; below, courtesy of the Hayward Area Historical Society.)

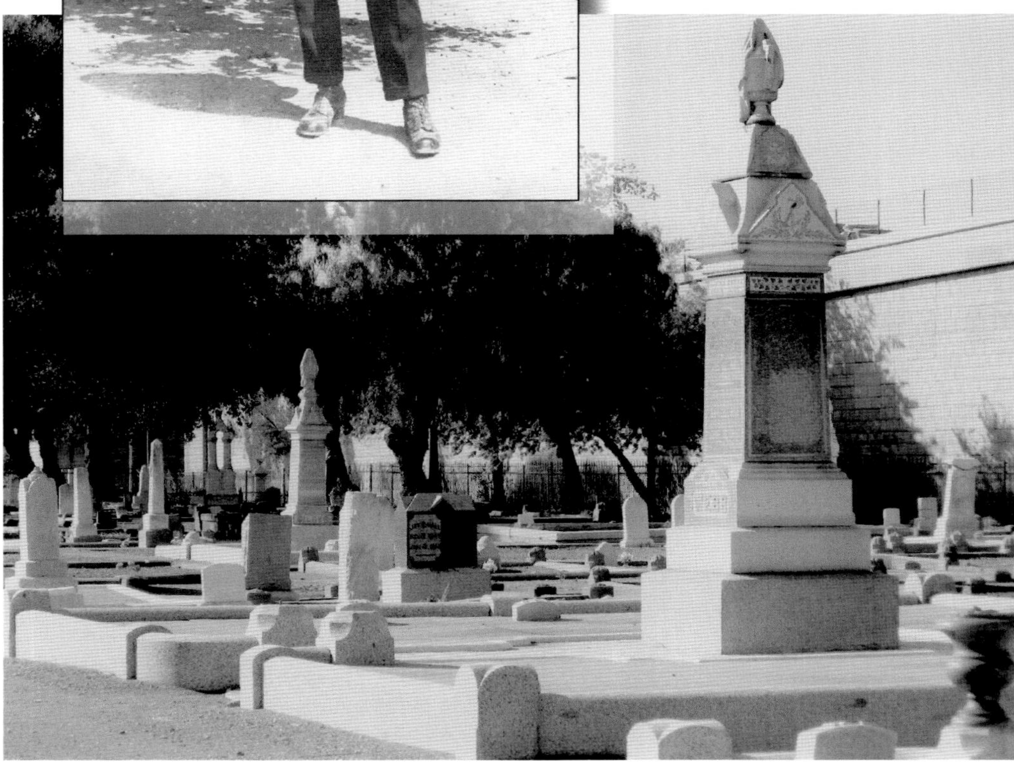

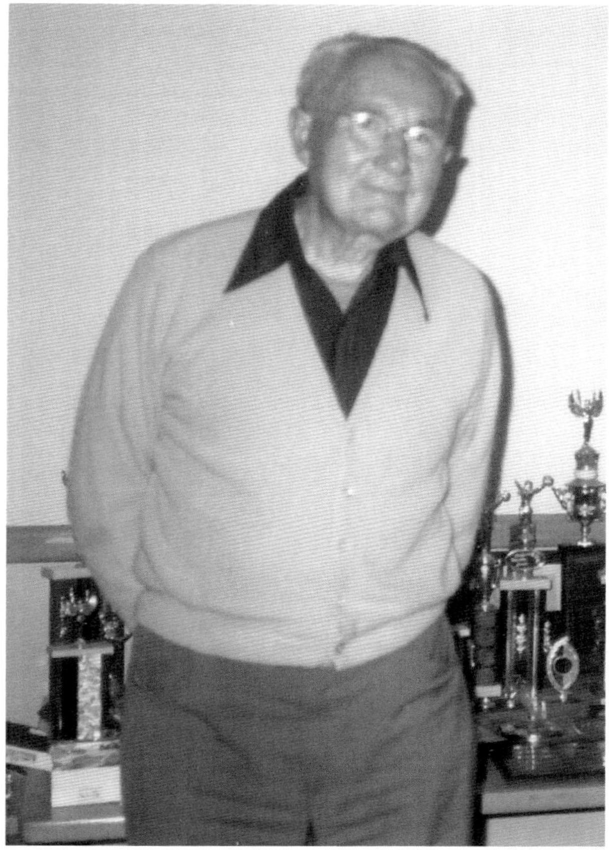

Blacksmith's Son
William Teubert Smith's father, William Z. Smith, came to San Lorenzo in the late 1800s. He rented a room at Herman Teubert's boardinghouse while working at Smyth's blacksmith shop and married Frederica Teubert. When the blacksmith shop was demolished in 1930, he bought the equipment and built a shop by the boardinghouse, the building, pictured below, still stands on Albion Avenue. William, known as Teubert or Tubie, was born in 1905. He attended San Lorenzo Grammar School and graduated from Hayward Union High School in 1917. In 1932, Teubert, shown here, married Lucille Thorup Smith. When he retired from the Crocker-Anglo Bank of Hayward in 1970, he volunteered at the Hayward Area Historical Society Museum and attended the San Lorenzo History classes. Teubert liked to share his pictures and memories of growing up in San Lorenzo. (Both, author's collection.)

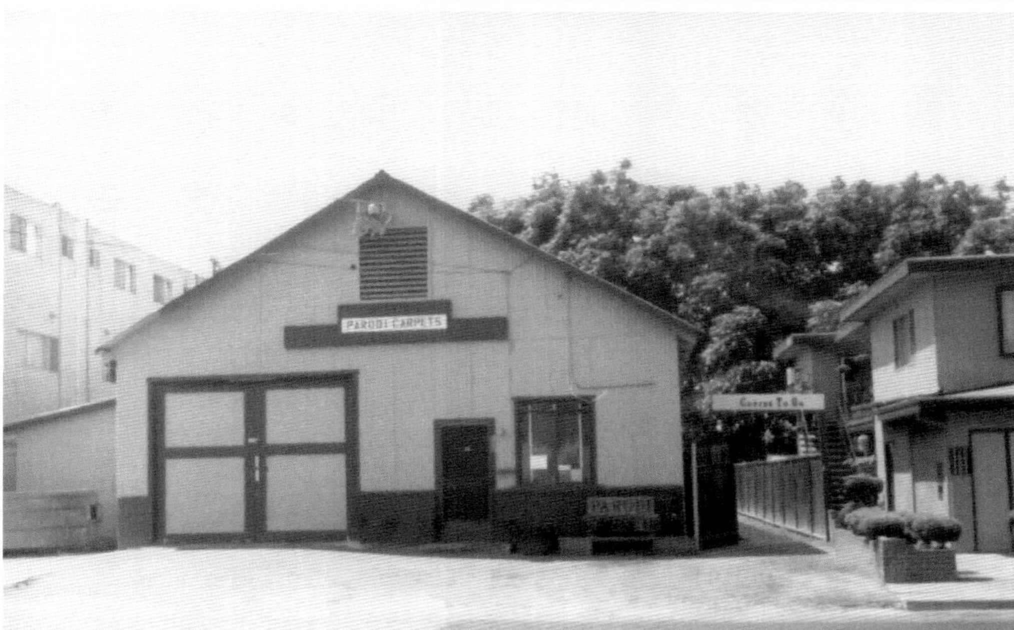

The Post Office Saved

Gertrude Mooney was the postmaster of San Lorenzo from March 18, 1942, until her retirement in 1963. She is pictured here with her husband, Bernard "Dutch" Mooney, and sons, Bernard (left) and Robert (right). When she became postmaster, San Lorenzo was a farming area with 1,500 families. It had a third-class post office with postage sales averaging $2,000 yearly. She lived by the post office and was the entire staff. A rural carrier from San Leandro delivered the mail. She hired her neighbor Mary Videll in November of 1942 as her clerk. When the David D. Bohannon Organization built 1,459 homes in San Lorenzo in 1944, Mooney and her clerk were deluged with mail. They worked with the help of volunteers from 6:00 a.m. to midnight daily to serve the community. Residents of the new village stood in line daily to get their mail. Gertrude pleaded with Washington, DC, to reclassify the post office so more carriers and clerks could be hired. But the post office regulations based reclassification on revenues of the previous years. The federal agency suggested that San Lorenzo be taken over as a branch of the San Leandro Post Office, which was already a first-class post office and immediately eligible for more personnel. Gertrude's answer was NEVER! That would have meant the loss of San Lorenzo's identity. She joined the old-time residents and newcomers in circulating a petition against the proposed annexation. Gertrude went directly to Washington, DC, to plead her case for San Lorenzo, and San Lorenzo residents won! On July 1, 1945, San Lorenzo became a second-class post office with three new mail clerks and three mail carriers for home delivery. Gertrude's husband, Bernard, was added to the staff as the first parcel post worker. Men who lived in the new subdivision of San Lorenzo Village delivered packages in their spare time to help aid the mail service. On September 3, 1946, the staff moved to an empty store in the San Lorenzo Village shopping center. Her staff of 45 men and one woman, Mary Videll, served the homes and businesses. There are two streets in the Hesperian Gardens housing area of San Lorenzo named Mooney and Videll to honor the two postal women. (Courtesy of Barney Mooney.)

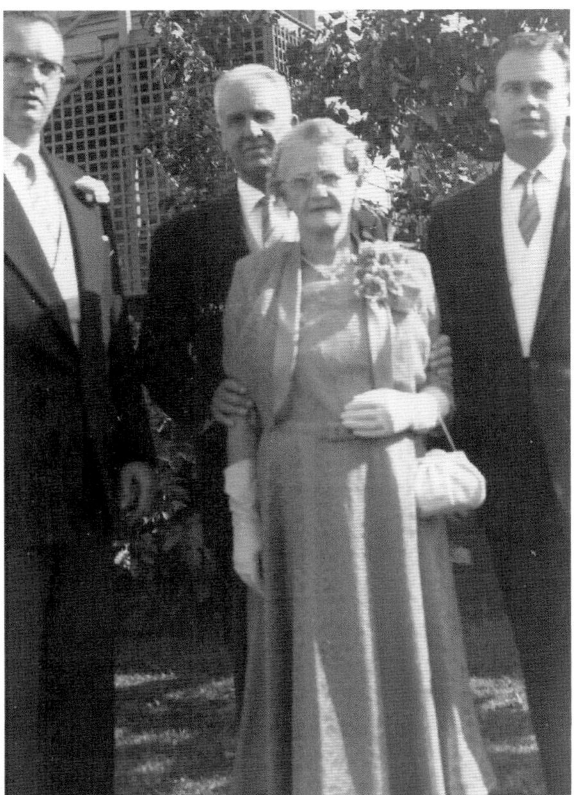

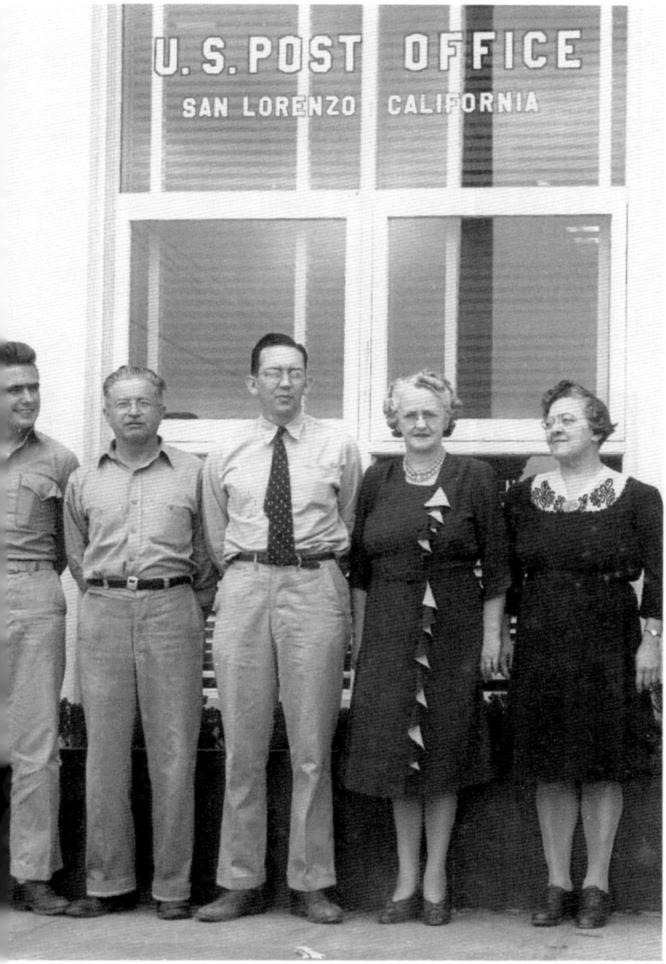

The Grove

Mary Rodgers Videll's father, Manuel Rodrigues, sailed from the Azores Islands, Portugal, to New York in 1876 and settled in San Lorenzo. One of the first changes was his name. It was pronounced and spelled "Rogers;" he accepted "Rodgers." In 1911, Mary's father purchased the San Lorenzo Grove from the Oakland Traction Company and continued to operate the amusement park with its pavilion. Mary met her husband, Frank Videll, at a pavilion dance. Her father converted the property to orchards in 1920. The Vidells lived in the caretaker's house until Frank built a house on the corner of the property with the pavilion lumber, pictured below. Both houses remain at the same location. Postmaster Mooney (second from the right) hired Mary (first from the right) in 1942 as the first San Lorenzo postal clerk, where she remained until 1963. (Left, courtesy of the Hayward Area Historical Society; below, author's collection.)

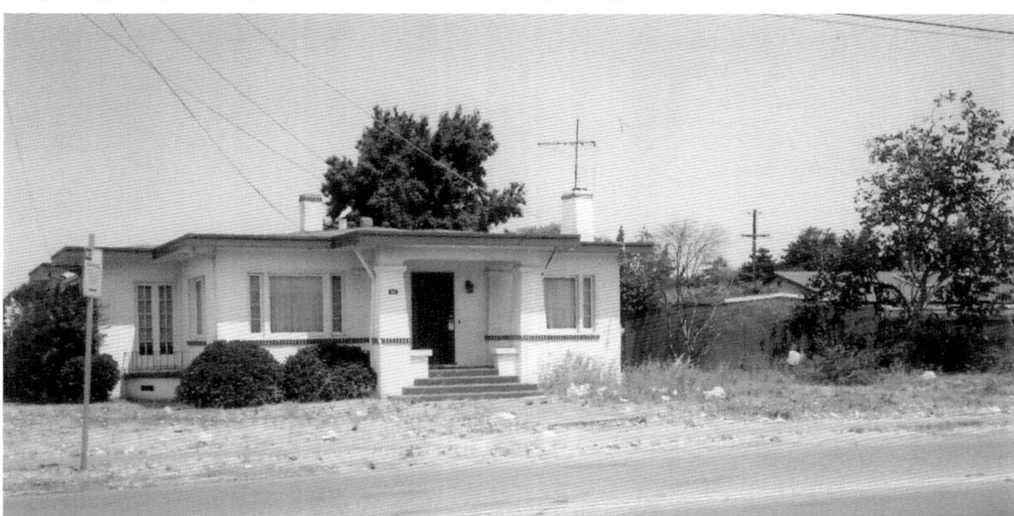

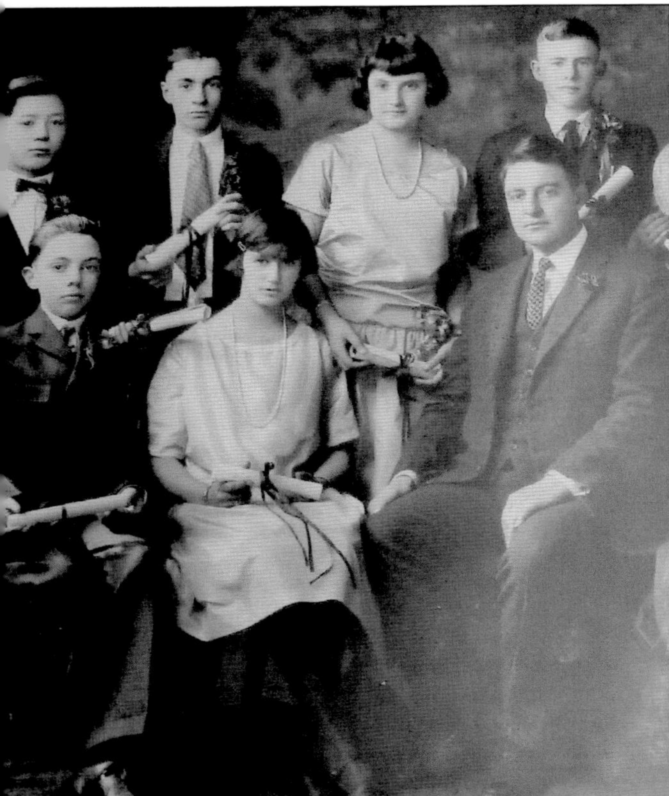

First Superintendent
Clyde E. Lawson from Boonville, California, graduated from Ukiah High School in 1908. After obtaining a teaching degree, he married and moved to San Lorenzo to teach at the San Lorenzo Elementary School in 1914, later becoming principal. Clyde is shown here with some of his graduates in 1922. When two elementary schools were built, Clyde was appointed superintendent. In 1948, with six elementary schools, he submitted his surprise resignation and said, "This will complete 34 happy years of service." (Author's collection.)

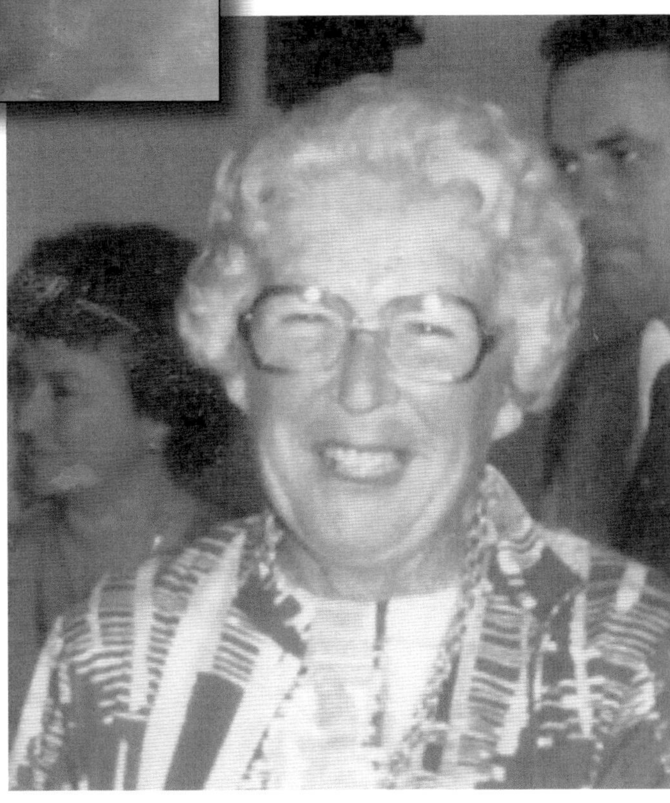

Forty-six Years of Service
Evelyn Poston was born and raised in San Lorenzo. After graduating from business school, she was hired by her neighbor, Supt. Clyde Lawson, as his only secretary in the district office; his wife had just quit. The office was located in the second elementary school on the same site where Evelyn had attended school in the early 1900s. She was secretary for all superintendents until retiring. (Courtesy of Bonnie Petersen.)

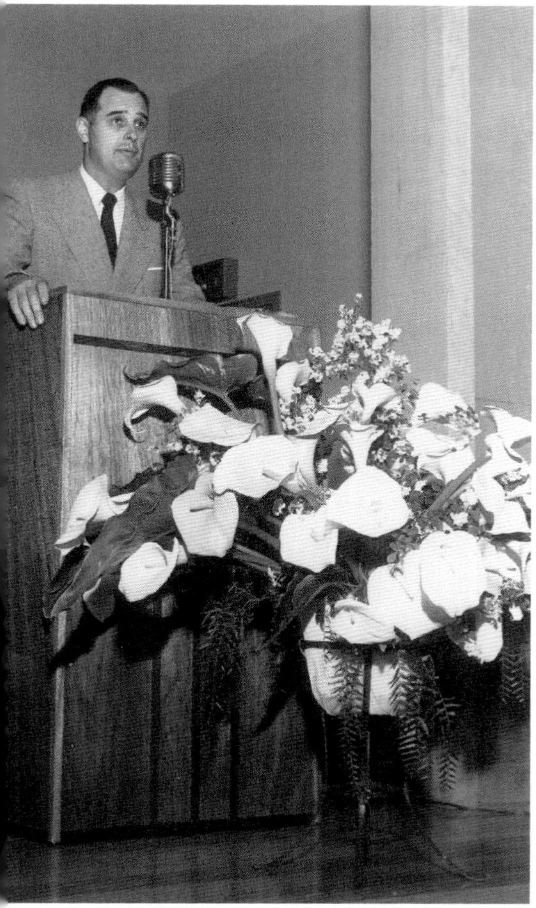

Second Superintendent
Upon the unexpected resignation of Superintendent Lawson in 1948, Paul D. Ehret, the principal of David E. Martin School, was appointed. The agricultural areas were being replaced with homes, creating the need for more schools. He led the district through a period of phenomenal growth, from six elementary schools to 20 elementary, four junior highs, and three high schools. He retired in 1975. (Author's collection.)

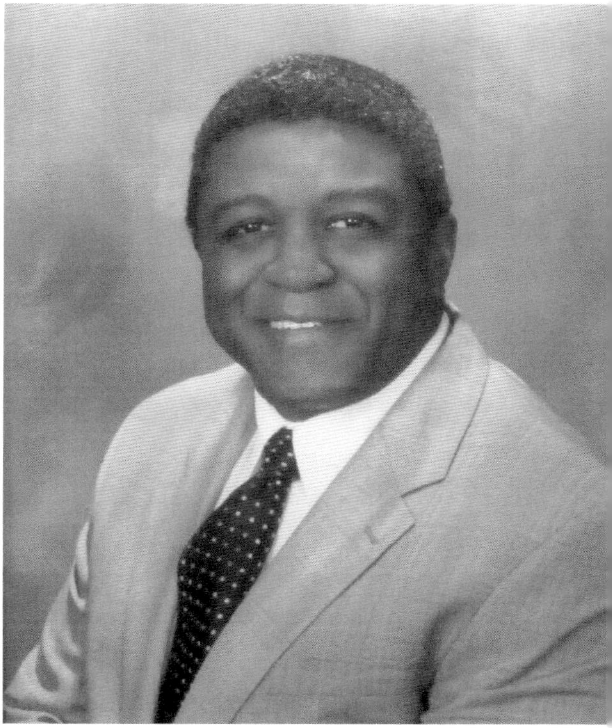

The Seventh Superintendent
Dr. Dennis Byas became the San Lorenzo Unified School District superintendent in 2007. He attributes his very successful career to the hard work of the students, staff, community and school board leadership. Under his leadership, the district has won numerous awards, grants and been extremely successful in increasing student attendance, academic performance and the highest number of students attending college. The district has significantly reduced student suspensions, expulsions, and dropout rates. (Courtesy of the San Lorenzo Unified School District.)

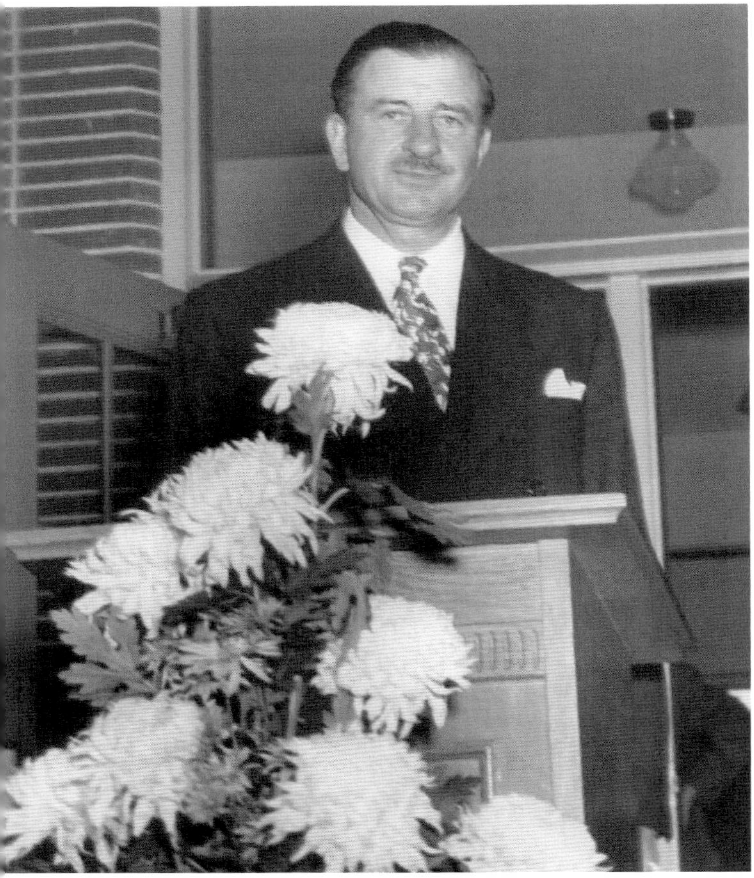

Village Developer

The Bay Area housing shortage during World War II brought David D. Bohannon, master builder, to San Lorenzo. He began his real estate career in 1925 and created a real estate and land development organization in 1928. He began building homes in 1934 until World War II, when materials were restricted to war production. In 1944, David located a large plot of farmland in San Lorenzo to build housing for war workers. He was an innovator, perfecting the "California Method" of on-site construction. With the slogan "Every House a Garden Spot," the San Lorenzo Village erected about 1,500 homes in only 500 days and was complete with shopping and neighborhood services. The village was a truly planned community, shown below in 1946. For his accomplishment, David Bohannon was inducted into the Builders Hall of Fame. (Left, author's collection; below, courtesy of Hayward Area Historical Society.).

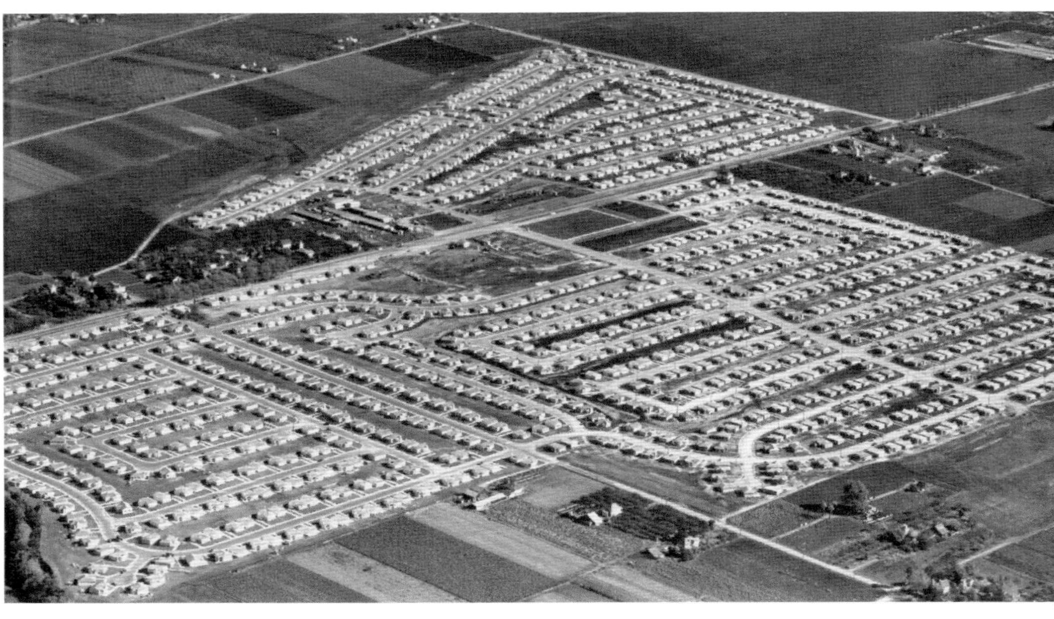

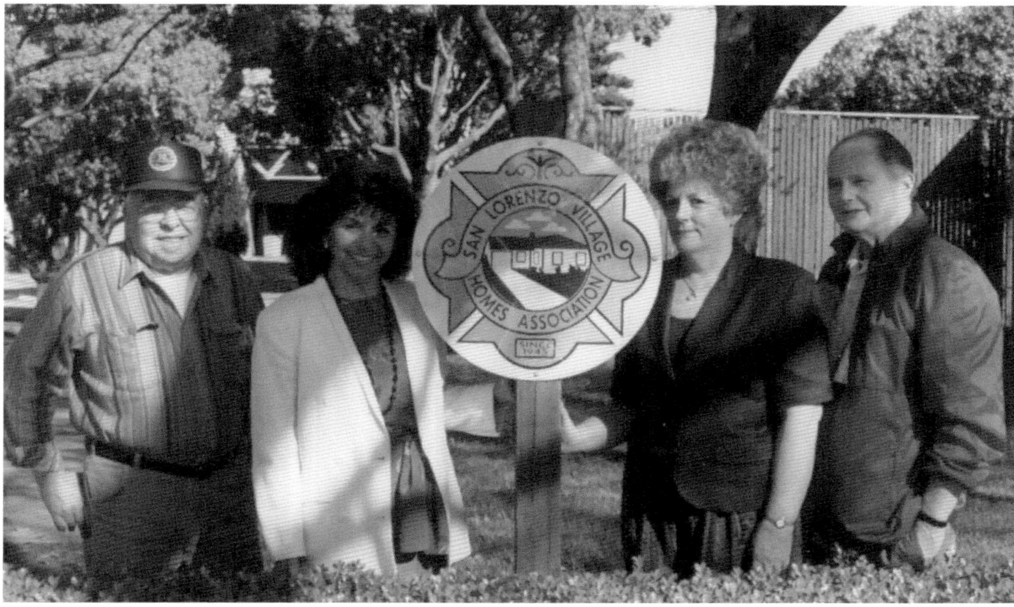

Homes Association
When David D. Bohannon built the planned community of San Lorenzo Village in 1944, covenants, conditions, and restrictions were incorporated into the deed of each home. A nonprofit corporation was formed to enforce these rules. The San Lorenzo Village Homes Association was established in 1945. It is governed by a five-member volunteer board of directors. The association is still active today after more than six decades. Pictured here is the 1996 board of directors. (Courtesy of the San Lorenzo Village Homes Association.)

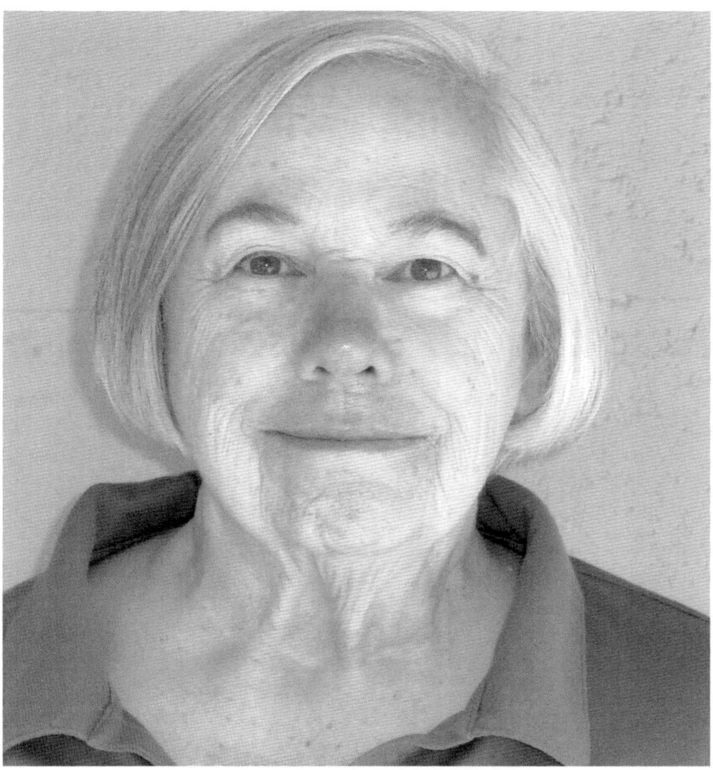

Homes Association Director
Nancy Van Huffel became a legend not only as the first woman administrator for the San Lorenzo Village Homes Association for 23 years but also in Alameda County where she volunteered on many committees, commissions, and projects. After her retirement in 2011, Nancy continues to stay actively involved with the League of Women Voters, Eden Area, and volunteers for the Alameda County CASA program working with foster children. (Courtesy of Nancy Van Huffel.)

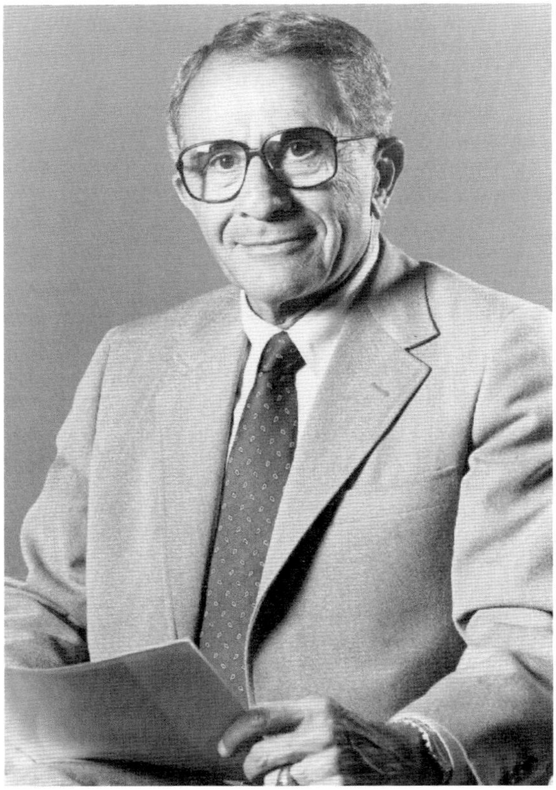

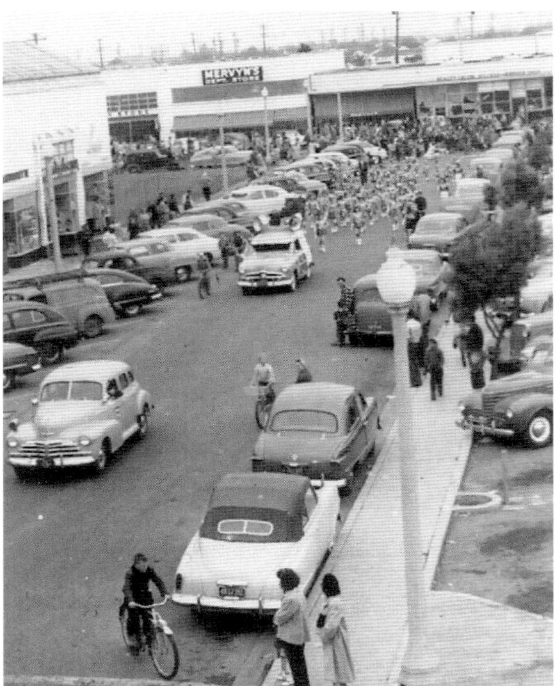

Mervyn or Mervin

Mervin Morris arrived in San Francisco in 1949 looking for a vacant building to open a store. His broker sent him to San Lorenzo Village where he purchased a store for $25,000. After remodeling, Mervin noticed his name was misspelled on the sign. The architect had changed the "i" to "y" because it "looked better." On July 29, 1949, he opened a specialty department store with two employees. Soon, the successful store moved across the street to a larger building. By 1974, Mervyn's expanded to a chain of 48 stores and 4,000 employees. Mervin merged with Dayton Hudson in 1978 and he resigned as chief executive officer. The San Lorenzo store moved to Hayward, but Mervin never forgot the community. He donated to the San Lorenzo school district's programs and scholarships. He also donated the tennis courts in the Mervin Morris Park.

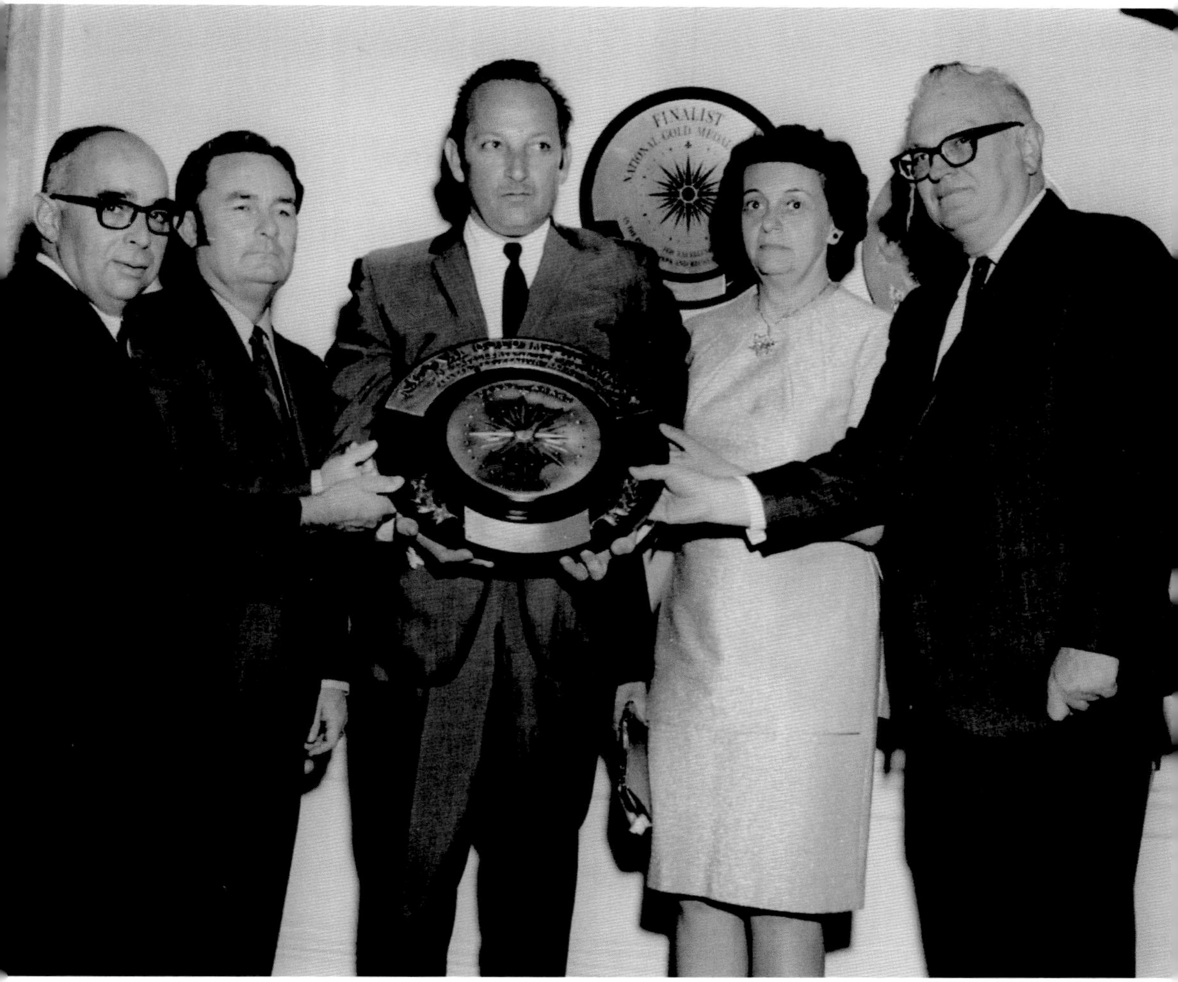

Community Center
Kenneth Aitken was born in San Jose, California. His family moved to Los Angeles where he graduated from Belmont High School in 1934. During World War II, he was an accountant for the federal government in Washington, DC. In 1944, Kenneth and his wife, Corrine, moved to San Lorenzo Village. They were active in the community. Corrine was the first woman elected to the San Lorenzo Elementary School Board in 1954. Kenneth was elected to the San Lorenzo Village Homes Association Board and to the Hayward Area Recreation and Park District Board of Directors. Pictured here with other district board members are, from left to right, Julio Bras, Douglas Morrisson, Jim Robbins, Meda Sores, and Kenneth. In 1992, a community center was rededicated as the Kenneth C. Aitken Senior and Community Center in honor of his distinguished and outstanding 32 years on the recreation board.

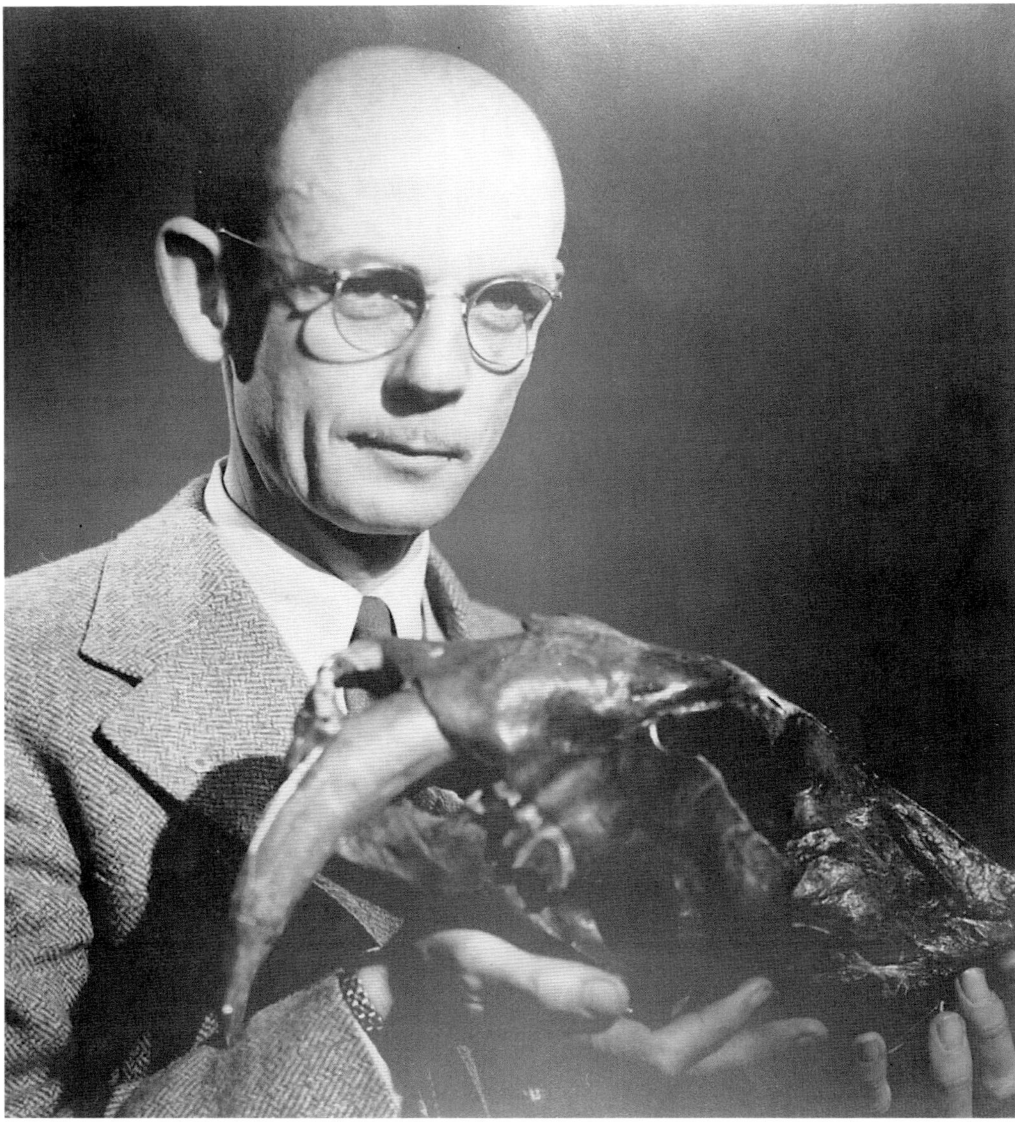

Science Consultant and Museum

In 1953, Wes Gordon was assigned to San Lorenzo Elementary School District as a curriculum consultant from the Alameda County Education Department. His background included classroom teaching, special education, and supervision, and he was a specialist in science and science education. He was hired in 1954 by the district to be the first science consultant. Wes had a science museum with fossils and natural science exhibits at David E. Martin School until the 1970s. The museum moved to the closed David D. Bohannon Junior High School and was renamed the Wes Gordon Museum. When the junior high school was reopened, Wes's family moved the museum collection to the Children's Nature History Museum in Fremont. Wes Gordon's work with the "Boy Paleontologists" in the east and south bay achieved national recognition and was featured in national professional publications, including *LIFE* magazine and the *American Magazine*. He was a member of numerous scientific and educational societies.

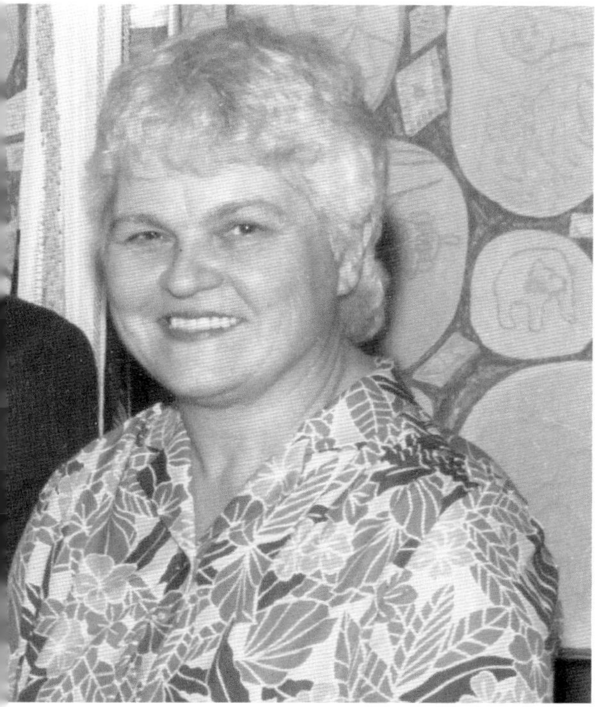

Community Volunteer
As a resident of the San Lorenzo Village since 1961, Dorothy Partridge is a participant in committees, councils, boards, projects, and organizations. Prior to being elected to the San Lorenzo Unified School District Board of Education for 17 years, she was active in school district committees and received many awards. Dorothy was a member of the Alameda County Library Commission, sheriff's advisory committee, San Lorenzo Library Advisory Committee, and San Lorenzo/Ashland/Cherryland Youth Collaborative. She was a cofounder of the San Lorenzo Area Youth Resources Group, Bobby Sox team manager, and director of the San Lorenzo Village Homes Association. Bicycle paths, "Project Clean," and limiting truck traffic in San Lorenzo Village streets are just some of the projects Dorothy coordinated. Some county ordinances are a result of Dorothy's participation. She is a communicator and involves others in the unincorporated community.

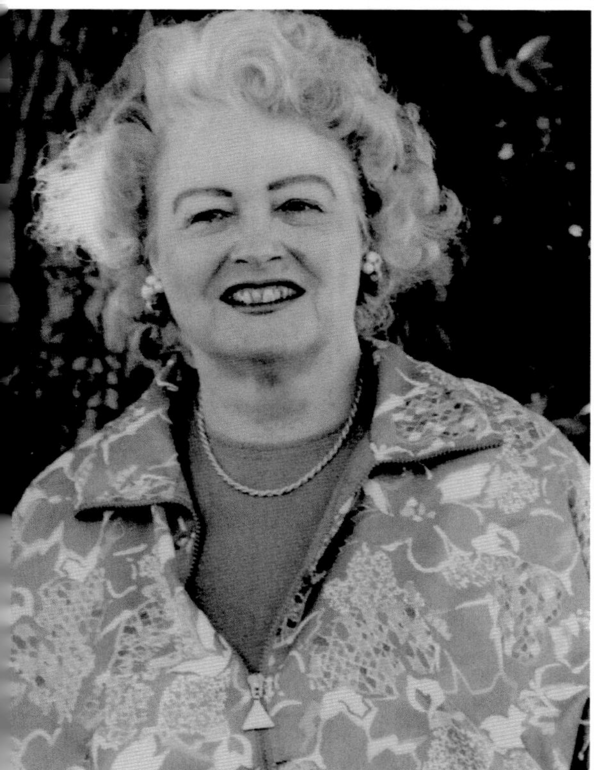

Community Preservationist
Esther Jorgensen made history in 1973 as the first woman elected to the San Lorenzo Village Homes Association Board of Directors, and set a record serving 15 years. She was elected president of the board three times. When the association was without a paid administrator, she and director Frank Peixoto took over the office. They did all the work until an administrator was hired. In 1954, Esther, her husband, and sons moved into a split-level home in San Lorenzo Village behind McConaghy House. When Esther saw a notice that the beautiful house would be demolished, she worked to save it. When it became the historical museum house, Esther was a docent. She was on the Hayward Area Historical Society Board and gave McConaghy House reports to the Hayward Area Recreation and Park District, owner of the house. (Courtesy of Esther Jorgensen.)

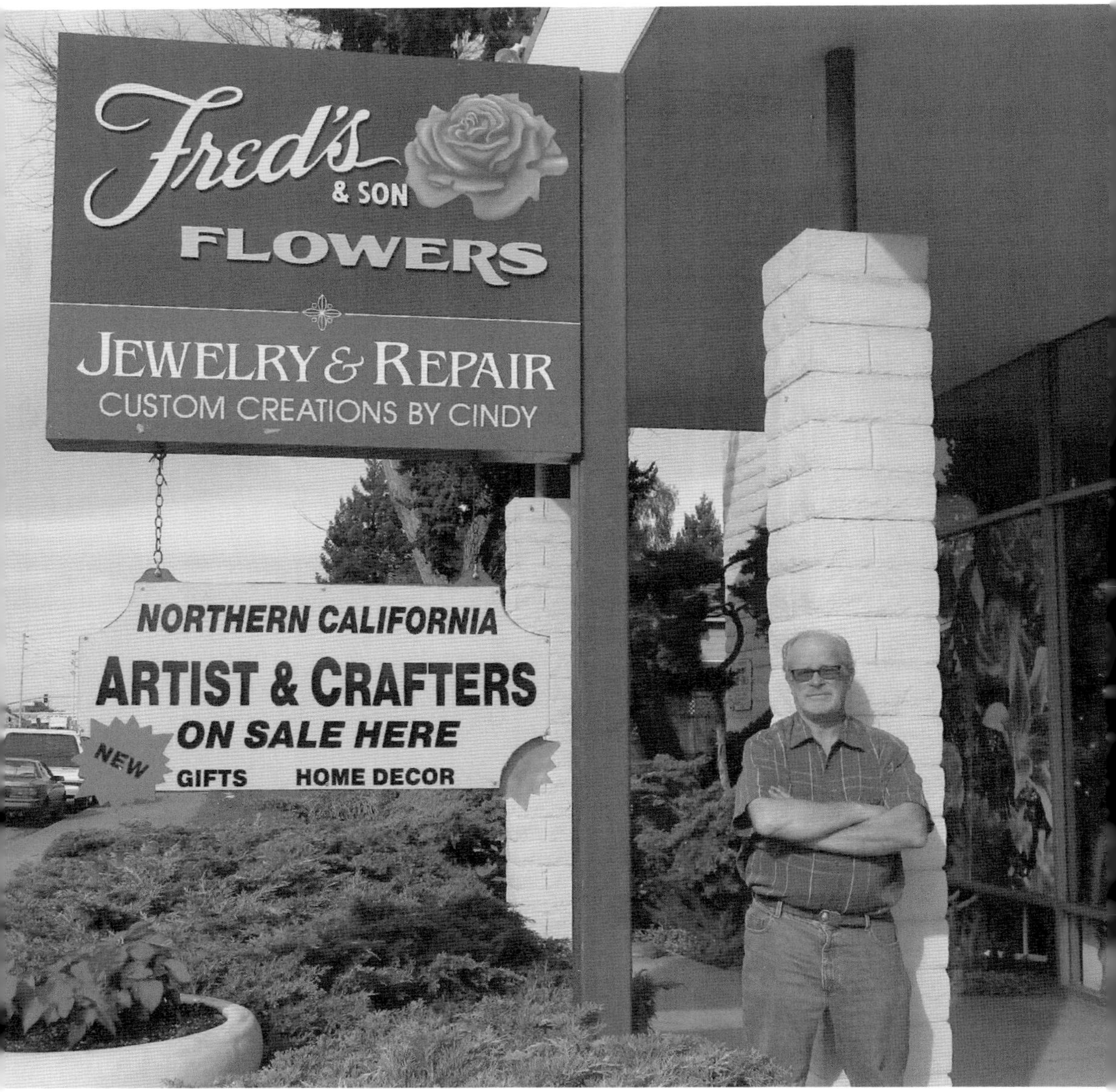

Oldest Business

In 1941, Richard Kraus's parents, Fred and Lucille, purchased a flower shop in San Lorenzo and began Fred's Flowers. When the original shop was demolished in 1947 for a freeway exit, Fred purchased property with a house and built a new shop and nursery across from the McConaghy House. After graduating from Sunset High School, Richard enrolled in an ornamental horticulture program at the City College of San Francisco. While attending college in 1968, he was drafted into the Army. Discharged after being wounded, he completed his degree at Chabot College. When Richard's mother died in 1974, he assumed her responsibilities as artist, creator of floral designs, and public relations. His father grew the flowers until his death in 2002. Richard has continued the business. He donates flowers for community functions and received the 2011 Historic Business Award from the Hayward Area Historical Society. (Courtesy of Richard Kraus.)

The Sandwich Program

For Tom Vierra, it all began with a desire to do some type of volunteer work. While conversing with some members of the St. Gerard Women's Group who were hosting a reception for a visiting priest from Africa at St. John's Catholic Church, he learned of the sandwich program. Tom was advised to see Mary Baca who began the program. The sandwiches are made at the church kitchen for the poor and homeless. Individuals and businesses donate money and food to continue the program. Tom began in 2004 and later accompanied Mary every Monday, Wednesday, and Friday to deliver the sandwiches at a park. Sometimes clothes are delivered. Doing something for the poor is very rewarding. Due to Mary's health, Tom is now in charge of the program. Tom is pictured here with fellow volunteer Jackie Freitas. (Author's collection.)

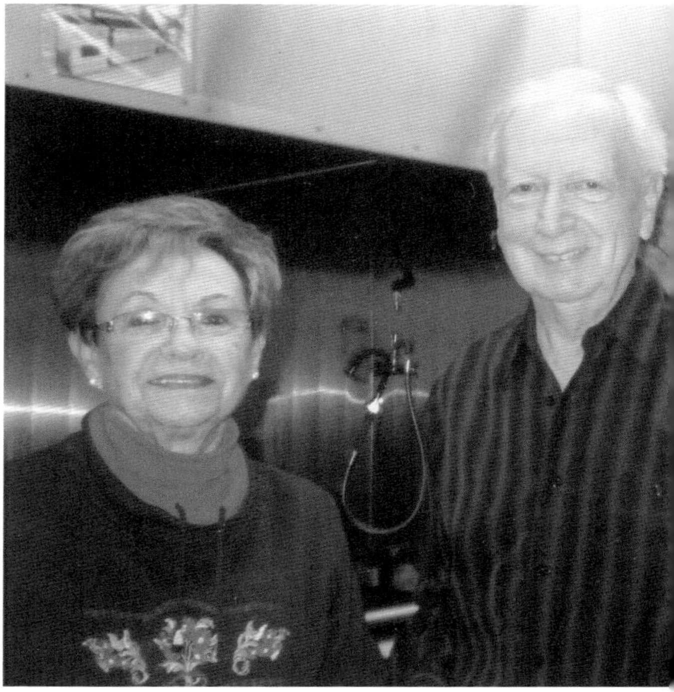

"Being Involved"

"Being involved" is Maybelle Rasmussen's motto. Born in 1918, Maybelle grew up in the area and attended local schools, including Hayward Union High School. At San Jose State, Maybelle received her bachelor's of arts degree and an elementary teaching credential with majors in music and natural history in 1941. Her teaching career began in Monterey, California. She married Lloyd Rasmussen in 1946. They had one daughter. While Lloyd was in the South Pacific for three years, Maybelle went back to teach in Hayward. Her Hayward teaching career in science totaled 31 years. Maybelle participates in many organizations and continues her hobbies. She started playing the piano at age 10 and today plays for the retired teacher organization. She enjoys painting watercolors on location and has displayed her art locally. Astronomy and geology are other hobbies. Maybelle certainly lives her motto. (Courtesy of Maybelle Rasmussen.)

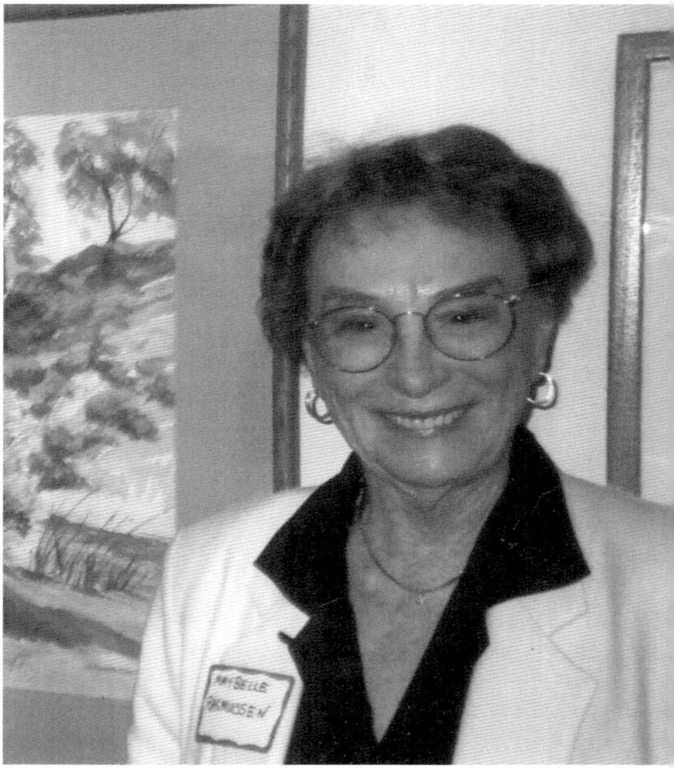

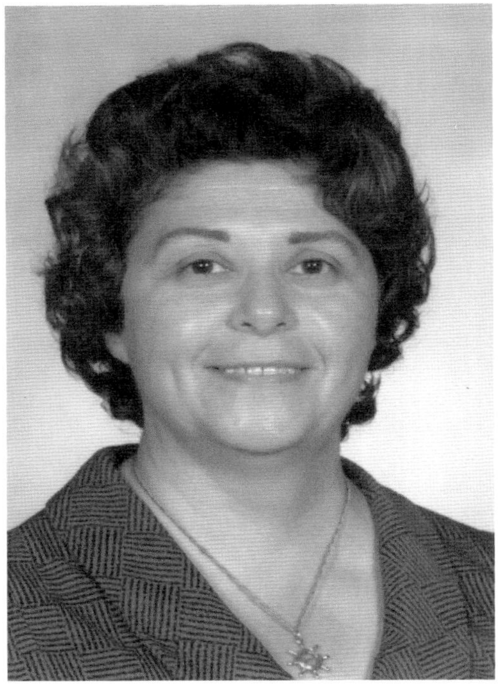

Historian and Volunteer

Doris Marciel, is a third-generation native of San Lorenzo. Her great-grandparents, originally from the Portuguese Azores Islands, purchased property with a house in 1875, which was where her grandfather and mother were born. Doris attended San Lorenzo Elementary School and San Lorenzo High School. After graduating from San Jose State College in 1960 with a major in education and minor in recreation, she received a bachelor of arts degree and general elementary credential. She began teaching elementary grades in the San Lorenzo Unified School District and also worked part-time for the Hayward Area Recreation and Park District. Doris taught kindergarten through sixth grade for 38 years, San Lorenzo history for 25 years at the San Lorenzo Adult School, and spent 40 years as a playground director and teenage coordinator for the Hayward Area Recreation and Park District. San Lorenzo history is her passion. She has written articles for websites, newspapers, calendars, and the Hayward Area Historical Society's *Adobe Trails* newsletter. She wrote the book Images of America: *San Lorenzo* and the *A-Z of San Lorenzo* booklet for elementary students compiled by the Hayward Area Historical Society. Doris displays San Lorenzo history at the Alameda County Library, San Lorenzo Branch. She selected the sites and wrote the information for the historical sidewalk plaques on Lewelling Boulevard and conducts historical walks. She has a private San Lorenzo History Museum in her great-grandparents' house. Doris is a member of the California Retired Teachers Association, the Epsilon Omega Chapter of Delta Kappa Gamma, Hayward Hill and Valley Club, Hayward Area Historical Society, Cherryland Community Association, Alameda County Historical Society, League of Women Voters, the Ashland Redevelopment Citizens Advisory Committee, the Mount St. Joseph's Cemetery Committee, and the Hayward Centro Board of Directors for the Centro Social Msgr. Julio A. Martins Children's Day Care Center located in Ligares, Portugal. As a volunteer for the Hayward Area Historical Society, she oversaw the San Lorenzo Pioneer Cemetery for more than 20 years and wrote a series of articles titled "Who is buried in the San Lorenzo Pioneer Cemetery?" and "Why This Name?" for streets and buildings. Doris received the Hayward Area Recreation and Park District Board of Directors' Award in 1999 and the Hayward Area Historical Society John Sandoval History Award in 2001 and was nominated by the Southern Alameda County Retired Teachers of CalRTA for the Hayward Volunteer Award in 2010, and the Hayward Area Recreation and Park District's Battle of the Bands award in 2013. (Author's collection.)

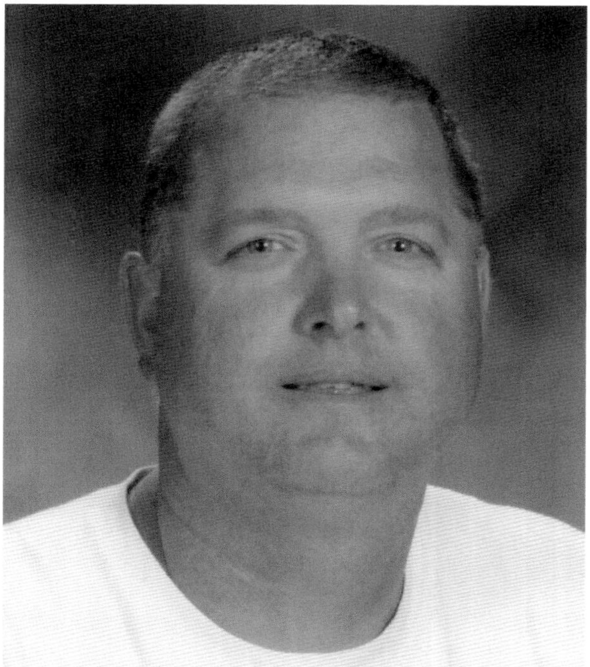

The Sports Hall of Fame

Tom Longaker, varsity basketball coach and athletic director at San Lorenzo High School, founded the San Lorenzo High School Sports Hall of Fame in 2006. He wanted to recognize and honor the athletes, coaches, and teams in San Lorenzo High School history with an awards dinner every two years. The inductees' names are imprinted on a permanent banner for every year's group. The banners are displayed in the gymnasium. (Courtesy of Tom Longaker.)

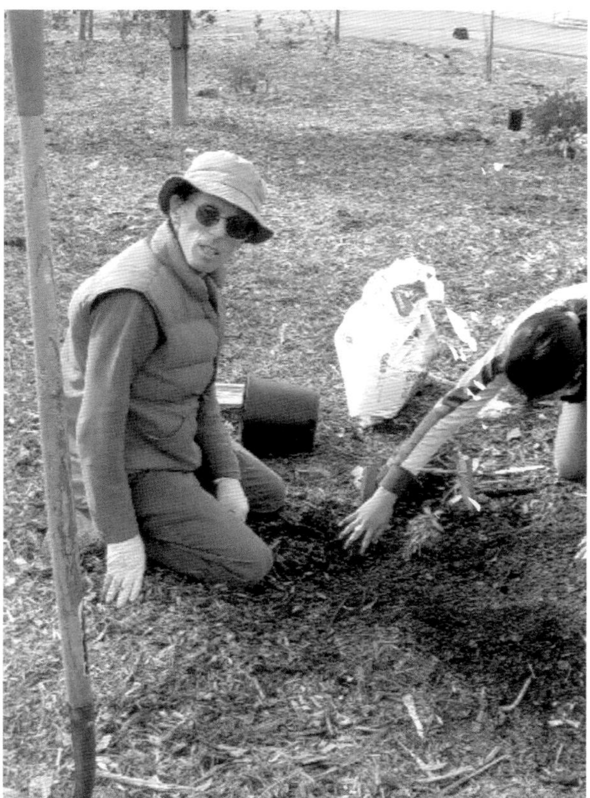

Green Academy

Alan Fishman, creator of the Green Academy at San Lorenzo High School, teaches the environmental leadership class. The program is dedicated to preparing students for the growing industry of green employment. Through Alan's efforts, San Lorenzo High is the only public school in the Bay Area to contain a one-acre botanical garden with 60 species of native plants. Alan began and hosted the "Bringing Back the Native Garden" tour. (Courtesy of Alan Fishman.)

Real Estate and History
Tom and Cathy Clements of the Village Realtors celebrate San Lorenzo history in many ways. They purchased the "Heidi House" from Evelyn Heidi, agreeing to keep it historical for their office. At the front of the property is the "All Wars Memorial Monument" to honor men and women veterans of the area. They also publish a calendar with many months dedicated to San Lorenzo history. (Author's collection.)

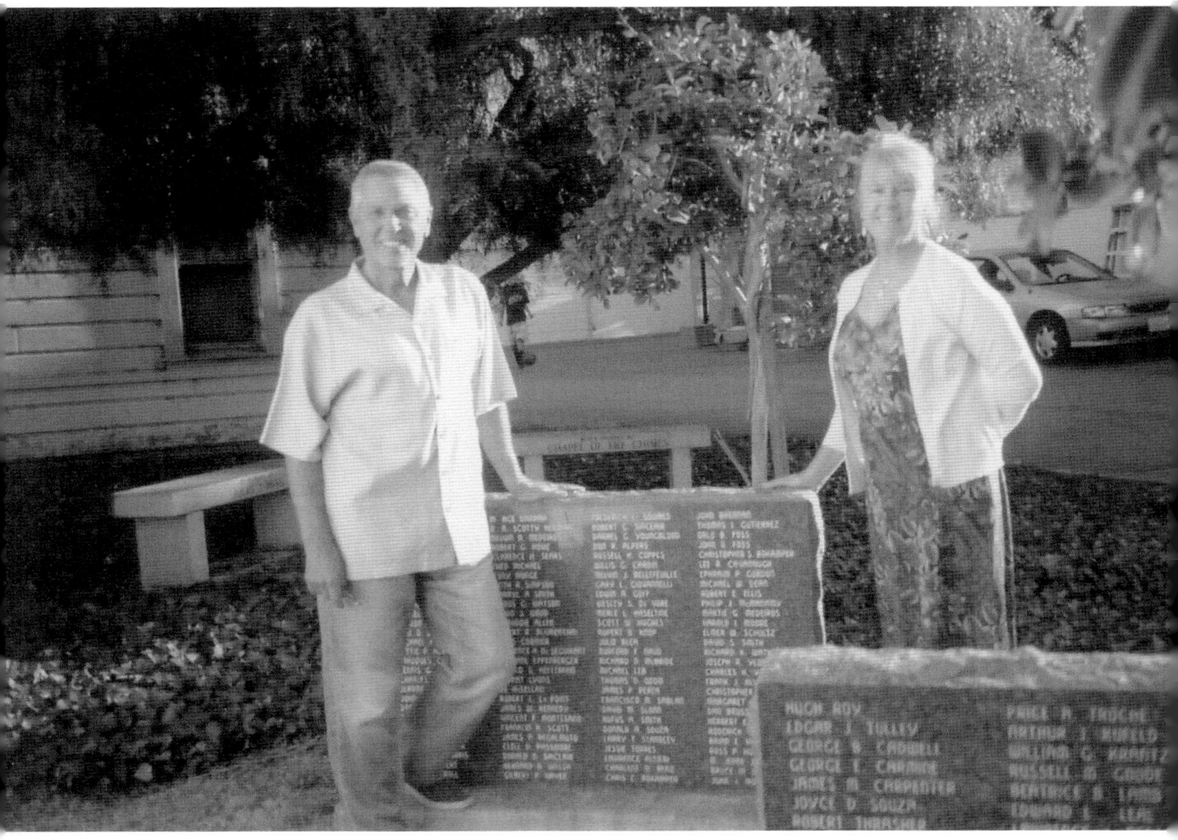

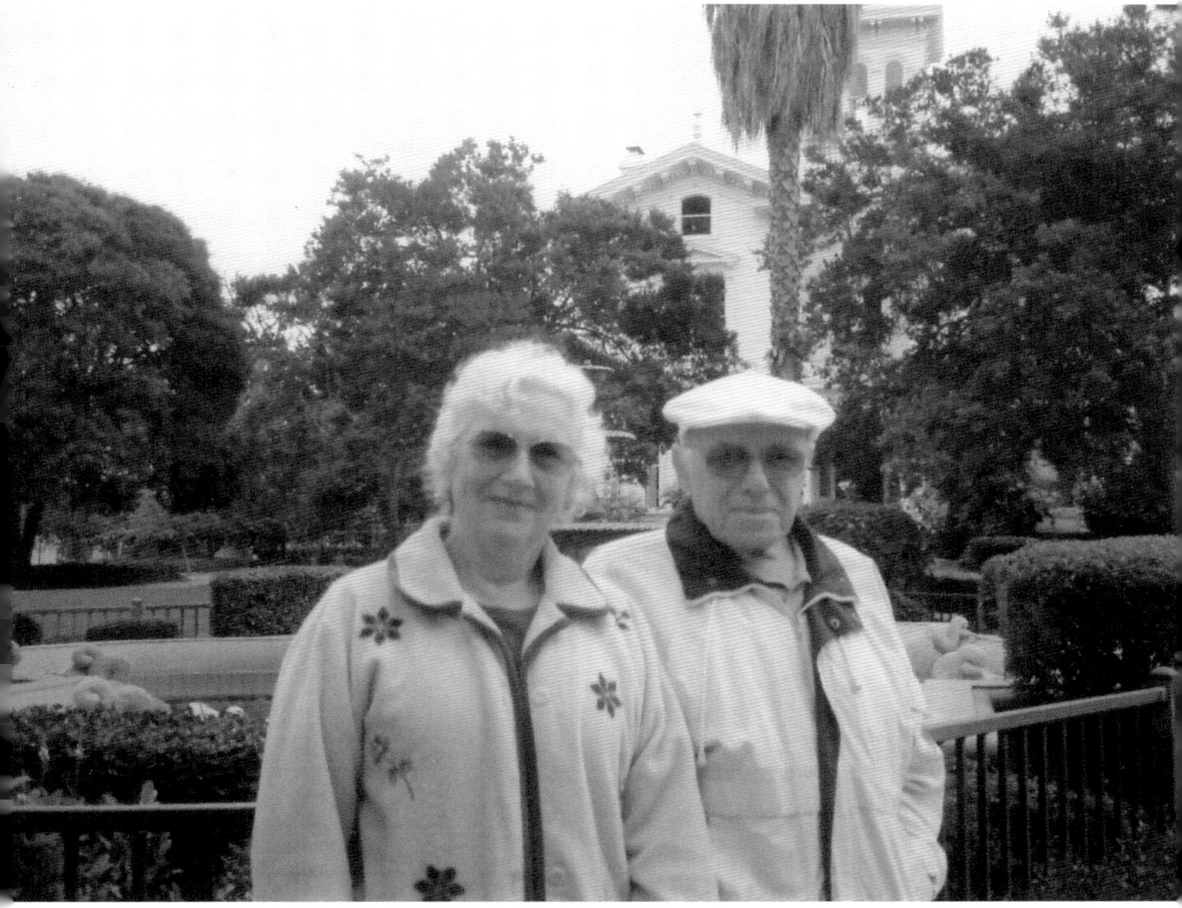

Saving a Fountain
In 1996, Robert and Erica Campisi volunteered their time to restore the fountain that welcomes visitors to the Meek Mansion. Retired plumber Robert researched images to ensure the fountain was historically accurate and retrieved the center bowl of the fountain from the basement of the mansion. The couple is pictured here in front of the fountain and mansion. (Author's collection.)

Native American

Deanna Olney Espina was a member of the Yakima Nation and was born in San Francisco during the government's American Indian Urban Relocation Program. She lived 52 years in San Lorenzo. Her mother grew up on the Washington Yakima Reservation. In 1974, Deanna was the Native American Community Relations Representative for the San Lorenzo Unified School District under the Title IV Indian Education Program to provide liaison services to the home, school, and community; to work with school personnel in developing strategies for improving the education of Native American students; and to participate in all presentations relating to Native American culture and history. In 1983, Deanna became the Native American and Education Specialist for the school district to maintain a funded project under the Indian Education Act. Deanna established a Native American Museum in the school district where more than 35,000 students attended presentations during her management of the program. The museum contained samples of wild foods, handcrafted clothing, musical instruments, jewelry, pictures, and Native American houses. This was not required in the Indian Education Program, but Deanna was committed to not only improve the academic progress of the Native American students but to also raise the community's awareness of the history and richness of the Native American culture. Her students gave demonstrations in dance, Indian foods, crafts, and games. Deanna also taught a series of adult classes on Native Americans as part of the San Lorenzo Unified School District's Project Awareness Indian Education Program. On May 12, 2010, Congressman Pete Stark addressed the House of Representatives declaring Deanna's contributions to the community. The speech is permanently listed in the congressional record. Her achievements and honors are many. She was a founding member of the Bay Area Indian Education Council, recognized as Administrator of the Year by the National Indian Education Association, received the Distinguished Educator of the Year for Indian Education from the State of California, and received the Indian Education Showcase Award from the federal government for one of the best Indian Education Programs in the country. Deanna was one of the first Native American women elected to the National Board of the YWCA. She was also a founding member of the Oakland Museum's Cultural and Ethnic Affairs Guild. (Courtesy of Joe Espina.)

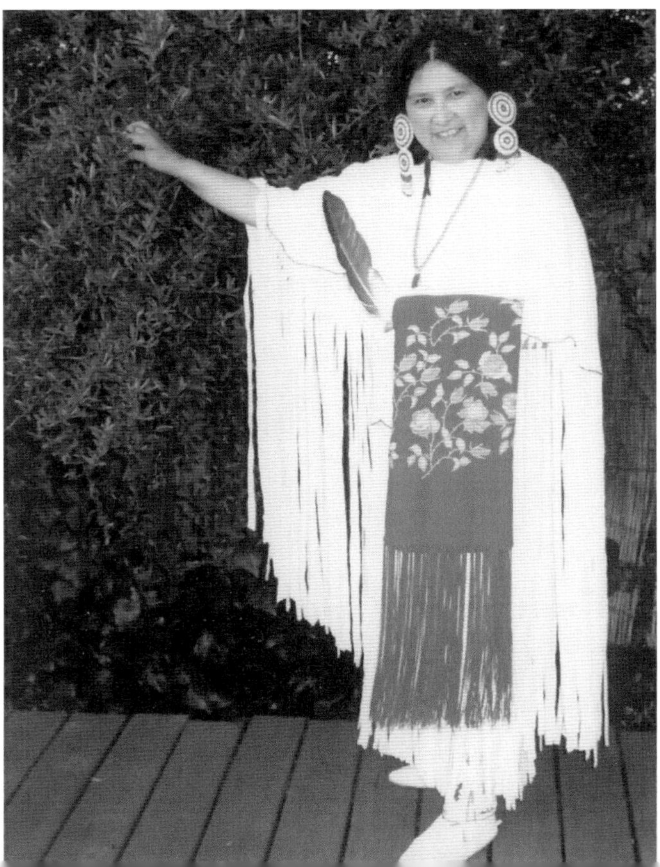

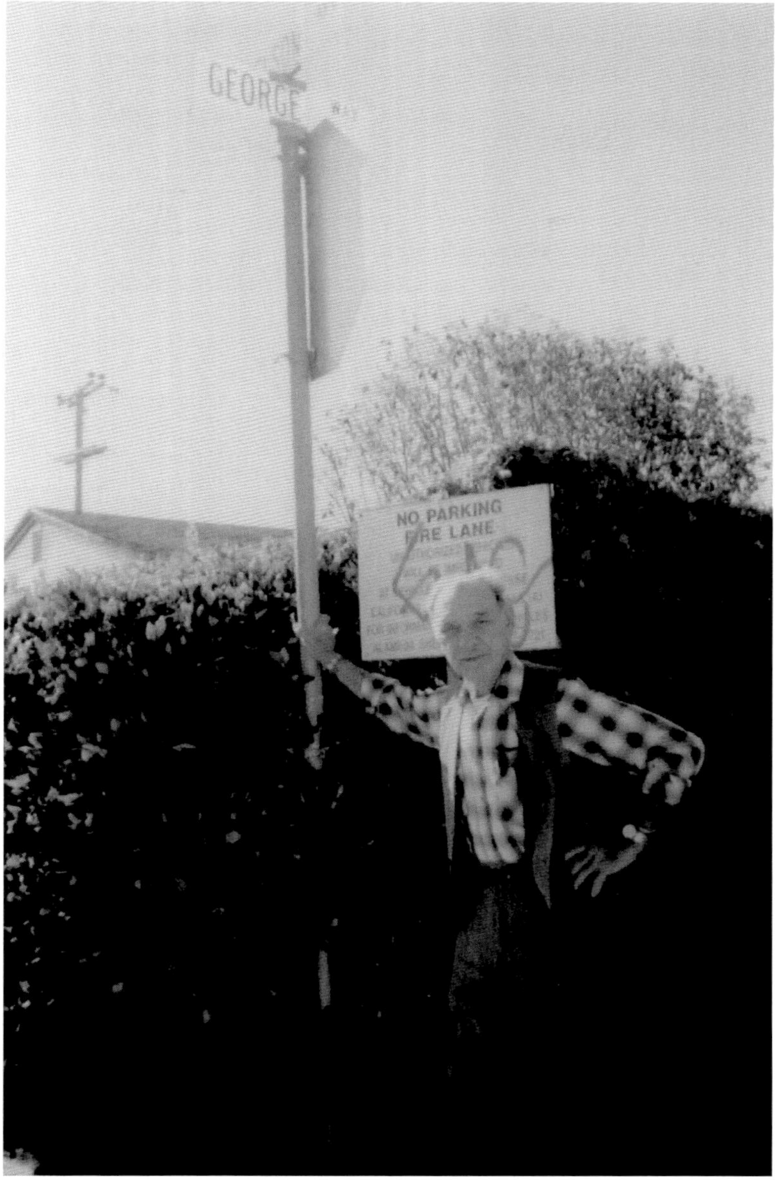

Flower Nursery
George Gianelli's parents came from Genoa, Italy, in 1913 with two children and established a carnation nursery and residence in San Lorenzo. George was born there in 1924. After his parents' deaths, he and his brother continued the business, called Gianelli Nursery. He was a partner in the San Francisco Flower Growers Association and an active member of the San Francisco Flower Market. He served in World War II as an Army staff sergeant in Europe. George married Lola Pollastrini in 1953. They had three children and lived on the property. George was a member of the Moose Lodge of Castro Valley, the IOOF Lodge of San Leandro, and the Hayward Area Historical Society and was past president of the Buon Tempo Italian Social Club. In 1987, the nursery was sold to developers for homes. The street leading into the development is called George Way. (Courtesy of Lola Gianelli.)

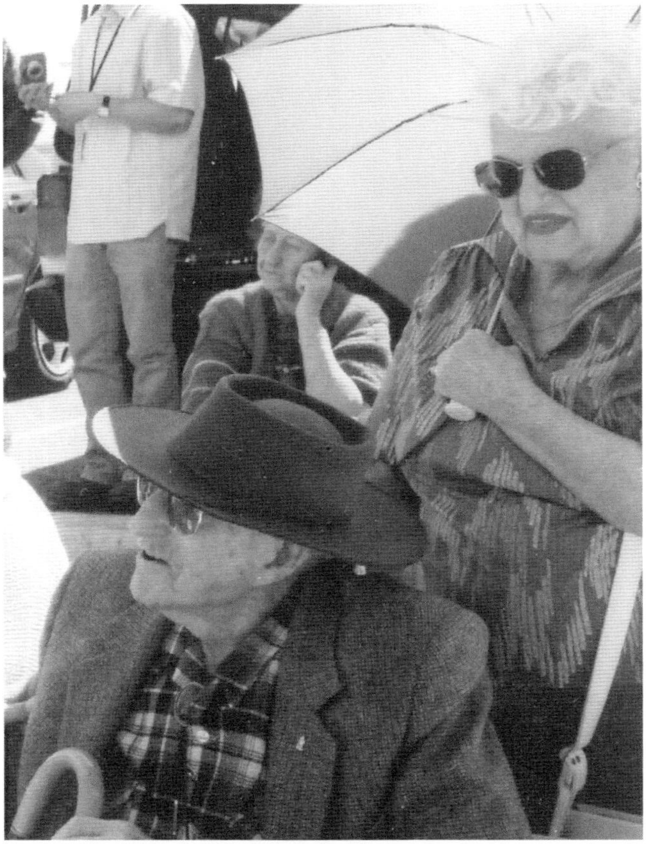

Pioneer Family
In 1900, the Rodrigues family purchased 12 acres of farmland from James Quigley's family along Telegraph Road, now Hesperian Boulevard. They lived along the dirt and gravel farm road and raised three children: Ignatius, Allance, and Violanta. The family grew strawberries, rhubarb, currants, apricots, tomatoes, and figs. Ignatius, called "Nish," was born in 1906. He and his siblings walked on Telegraph Road to attend the San Lorenzo Grammar School. The Rodrigues family farmed until the land was purchased for San Lorenzo Village homes. In 2006, at age 100, Ignatius renamed the farmer's lane "Quigley Road." He and his wife, Lorraine, attended the dedication, pictured above. Nish told many stories of his childhood and the farm. He and his wife are no longer living, but his sister Violanta, born in 1909, lives in her San Lorenzo home. (Author's collection.)

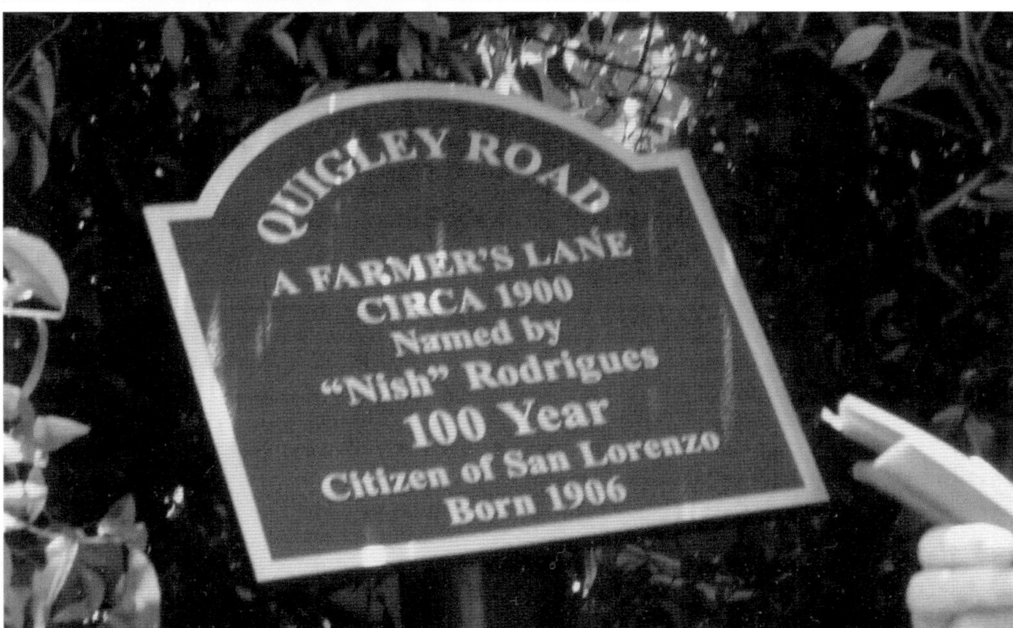

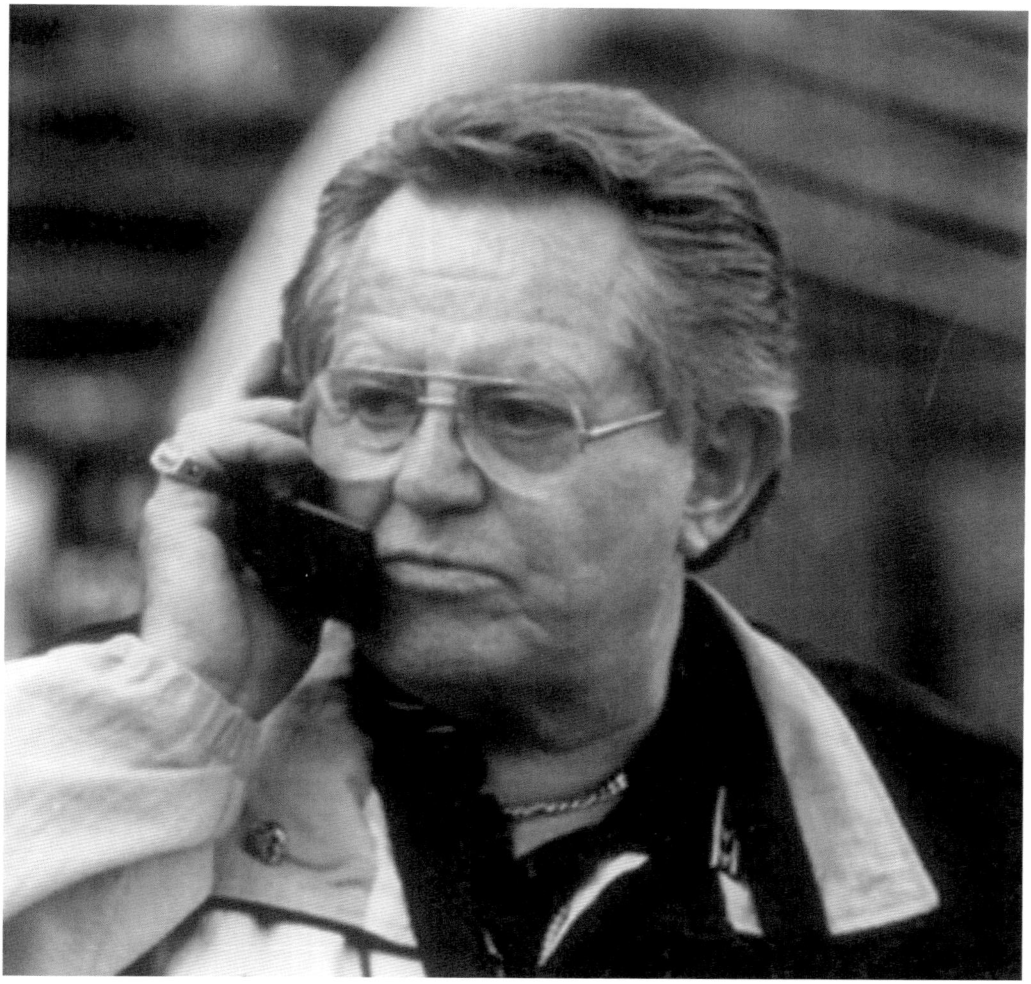

Photography
In the 1930s, Frank R. Denevi's family lived on Bockman Road, where the house still remains and Bohannon Middle School is located on the former flower fields. His father cultivated flowers for the San Francisco wholesale flower market. Frank attended Sunset Elementary and Hayward Union High School. After graduation, he went to college in San Francisco. While at Hayward High, he was given the challenge of producing the high school newspaper and taking pictures of all the teams and events, which were made into a successful publication. From that time on, his love for photography became his lifetime passion. In 1959, Frank opened his first studio in San Lorenzo called Denevi's Studios. He was a portrait and wedding photographer. He eventually opened stores in Dublin, Berkeley, Cupertino, and San Jose. The name was changed to Denevi Camera. His present business is Denevi Digital Imaging, located in Hayward, offering the service to archive one's memories to the digital age before they fade away. In 1970, Frank began taking pictures for the Oakland Raiders football team. He has images of every Oakland game for 44 years as well as three Super Bowls. He was a judge for the Raider cheerleaders and began the Oakland Raider Lineman's Club. For 10 years, he worked with Al Losale on the KGO radio show *Ask the Raiders*. In 1976, he was a sponsor for the team. Frank and staff print the luggage tags, Raiderette calendars, and staff photographs for the team. His office contains a museum of Oakland Raiders memorabilia he has collected over the years. Frank has generously donated to the San Lorenzo Unified School District and the San Lorenzo Village Homes Association. (Courtesy of Frank Denevi.)

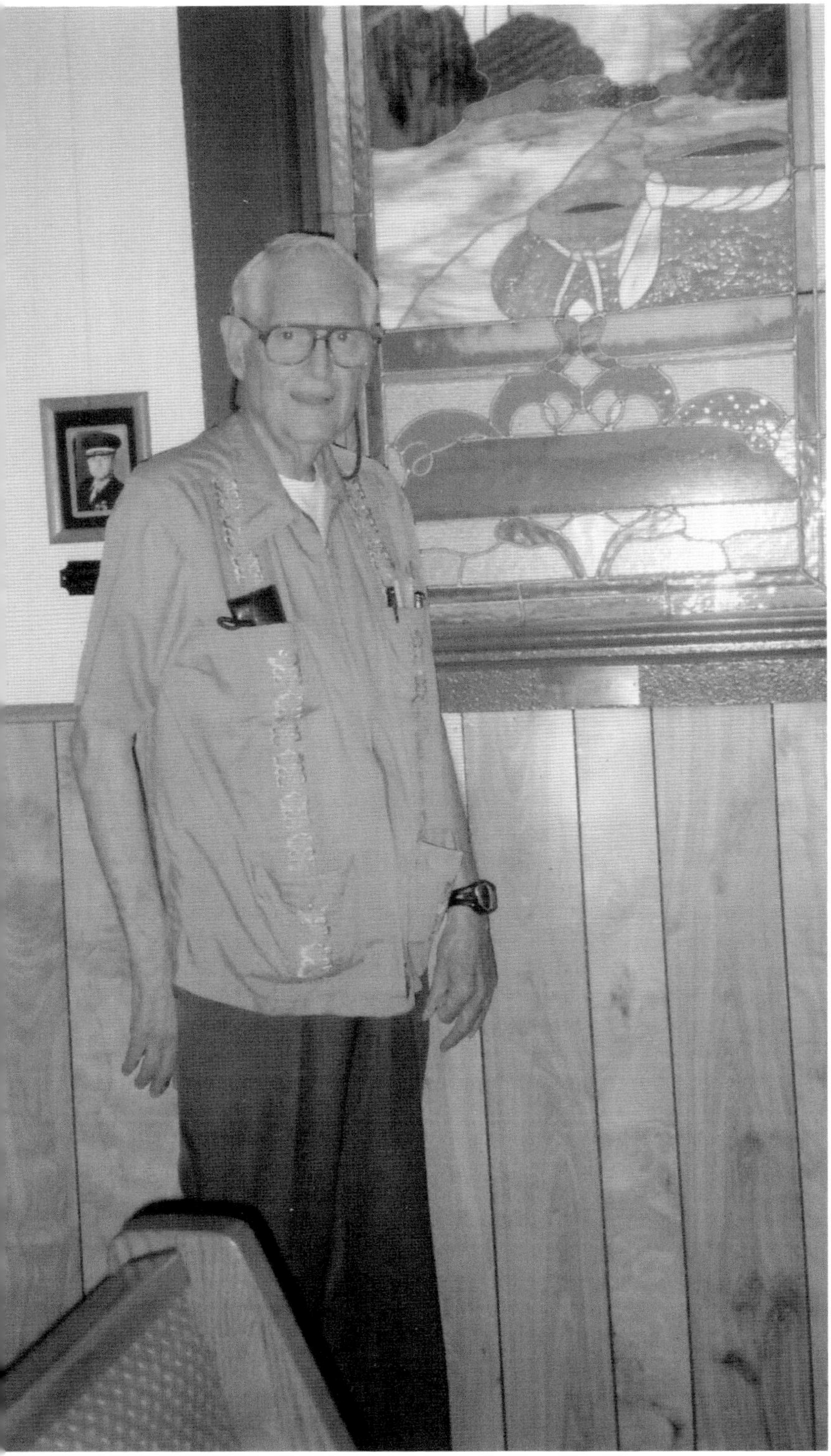

Stained-Glass Windows
The First Southern Baptist Church had one stained-glass window. In 1989, Rene Dubois had a dream to have more stained-glass windows. She felt compelled to do one behind the baptistery after surviving nine surgeries in one year, including the amputation of her legs. With the help of stained-glass classes and a special table made to fit her wheelchair, Rene designed the 13 windows from the Testaments. She completed her first window in three months. The day the first window was dedicated in 1991, Rene went to the hospital. John King, a member of the church, visited her. She asked him to continue with the windows. He promised to complete her project. Twenty-five days later, she passed away. John, with the help of stained-class students, completed the windows in 1993. (Author's collection.)

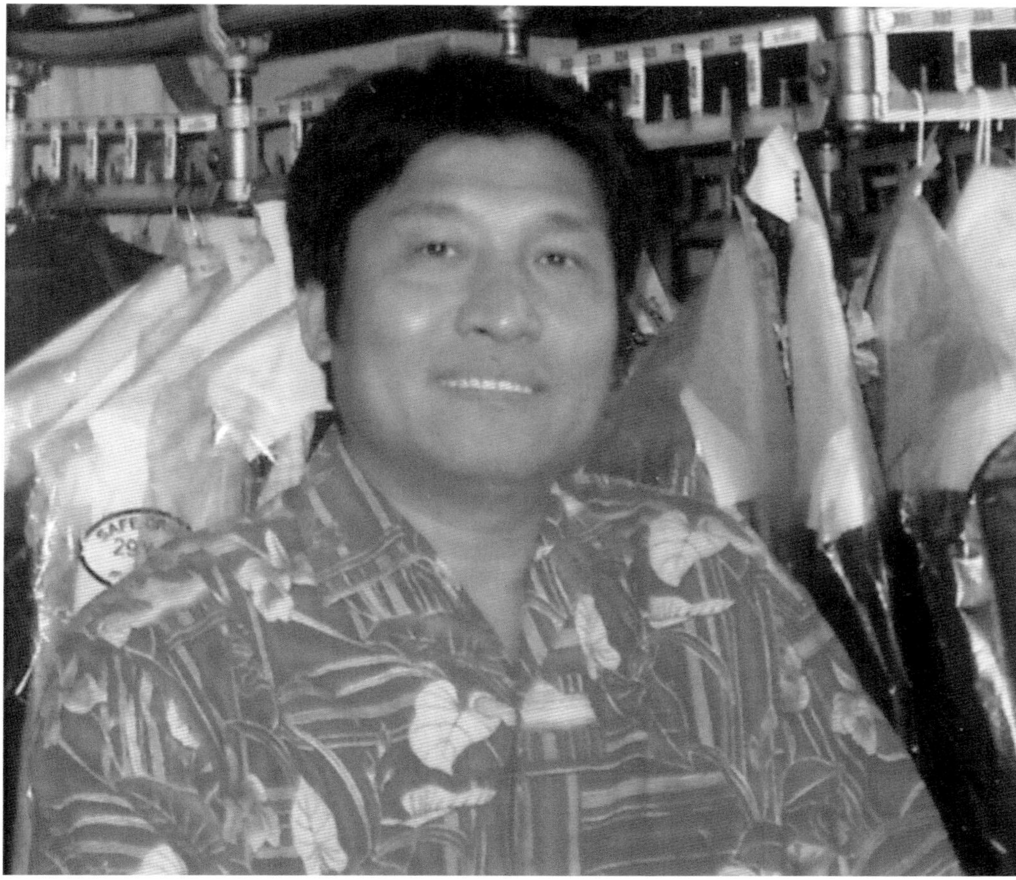

Green Cleaners
Sung Han Lee was born in Korea. His family immigrated in 1977 to the United States and settled in Sunnyvale when he was 19 years old. As the oldest son, he went to college and worked. Sung's parents wanted him to go into business. Many of his father's friends were in the dry cleaning business, so Sung went to dry cleaning school in San Jose, passed the state board exam, and received a license. In 1982, at the age of 23, Sung opened the Hesperian Cleaners in San Lorenzo and became active in the community. Sung has sponsored a San Lorenzo Little League team since 1983 and is on the Lorenzo Theater Foundation Committee. In 2007, he converted the dry cleaners to green technology by eliminating the traditional cleaning solvent Perchloroethylene and other toxins. This offered healthier alternatives to customers for garment cleaning with no hazardous waste generated. As the first green dry cleaners certified in Alameda County, Sung received the Bay Area Green Business Program Award in 2007. From Acterra, a nonprofit organization, he won the Environmental Business Award in 2008 for having the only green dry cleaners in the Bay Area and nationwide. From 2007 to 2009, Hesperian Cleaners was the demonstration site for the state of California. Sung showed other dry-cleaning business owners how to convert to green technology called "Professional Wet Cleaning." The State of California awarded him the Excellent Small Business Award in 2009. The Water Smart Award was given to him by the East Bay Municipal Utility District for conserving water usage and demonstrating these practices to other businesses. From Alameda County Supervisor Wilma Chan, Sung received commendation for showing leadership in the green movement. In 2011, Sung was inducted into the Hall of Fame of Environmental Business People. He also participated in the Environmental Mega Trend Museum Exhibition. As an avid collector of orchids, Sung conducts orchid classes for the community and adult school. (Author's collection.)

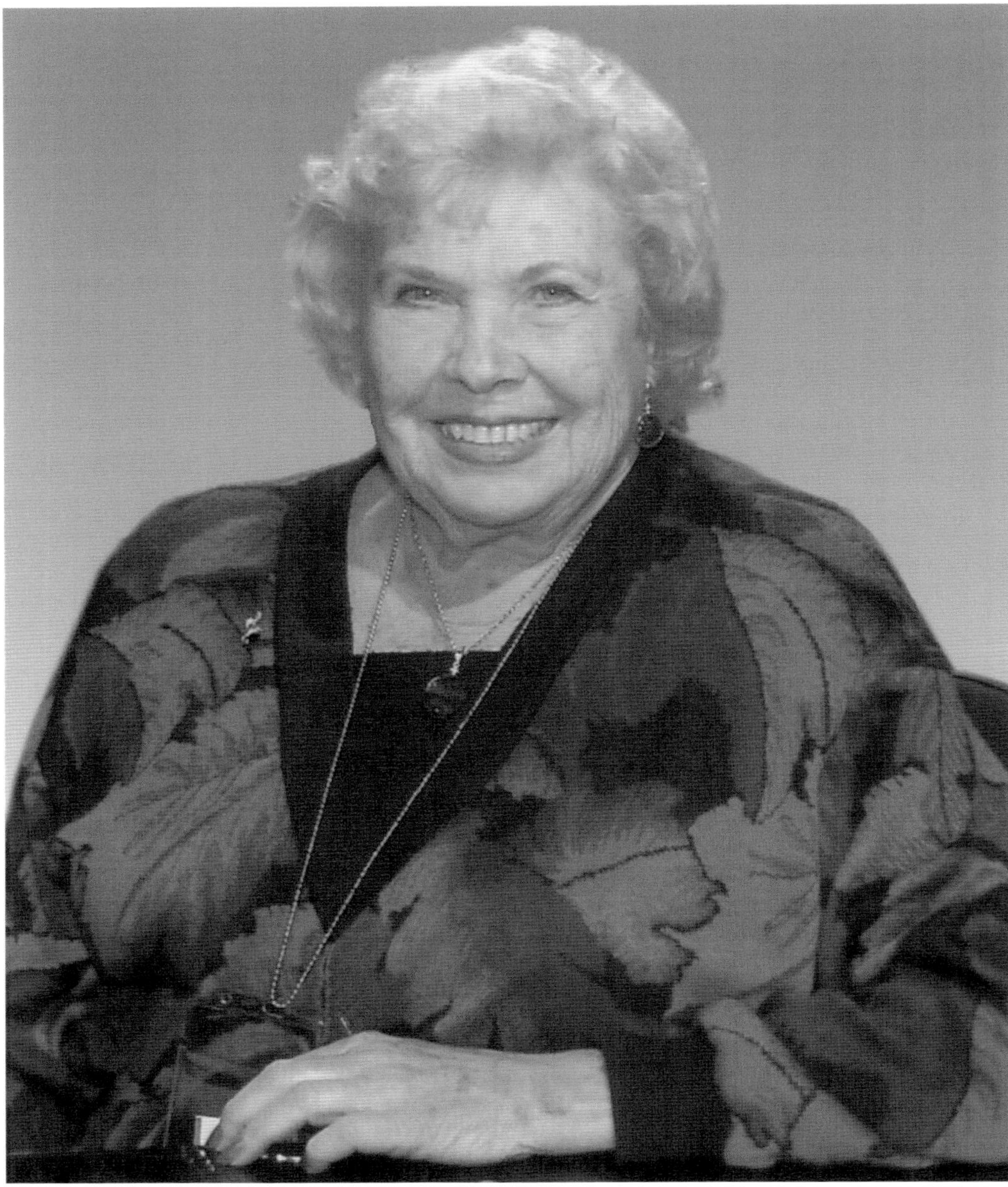

Traveling and Volunteering
Because of her love of travel, Donna McCarty became the tour leader for the Hayward Travel and Culture Club. She escorts seniors all over California, the United States, and the world. Traveling alone for one year around the world, she taught swimming in Hawaii and Greece. Donna has traveled to all seven continents. A California native, Donna was born and raised in Cherryland. Her father and uncles built the home she grew up in, the ninth house on the Meek property. After graduating from Hayward Union High School, Donna continued her education at San Jose State for a degree in physical education and taught junior and senior high school physical education for 30 years. Donna received awards for volunteering as a docent at the McConaghy House, Dunsmuir House, Chairman of Meek Estate restoration, and the California Retired Teachers, Division No. 59. (Courtesy of Donna McCarty.)

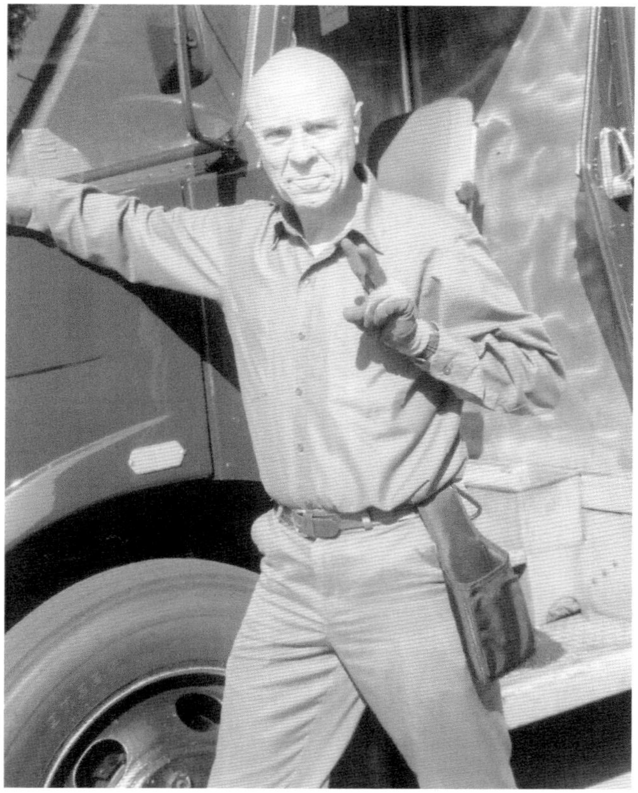

Safety, Service, and Song

Keith Barros has lived in San Lorenzo Village since 1976. He is well known as a San Lorenzo and Eden Area community activist, especially in safety. Many years ago, he began his activism in stopping the county public works and the highway patrol from raising the speed limit on some busy streets near the schools. He also volunteers for community projects. He is a supporter of the movement to save the historic Lorenzo Theater, was instrumental in creating the Alameda County Board of Zoning Adjustments, and successfully led the first recall election of a San Lorenzo Village Homes Association director in 2003. The San Lorenzo Village Homes Association Board designated Keith as San Lorenzo's "Community Hero," and he represented San Lorenzo in the Alameda County Fair Parade. As a longtime UPS driver, Keith has been a relentless advocate for safety. His advocacy has resulted in the installation of speed bumps, school zone signs, and a traffic light at a local school crossing. Keith was pictured in the local newspaper and nationally in the Teamster magazine for his efforts to change inconsistent speed limits on Lewelling Boulevard and return it to 25 miles per hour. As a safety advocate at work, he was the first chairman of the UPS Oakland Metro Safety Committee and a facilitator at annual UPS District Safety Conferences held throughout Northern California. Keith has also written and performed over 30 song parodies, some with videos for UPS, the Teamster Western Conference Convention in Las Vegas, and for the San Lorenzo community. Some of the local parodies were for the Lorenzo Theater Foundation, San Lorenzo Library's 100th birthday, retiring directors and board members, a county supervisor, and one paying tribute to San Lorenzo set to the tune of "New York, New York." Some of the lyrics are: "Start spreading the news. / We're not going away. / We'll make a better place of it. / San Lor-en-zo! / Our troubles will go / 'cause we'll chase 'em away / We're going to make our stand in it. / San Lor-en-zo! / I like to wake up after getting a quiet night's sleep / and see my street get cleaned up by our guy on the sweep. / We little townfolks are all gonna stay / and make a brand new town of it, San Lor-en-zo. / It's gonna happen now / and I'm gonna Tell ya how. / It's up to you / San Lor-en-zo!" (Author's collection.)

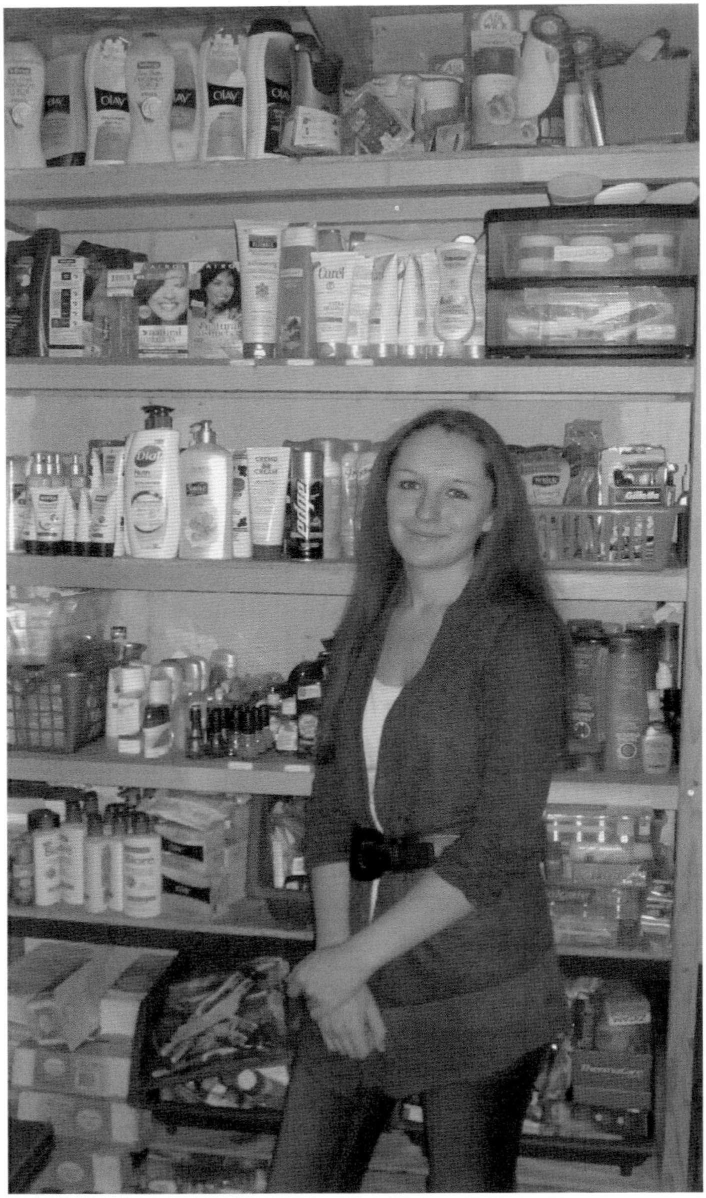

Coupon Hobby

Mary Bossley, began clipping coupons as a teenager to save her family money. She never knew there was a whole community of "coupon people." After researching, Mary found many coupon websites and forums where collectors gather. Part of Mary's schedule includes an hour on Sundays clipping from newspapers, and six hours per week filing the coupons alphabetically before going shopping. She has many bins of items, anything from shampoo to paper towels. The items her family does not use or are in excess are donated to the homeless, women's shelters, senior citizen homes, Goodwill, and the Salvation Army. Coupons are never thrown away. Mary sends unused ones overseas to military troops. They can use them up to six months past the expiration date at the military commissary. Mary shares her couponing secrets with others at sessions at the local library. (Courtesy of Mary Bossley.)

INDEX